THE TRIALS OF OSCAR WILDE

THE TRIALS OF OSCAR WILDE

Deviance, Morality, and Late-Victorian Society

MICHAEL S. FOLDY

YALE UNIVERSITY PRESS
NEW HAVEN AND LONDON

Set in Adobe Minion
Printed in Great Britain by Redwood Books, Wiltshire

Library of Congress Cataloging-in-Publication Data

Foldy, Michael S., 1953–
     The trials of Oscar Wilde: deviance, morality, and late-Victorian society/by Michael S. Foldy.
     Includes bibliographical references and index.
     ISBN 0–300–07112–4
     1. Wilde, Oscar, 1854–1900—Trials, litigation, etc.   2. Homosexuality and literature—Great Britain—History—19th century.   3. Literature and society—Great Britain—History—19th century.   4. Trials (Sodomy)—England—London—History—19th century.   5. Great Britain—Social conditions—19th century.   6. Great Britain—Civilization—19th century.   7. Authors. Irish—19th century—Biography.   8. Gay men—Great Britain—Biography.   I. Title.
PR5823.F65   1997
828'.809—dc21   97–24369
[B]   CIP

A catalogue record for this book is available from the British Library.

10 9 8 7 6 5 4 3 2 1

For permission to reprint extracts from copyright material the author and publishers gratefully acknowledge the following: Merlin Holland for *Letters of Oscar Wilde* (1962) edited by Rupert Hart-Davis, © The Estate of Oscar Wilde; Little Brown and Co., UK for *The Diary of Beatrice Webb, vol. 2: 1892–1905, All the Good Things of Life* (1983) edited by N. and J. Mackenzie; The Historians' Press for *The Destruction of Lord Rosebery* (1986) by David Brooks; William Hodge and Co. Holdings Ltd. for *The Trials of Oscar Wilde* (1962) by H. Montgomery Hyde.

To Elizabeth, who has enlarged my world in so many different ways, and to my father, who was always behind me one hundred percent

CONTENTS

ACKNOWLEDGMENTS

Although I am solely responsible for the analysis and opinions expressed in these pages, there are several people I wish to thank for helping me to realize this book. My greatest debt is to Philippa Levine—the best reader, editor, and advisor one could ever hope to have—for helping me to sort out and, in some cases, to discover what it was that I wanted to say about Wilde and the trials. I am grateful for the unflagging energy, generosity, and support that she has extended to me from the beginning. To my wife, Elizabeth, I owe thanks of a different sort, for putting up with my single-minded absorption in the project, and for the love and encouragement which sustained me throughout the course of the writing. I also owe a debt to Mauricio Mazon for reasons usual and unusual, and I thank him for his friendship and for the many things I have learned from him. Several others have assisted me and/or inspired me over the years as this and other projects have taken shape: Margo Bistis, Barry Glassner, Lloyd Moote, Eyal Chowers, Richard Allen, Kent Casper, and Carsten Seecamp. Special thanks go to my friend, Bethe Allison, and to my mother, Alice Foldy, for their consistent support over the years.

Publishing this book with Yale University Press has been a pleasant experience for me and I am particularly indebted to those individuals at the London office who took my manuscript and helped me shape it into a book: to Robert Baldock, whose stewardship of the project has been marked by the utmost kindness, sensitivity, and professionalism; to Candida Brazil, who has overseen the copy-editing of the manuscript with great efficiency and good cheer; to an unknown reader whose comments helped me to address some crucial lapses in the original manuscript; and finally, to Charles Grench of the New Haven office, who started the ball rolling by expressing an interest in my initial manuscript. To all I offer my warmest thanks.

INTRODUCTION

The British Crown's prosecution of Oscar Wilde in the spring of 1895 was one of the most sensational criminal trials of the Victorian age. Wilde's prominence as an artist and celebrity was one reason; the nature of the alleged crime—sodomy—was another. Up until that point, the eighteen-nineties had been Wilde's decade. His singular personality dominated the most exclusive dining tables and the most fashionable drawing rooms of London, and he was an important and recognizable public figure on three continents.

In 1913, the noted cultural historian Holbrook Jackson observed that prior to 1890, Wilde "might have passed away without creating any further comment than that which is accorded an eccentric poet who has succeeded in drawing attention to himself and his work by certain audacities of costume and opinion."[1] In 1890, however, Wilde began an incredible five-year run of virtually uninterrupted critical successes that served to cement his reputation as a brilliant wit, literary stylist, and master of the English language.[2] When the Queensberry libel trial began in late March of 1895, Wilde had two smash successes playing in the fashionable West End: *An Ideal Husband* at the Haymarket Theatre, and *The Importance of Being Earnest* at the St. James's. But as Wilde's first criminal trial stretched into April, and the second into May, the daily press coverage of his sex scandal quickly upstaged the plays, and growing public pressure soon forced them to close.

Wilde's literary career was effectively ended by his conviction on the (lesser) misdemeanor crime of committing "acts of gross indecency between men" and subsequent two-year imprisonment. The three years between his release from prison in 1897 and his death in 1900 were spent living in poverty, shame, and, most sadly of all perhaps, unproductivity. He lived on the Continent in a self-imposed exile from England, his adopted homeland and the site of his many glorious triumphs, where his works were no longer produced, and where his Christian name, "Oscar," now served as a euphemism for a male homosexual.[3] During the period of the three trials which forms the focus of this book, from late March to late May of 1895, Wilde endured suffering and humiliation, and lost virtually everything he held dear: his freedom, his marriage and access to his children, all of his wealth and possessions, his reputation, and, for all intents and purposes, the will to live and to create.

A quick perusal of the "facts" would certainly lead one to think that the main issues of the case against Wilde were technical and legal. In broad outline, the "facts" were these: Wilde, a well-known and respected talent, if an unpopular public figure, was publicly accused by the Marquess of Queensberry, the father of Wilde's "lover" and companion, Lord Alfred Douglas, of being a "sodomite." To defend his reputation, Wilde sued Queensberry, a notoriously crude and cantankerous peer of the realm, for libel.[4] During the libel trial, testimony was elicited which implicated Wilde in a series of same-sex affairs with a number of working-class youths. Following Queensberry's acquittal on the libel charge, Wilde himself was indicted for violating section 11 of the 1885 Criminal Law Amendment Act, which criminalized "acts of gross indecency between men," even those consensual acts committed in private. For a variety of reasons, Wilde's first criminal trial ended in a hung jury, but following a second trial, Wilde was convicted and sentenced to two years' imprisonment with hard labor, the harshest sentence permitted by law.

If the number of recent titles is any indication, there has been, in the past decade or so, a huge resurgence of interest in Oscar Wilde, especially from within the academic community. There has been a "definitive" critical biography,[5] several interpretive studies,[6] a psychoanalysis of Wilde and his works,[7] an inspired consideration of Wilde's audiences,[8] and a whole slew of works, all of them excellent, and some of them brilliant, that tackle the issue of Wilde's "sexual deviancy" from one viewpoint or another.[9] Many of these books refer to the trials as well, most of them in a peripheral way, and one of them, Ed Cohen's, very directly and specifically.[10] I would like to say at the outset that the present work has benefitted greatly from all of these studies.

The purpose of the present study, however, is not to re-cover old ground, or to rehash tired debates about Wilde's "guilt" or "innocence," or once again to portray Wilde (rightly, in many respects) as an unnecessary "victim" of an intolerant society and a repressive legal code. I am less interested than Ed Cohen, for example, in the Wilde trials as a major landmark case in the history of (the repression of) homosexuality in England. I am also less concerned than Alan Sinfield, for example, with "reading" the Wilde trials in light of a contemporary (nineteen-nineties) agenda of gay cultural politics. Wilde's sexual desire, his "passion for passion," as it were, as well as his preferences for certain sexual practices and particular sexual objects, do play a significant role in the present study, but they do not play the only role, or even the most decisive one. I am very interested in Wilde's "deviancy," to be sure, for Wilde's "deviancy" is undoubtedly the key issue of the trials. Where this study differs from others is in trying to reach a broader understanding of the many contributing factors that constituted Wilde's "deviancy" within the context of late-Victorian society. As an historian, I have been especially preoccupied with reconstructing Wilde's "deviancy" from two primary perspectives: as Wilde himself described it, and as the State and many (if not most) of his own contemporaries described it.

This exploration has been motivated by a desire to identify and explain precisely what it was about Wilde that seemed to threaten and outrage a late-Victorian society that, much like our own, was exposed routinely to shocking public scandals, especially sex scandals, many of which involved notable persons. When I first encountered the trials, it was difficult for me to understand why the public's reaction to Wilde was so hostile, and moreover, why it remained so for several generations after his death. It has taken the greater part of the twentieth century to rehabilitate Wilde's literary reputation, principally because as a result of the trials, the public's reception of his artistic works was thereafter tainted by the knowledge of his homosexuality. Today, however, in certain artistic and literary circles, Wilde has been resurrected as a counter-cultural hero, and as such enjoys a current vogue within contemporary "pop" culture. Although this is certainly cause for celebration, I still felt the need to explain how he had come to be so vilified in the first place. Surely this process of erasing Wilde from the cultural memory began with the trials, but how had it happened, and why did it happen as it did?

In this book I have endeavored to represent the trials within the context of the different forces and trends that were moving British politics and society, and of the views, values, and attitudes that were expressed by Wilde's contemporaries. I believe that the very potent constellation of dangers and threats that Wilde (as a result of the trials) came to represent, not just to England, but also to Britain and the Empire, can be grasped only by understanding contemporary social and political realities and the prevailing views, attitudes, aspirations, and fears of the English public. Ultimately, this book represents a dual effort: to reconstruct Wilde as the social and cultural symbol he became in 1895, and to reconstruct the popular *mentalité*, or consciousness, that perceived the symbol.

Methodologically, this book falls into the general category of the "micro-history." Micro-histories generally examine the complexity of relatively small-scale or "minor" historical events. The many facets of the small event serve as different lenses onto the larger social and cultural processes which envelop it and of which it is a part. This approach has been associated historiographically with Emmanuel Le Roy Ladurie, Natalie Davis, and Carlo Ginzburg in their cultural histories of the late medieval and early modern periods, and has yielded startling results. I have tried to approach the modern period in a similar

way. My study has been inspired and informed by the methods and ideas of
many thinkers representing a variety of disciplines, among them: the cultural
anthropology of Clifford Geertz and Mary Douglas; the hermeneutics of Hans-
Georg Gadamer; the social theory of Emile Durkheim, Georg Simmel, Daniel
Bell, and Pierre Bourdieu; the history of science and medicine of Georges
Canguilhem and Michel Foucault, the psychoanalytic self-psychology of Heinz
Kohut; the reception theories of Wolfgang Iser and Georges Poulet; and the
critical/social theories of Fredric Jameson, Susan Sontag, Guy Debord, Jean
Baudrillard, and Mikhail Bakhtin.

The substance of the first two chapters has been reconstructed from the trial
testimony which was printed more or less verbatim by the major London
newspapers. I rely primarily upon the *Daily Telegraph* and the *Star*, for their
coverage was the most comprehensive. The dialogue that was considered
improper or inappropriate to print because of its content is found in H.
Montgomery Hyde, *The Trials of Oscar Wilde*. I have relied on Hyde throughout to supplement the accounts of the *Telegraph*, the *Star*, and the other
London newspapers, in order to provide a more complete picture of the trials
and related events.

Hyde reported that the official Court shorthand writers and compilers of the
Central Criminal Court Sessions Papers "declined to print the proceedings of
any of the [Wilde] trials on the ground that the details disclosed by them were
'unfit for publication.'" Hyde's version of the trial is itself a patchwork of newspaper accounts, the remembrances of five people (including Lord Alfred
Douglas and Sir Travers Humphreys, Wilde's co-counsel) who were present
for part or all of the proceedings, and what are purported to be unexpurgated
accounts based on these unpublished "original shorthand reports." Hyde relies
especially on Stuart Mason's (also known as Christopher Sclater Millard,
Wilde's bibliographer) *Oscar Wilde: Three Times Tried*, London, 1912, and on
Charles Grolleau's *The Trial of Oscar Wilde*, Paris, 1906. Neither of these ver-
sions strictly corresponds as to the exact chronology of the testimony, the
words employed, or the phrasing of the sentences. This might be expected since
they were constructed long after the trials were over. They are, however, similar
enough in substance and tone to warrant their acceptance as "reliable" sources.

I have chosen to rely on Hyde rather than Mason or Grolleau primarily for
aesthetic reasons. Hyde's text has greater clarity and more stylistic merit, and
since it most closely follows the newspapers, it is also the easiest to correlate.
Throughout, I have striven to interpret my sources in good faith, and done my
best to decode the ideological biases of the various commentators. The narrative overview of the trials thus constructed represents more than just a synop-
sis, but it should by no means be construed as comprehensive. I have tried to
strike a middle ground between Richard Ellmann's expeditious handling of the
trial in his otherwise magisterial biography of Wilde, and the overwhelming

wealth of detail in Hyde's invaluable book. This study attempts to convey a sense of the structure, the color, and the tone of the proceedings, and to emphasize what I see as the substantive highlights. My idea was to present enough substance to engage the reader's interest without, however, burdening him or her with unnecessary matter. It is hoped that throughout there is both sufficient context to orient the reader in time and place, and points of reference to inform the analytical sections which follow the narratives.

The book is organized in the following way. Chapters One and Two present a relatively straightforward narrative overview of the three trials. In addition to outlining the substantive issues, they highlight the legal maneuvering both inside and outside the courtroom, the strategies of both prosecution and defense, and the biases of the judges. The first chapter includes a speculative section on the relationship between Queensberry and Lord Rosebery, the Prime Minister during this period. Rosebery was suspected by some contemporaries of being a practicing homosexual, but this allegation has proved impossible to substantiate. Lord Alfred Douglas suggested at the time that the government would never have gone to such lengths to prosecute Wilde if not for pressure exerted by Queensberry upon some highly placed person or persons.[11] Suspicions have fallen on Rosebery for several reasons, but no direct evidence exists. It is known that Rosebery suffered what might today be termed a "nervous collapse" from late February to early May of 1895—a period which curiously overlaps with the dates of the Wilde trials. In this section I employ psychohistorical methods to explore this apparent "coincidence."

Chapter Three examines the trial coverage in the press and the reception of the trials by the reading public. I analyze the content of some representative editorials and reader-responses to the proceedings (in the form of letters to the editor) which were published in the correspondence columns of the major metropolitan newspapers. The relatively recent innovation of the correspondence column and the emergence of the "sex scandal" as a sub-genre of crime reporting are contextualized within a brief historical overview of the "New Journalism" and its impact upon Victorian society. From a larger perspective, this chapter also tries to represent the Wilde trials as a case study in order to examine the various ways in which the press was able to reflect, shape, and distort public opinion at this particular moment in its own evolution as an institution.

Chapters Four, Five, and Six represent the heart of the study. Chapter Four situates the trials within the prevailing cultural and intellectual climate which I describe as "heterosexist" and "homophobic." In this chapter, I discuss "heterosexism" and "homophobia" as dynamic and transitive historical phenomena which are culturally specific and socially constructed. I argue that the mechanisms of restraint and the structures of repression, which represent the reification of "heterosexism" in virtually every modern society, comprised a very powerful (if very discreet) social presence within English society before the trials, and that this presence became even more powerful, and even more obvious, as a direct result of the Wilde trials. I further suggest that the late nineteenth-century variant of "homophobia" was the historical correlative of the late nineteenth-century "redefinition" of the "homosexual" according to medical and scientific criteria. This chapter also explores the ways in which the prevailing "heterosexist" and "homophobic" attitudes were generally supported and reinforced by both popular and professional discourses on "decadence," "degeneration," and "sexual inversion."

Another goal of this chapter is to explore the paradox of the codification of fairly strict laws that prohibited same-sex practices and yet the general reluctance on the part of officials to enforce them, and on the part of society to demand that these laws be enforced. In response, I suggest that the milder, more tolerant attitudes toward sexual and gender deviance usually associated with the "early modern" period generally prevailed in British society well into the eighteen-nineties, and that it was only in the wake of the public outrage that accompanied the Wilde trials that these traditional attitudes toward same-sex practices and male effeminacy were radically transformed, almost overnight, becoming much harsher and more intolerant in the process.

Chapter Five changes course somewhat and explores the meaning and symbolism of the trials from Wilde's point of view. I examine Wilde's justification of his work and behavior and his various appeals to the authority of art, literature, and philosophy. I also contextualize Wilde's denial of his homosexuality within the personal philosophy expressed in his critical works. In addition this chapter represents an attempt to theorize Wilde's identity and desire, and an effort to understand the connection between Wilde's artistic and sexual activities. Rather than considering Wilde's life and works through the prism of his homosexuality, as has been done repeatedly within the current literature on Wilde, I have sought instead to try to understand Wilde's sexuality through his own philosophy of aesthetics. In this sense, Chapter Five represents the effort to integrate Wilde's ideas and his sexuality, as it were—rather than considering them as separate but parallel issues. In doing so, I have tried to construct a portrait of Wilde as an historical subject which accepts and explores the many contradictions contained within a very complex and multi-faceted personality, and which emphasizes the importance of his sexuality without subordinating either his experiences or his ideas to a "totalizing" sexuality which overshadows all else and which obscures other equally important facets of his identity.

I believe that Wilde's mature aesthetic was crucial to the development and expression of his sexuality, and moreover, that his aesthetic was instrumental in informing and shaping his choices of sexual objects and gender roles. I argue that what was described as Wilde's "aberrant" sexuality was seen by contemporaries as an integral part and as a logical manifestation of his personal aesthetic, which I characterize as his "ontological aesthetic of dissent." I analyze the substance of Wilde's aesthetic views and suggest that it was precisely Wilde's "ontological aesthetic"—and his committed practice of it—that threatened to subvert the values and structures of late-Victorian society. In looking at Wilde's desire, I discuss the class basis of Wilde's aesthetic, and contrast the idealized Hellenic conceptions of pederasty with the social and cultural implications of Wilde's sexual exploitation of working-class youths. In addition, I explore the aesthetic roots and the symbolism of Wilde's sodomitical pursuits, and situate them within a Sadean discourse on the "metaphysics of sodomy."

Finally, Chapter Six foregrounds the trials against the historical background of the eighteen-nineties. In a general sense, I depict Wilde as personifying the "onslaught of modernity" with its concomitant threats to traditional moral values and its challenges to traditional gender roles and sexual identities. More particularly, however, Wilde and the issues of the trials are considered within the context of the high-profile "social purity" movements of the eighteen-eighties and nineties, and viewed against the emerging social and political doctrine of "new liberalism." I argue that both "social purity" and "New Liberalism" should be regarded broadly, within the context of popular views on social structure and the purpose of societies, as movements of "cultural revitalization" which were responding to serious and widespread feelings of real (or perceived) decline in the morality, prosperity, and Great Power status of the nation. More importantly, I show how the rhetoric of the social purists and new liberals, which specifically linked issues of moral and physical health, had been absorbed into popular debates concerning one of the great questions of the age, namely, the question of the "health" or "condition" of England. Ultimately, I locate the meaning of the Wilde trials within the context of this public debate. I demonstrate that throughout the course of the trials, Wilde—whose literary works have always been regarded as quintessentially "English"—came himself to symbolize the very antithesis of "Englishness." In effect, Wilde came to represent a very potent threat to the "health" of Britain at a very critical juncture in that nation's history, and Wilde's conviction and imprisonment in turn represented a concerted effort on the part of "society" to address and cure a debilitating "sickness" and to reaffirm the existing moral order.

1 THE QUEENSBERRY LIBEL TRIAL

On the morning of April 3, 1895, the Marquess of Queensberry surrendered at the Central Criminal Court to be tried upon the charge of having unlawfully and maliciously published a defamatory libel against Oscar Wilde. The *Daily Telegraph* reported that the courtroom was crowded when Mr. Justice Henn Collins took his seat at half past ten.[1] Oscar Wilde sat at the solicitor's table until he was called into the witness-box, where he remained for the rest of the day. Wilde's cross-examination was still uncompleted when the Court rose for the evening.[2]

Wilde was represented by Sir Edward Clarke, Q.C., M.P., Mr. Charles Mathews, and Mr. Travers Humphreys. The Marquess of Queensberry was defended by Mr. Edward Carson, Q.C., M.P., and a former classmate of Wilde's at Trinity College, Dublin, by Mr. Charles Gill, and Mr. Arthur Gill.[3] The defense counsels were instructed by Mr. Charles Russell.[4] Mr. Besley, Q.C., and Mr. Monckton were also present in Court to observe the case on behalf of Lord Douglas of Hawick.[5]

Mr. Avory, the Clerk of the Arraigns, read the indictment charging Queensberry with having written and published a malicious and defamatory libel, to which the defendant pleaded "not guilty." With these preliminaries done, the case for the prosecution began. Sir Edward Clarke's opening statement noted that the libel had been published in the form of a card which had been left by Lord Queensberry with the hall porter at the Albemarle Club on February 18, 1895.[6] The card read, "For Oscar Wilde, posing as a somdomite [sic]."[7]

Clarke was simply stating the obvious when he maintained that the word itself had serious and injurious implications for the reputation and position of anyone connected with it. Although the word "posing" suggested that there was no commission of the actual offence—but rather that Wilde "appeared, or desired to appear" as a person who was inclined to commit "the gravest of all offences"—the slanderous intent was clear. The most pressing issue for Clarke, however, was Queensberry's insistence in his plea of justification that the statement was true, and moreover, that it had been published for the public benefit.[8]

After sketching Wilde's illustrious literary career as well as the history of his association with Lord Alfred Douglas, Clarke embarked upon a survey of the evidence that was to be presented by the defense. Although Wilde's counsel had been furnished with a copy of Queensberry's lengthy plea of justification which contained highly detailed evidence against Wilde, including the names of Wilde's alleged "victims," and the dates and places the alleged criminal actions occurred, both Wilde and Clarke were unaware that the defense had sequestered many of the named youths in another part of the building and that they had been brought there specifically to testify against Wilde.[9]

Had either Wilde or Clarke known that these witnesses were physically present in Court, it seems likely that the prosecution would have abandoned its case there and then. Privately, of course, many of Wilde's friends had been pushing for abandonment of the prosecution all along, believing that it represented sheer folly on Wilde's part.[10] But at this point in the case, Clarke still believed that Wilde was telling the truth, and on the basis of this belief, Clarke's strategy was to attack what he believed to be the substance of the defense's evidence against Wilde, which consisted primarily of Wilde's own published works. Queensberry's plea of justification singled out Wilde's "immoral and obscene" novel, *The Picture of Dorian Gray*. *Dorian Gray* was alleged by Queensberry to have been understood "by readers thereof to describe the relations, intimacies, and passions of certain persons of sodomitical and unnatural habits, tastes, and practices." Queensberry also cited Wilde's "immoral" maxims, entitled "Phrases and Philosophies for the Use of the Young," which Wilde had contributed to the Oxford literary magazine, *The Chameleon*.[11] Both works were accused in the plea of subverting morality, corrupting youth, and encouraging unnatural vice.[12]

The defense also planned to introduce into evidence two letters written by Wilde to Lord Douglas, both of which had been used in failed attempts to blackmail Wilde. In a tactical maneuver calculated to defuse any possible impact that might arise from a more dramatic presentation by the defense, Clarke elected to introduce one of the letters first. The letter, described as a "prose sonnet," read as follows:

> My own boy, Your sonnet is quite lovely, and it is a marvel that those red rose-leaf lips of yours should have been made no less for music of song than for madness of kissing. Your slim gilt soul walks between passion and poetry. I think

Hyacinthus, whom Apollo loved so madly, was you in Greek days.

Why are you alone in London, and when do you go to Salisbury? Do go there, and cool your hands in the grey twilight of Gothic things, and come here whenever you like. It is a lovely place—it only lacks you: but go to Salisbury first. Always, with undying love, yours, Oscar.[13.]

Clarke admitted that the wording of the letter might appear extravagant to those more accustomed to writing "ordinary letters" or commercial correspondence, but argued that Wilde was in no way ashamed of this letter or of the poetical feelings that were expressed within it. Clarke's differentiation between the "artistic" and "literary" qualities of Wilde's letter and the pedestrian prose that characterized the "ordinary" letters of the average person was intended to give the jury pause over the vast cultural gulf that separated them from Wilde, and to call into question the Court's ability to interpret "works of art." At the conclusion of his opening statement, Clarke challenged Carson to "get from [the literary evidence] anything that in the remotest degree suggests anything hostile to the moral character of Mr. Wilde."

Ironically, it is in the nature of a libel case for the prosecution to adopt a defensive posture. As the defendant, Queensberry had the responsibility to prove Wilde a liar. The burden of proof thus rested squarely with the defense. Once Queensberry's card was read, the prosecution had succinctly summarized the defense's case. Once the libel was stated, Wilde and his counsel had virtually nothing more to say about it, other than to emphatically and repeatedly deny its truth. So although it was Queensberry who was being tried, virtually all the evidence presented in the case was *against* Wilde. Wilde was unfortunately put into the awkward position of being forced to defend his own actions and intentions, all without the benefit of witnesses who could corroborate his own claims.

The prosecution's entire case consisted of the testimony of only two witnesses. The first witness was Sidney Wright, the hall porter at the Albemarle Club, who confirmed the receipt of the card from Queensberry. Wilde was the prosecution's only other witness, and he began imprudently by lying about his age. Clarke elicited selected information about Wilde's career and family which was calculated to establish Wilde's artistic talent, reputation, and social position as a gentleman. Wilde also told of his connection to Lord Alfred Douglas which dated back to 1891, and of his association with the entire Queensberry family. Wilde noted that he was on particularly friendly terms with Lady Queensberry, with Lord Douglas of Hawick, and also with the late Lord Drumlanrig. The fact was that Wilde had been on good terms with the entire family, save the Marquess. Wilde testified that he had not met Lord Queensberry before November 1892, and that he was aware of an estrangement between Queensberry and his son, Lord Alfred Douglas, an estrangement that extended to Alfred's mother as well.[14]

Clarke then asked Wilde about a specific series of incidents which occurred in 1893. At that time, two men, named Alfred Wood and William Allen, attempted to extort money from Wilde in exchange for the return of several letters that Wilde had written to Lord Alfred Douglas, which had been stolen.[15] Wilde recalled that Wood came to him first and returned copies of each of the letters. Wood claimed that Allen had stolen the originals from him. Wood asked Wilde for money, claiming that he needed the money to leave England because Allen had been threatening him with violence, presumably because he had double-crossed Allen. Wilde was melodramatic as he told the Court how he held the letters in his hand as he informed Wood that they were meaningless to him. Lacking meaning, Wilde said, the letters lacked value as well. Despite this, Wilde claimed, Wood's story tugged at his heart-strings, and he gave him £15 with the stated purpose that Wood should go to America and begin a new life. Shortly thereafter, Allen came to see Wilde, and a slightly different scene ensued. Allen argued that "a very curious construction could be put upon [one particular] letter." Allen told Wilde that someone had offered him £60 for the letter, and Allen had believed it might be worth even more to Wilde. Wilde told him point-blank that he ought to have accepted the other person's offer, and again asserted that the letter meant nothing to him, either sentimentally or monetarily. Once Allen realized that Wilde was clearly not going to let himself be blackmailed, he backed down from his demands. Wilde then said that as Allen was walking out the door, a feeling of compassion suddenly overcame him, and he ended up giving Allen a half sovereign. Sometime after that, Wilde explained, the affair ended completely when "a [third] man named Clyburn [sic]" returned the original letters to him. Wilde gave that man (Robert Clibborn) a half sovereign for his trouble as well.

With Wilde's version of the blackmail episode sufficiently explained, the final part of Clarke's examination-in-chief was concerned with establishing the chronology of Queensberry's persecution of Wilde. Queensberry had first met Wilde at the Café Royal in December of 1893, and shortly after that began publicly making disparaging remarks concerning Wilde's character and behavior. Queensberry wrote letters to his son, Lord Alfred Douglas, threatening to disinherit him if he did not drop Wilde as a companion.[16] At one point Queensberry came to Wilde's house and confronted him there, accusing him (and Lord Douglas) of having been kicked out of the Savoy Hotel for disgusting conduct, and threatening Wilde with public scandal if he did not stop seeing his son.[17] Wilde reported another instance in which Queensberry had planned to disrupt the opening-night performance of *The Importance of Being Earnest* at the St. James Theatre. Fortunately, Wilde learned of Queensberry's plan from a mutual acquaintance and had arranged for Queensberry's ticket to be cancelled and for police to be present.[18] Wilde also said he had seen several communications from Queensberry to various third parties which portrayed

Wilde's character in an unfavorable light. The final straw, however, which forced him to seek legal counsel and to initiate this prosecution was the card left at the Albemarle Club. The card contained a direct and public affront to his person which simply could not be overlooked without casting grave aspersions on his own character.

The "Literary Part" of the Case

The "literary part" of the case, as I will refer to it, consisted generally of Carson's cross-examination of Wilde on the nature of the relationship between art and morality. Specifically, Carson sought to elicit Wilde's views on several specific texts which were cited by Queensberry in his plea of justification: two poems written by Lord Alfred Douglas which had been published in *The Chameleon*; a story with a homoerotic theme, entitled "The Priest and the Acolyte," which had been widely attributed to Wilde;[19] two letters written by Wilde to Douglas, the first of which Clarke had already introduced into evidence (quoted earlier); Wilde's own "Phrases and Philosophies for the Use of the Young," which were published in the same issue of *The Chameleon* as the two poems by Douglas and "The Priest and the Acolyte"; and finally, Wilde's novel, *The Picture of Dorian Gray.*

In *The Trials of Oscar Wilde*, H. Montgomery Hyde claims that Carson's cross-examination of Wilde has long been regarded among students of advocacy in the English Courts as a brilliant forensic model, and that Carson's performance was "particularly impressive because he was suffering from an extremely bad cold at the time."[20] While it is undeniable that Carson's strategy was indeed brilliant, and that his tenacity was the perfect foil for Wilde's wit, it must also be noted that Carson's case on behalf of Queensberry was conducted from a position of tremendous advantage. Neither Wilde nor his counsel had any idea that detectives hired by Queensberry had provided Carson with damning evidence against Wilde, and moreover that they had managed to procure witnesses who were willing to corroborate that evidence. So whereas Carson was fully informed and prepared, Wilde and Clarke were operating under the illusion that Queensberry's case was unprovable. Clarke's ignorance was not culpable, however, as he operated, unwisely as he later found out, on the assumption that Wilde had been honest with him.

Although complaints against Wilde's literary works comprised only a very small part of Queensberry's original plea of justification, the "literary part" of the case dominated the majority of the trial proceedings at the Old Bailey. It is thus with good reason that the "literary part" of the case has claimed the lion's share of the critics' attention. However, it is important to note that while this aspect was exciting, entertaining, and highly provocative, it was ultimately not incriminating. The most the literary evidence could do by itself was to create an impression of possible wrongdoing. Despite Carson's superlative performance, Wilde more than held his own. In essence, his position was that the impression of wrongdoing conveyed by the literary exhibits represented little more than the spectrum of the various participants' subjective perspectives and values. However, the validity of Wilde's argument was eventually undermined by the presentation of hard evidence which corroborated the allegations contained in Queensberry's plea of justification. Once Carson dropped the bombshell and revealed that Queensberry had indeed found witnesses who were fully prepared to support his accusations against Wilde, Wilde's case effectively collapsed.

This information begs the question that if the literary aspect of the case against Wilde was indeed superfluous and unrelated to proving Queensberry's allegations, why did Carson not dispense with it altogether and go directly for the kill? Certainly, the literary evidence of the defense's case was instrumental in establishing a connection between Wilde's thoughts and his actions; but thoughts could not be tried in an English Court, could they? Even this, how-ever, was not crucial to Carson's strategy, for he knew that the physical evi-dence and the testimony of the defense witnesses would be truly damning.

The fact that Carson chose to toy with Wilde, as it were, and thereby to pro-long Wilde's inevitable agony, may only concur with Wilde's prescient remark that Carson's handling of the case would be inspired by the repressed hostility of an old rivalry that dated back to their school days at Trinity College.[21.] Yet the fact that Carson elected to attack Wilde's strength—his erudition and his wit—and so to lull Wilde into a false sense of security and superiority before burying him, so to speak, might suggest that Carson had some doubts about his own abilities vis-à-vis Wilde, doubts that could only be conquered by besting him on a fair field of play. It might also indicate an ambivalence on Carson's part in regard to Wilde, stemming from feelings of respect for him or even from the memory of past loyalties. But even though Carson clearly wanted to beat Wilde in Court, perhaps for personal as well as for professional reasons, it was appar-ently not his desire to see him punished for his crime.[22]

Carson began his cross-examination by attacking Wilde's credibility through his vanity, and immediately caught him in a lie about his age. As a former schoolmate, Carson knew exactly how old he was. During Clarke's examination-in-chief, Wilde initially gave his age as thirty-nine. With appar-ent discomfort he was forced to admit that he was forty-one. After thus embarrassing him, Carson alluded suggestively to the disparity between his age and that of Douglas. Douglas was twenty-four in 1895, and had been twenty when Wilde first made his acquaintance in 1891. Carson had no difficulty estab-lishing the fact that Wilde and Douglas had spent considerable amounts of time together at many different places from 1891 through 1895. Indeed, Wilde freely admitted it.

Moving on, Carson questioned him very generally about the contents of *The Chameleon*. Wilde was asked his opinion on some of the other pieces that were published in the issue that contained his "Phrases and Philosophies for the Use of the Young." First were two poems written by Lord Alfred Douglas, "In Praise of Shame" and "Two Loves."[23] After calling attention to the fact that the "two loves" in the poem referred to two boys, and that the last line of "In Praise of Shame" was "I am the love that dare not speak its name," Carson asked Wilde if he saw in the poems any improper suggestions. Wilde candidly said that he saw none whatsoever. Referring to another story in *The Chameleon*, "The Priest and the Acolyte," which recounted the tale of a priest who fell in love with his altar boy, Carson asked Wilde if he felt that *that* story was improper and immoral.[24] The story was far worse than immoral, Wilde retorted, it was "badly written."

Sir Edward Clarke objected to this line of questioning, of course, because Wilde was being examined upon works which he himself had not authored. Justice Collins overruled Clarke's objections, and gave Carson the latitude to examine Wilde on the reasons for his disapproval of "The Priest and the Acolyte," presumably because, in the judge's estimation, it went to the issue of Wilde's character. Carson repeatedly pressed him on the subject of whether or not he felt the story was "blasphemous." Carson's persistent rephrasing of the question flustered Wilde, who grew increasingly agitated at being unable to give a straight answer to Carson's question. Had Wilde responded truthfully to Carson's query—that is, had Wilde said the story *was* blasphemous, that it *was intended* to be blasphemous, and moreover, that he enjoyed reading it—this would have been to admit approval, complicity, prior knowledge of its publication, or all of the above, and thus to play into the hands of the defense. Unable to answer truthfully, Wilde instead dissembled brilliantly, deflecting the intent of Carson's pointed queries while simultaneously answering the questions superficially or tangentially.

In a representative exchange, Carson asked:

"Do you think the story blasphemous?"

WILDE: "I think the end—the death—violated every artistic canon of beauty."
CARSON: "That is not an answer."
WILDE: "It is the only one I can give."
CARSON: "I want to see the position you pose as."
WILDE: "I do not think you should use that."
CARSON: "I have said nothing out of the way. I wish to know whether you consider the story blasphemous?"
WILDE: "I did not consider the story a blasphemous production. I thought it was disgusting."
CARSON: "I am satisfied with that answer. You know that when the priest in the story administers poison to the boy that he uses the words of the Sacrament

of the Church of England?"
WILDE: "That I entirely forgot."
CARSON: "Do you consider that blasphemous?"
WILDE: "I think it is horrible—the word 'blasphemous' is not a word of mine."

As Carson's interrogation continued in the same vein and returned again and
again to the issue of blasphemy, Wilde's patience finally wore out. Although he
never conceded that "The Priest and the Acolyte" was blasphemous, Carson
ultimately forced him to admit that he "disapproved of the tone, the treatment,
and the subject from beginning to end."[25]

This sharply worded antagonistic confrontation briefly unnerved Wilde
even as it seemed to empower Carson. More importantly, perhaps, this
exchange set the pattern for similar exchanges for the duration of Carson's
cross-examination, which lasted well into the following day. Carson would
probe a point or an issue from every conceivable angle, and Wilde would constantly vary his responses, rarely if ever repeating anything he said word for
word. Carson took advantage of Wilde's penchant for creativity, and attacked
every variation of Wilde's replies, trying to exploit the different shades of
meaning inherent in each new word. This tactic was usually quite effective, for
in almost every instance, even though it was Wilde who drew most of the
laughs, it was Carson who scored most of the legal points. Ultimately, however,
it was Carson's tenacity, relentlessness, and persistence that exhausted Wilde
and exposed the transparency of his answers.

Carson's tactic of removing Wilde's statements from their intended aesthetic context, and reading them instead in relation to the "real" world, proved
to be highly effective. No matter how clever, witty, and entertaining Wilde's
responses were, they could not substantively counter the insinuating thrusts of
Carson's questions. Wilde's persistence in making wise remarks can be perceived as an effort on his part to "carnivalize the moment," that is, to devalue
the meaning of the proceedings, and to turn the whole thing into a joke. While
laughter, for Wilde as well as for Mikhail Bakhtin, represented a critical mode
of apprehending the world—in that it momentarily annihilated the world,
destroyed the familiar, and thus permitted a fresh glimpse of reality—when the
laughter subsided, the world, and Carson, were still there, as was the formal rit-
ual which resisted such laughter.[26]

By declining for aesthetic reasons to repeat the same answer twice, Wilde
presented the appearance of constantly changing his mind, and even of contra-
dicting himself. Also, and perhaps more importantly, Wilde's penchant for
altering his responses gave the impression that he was not particularly attached
or committed to any of them. Their terms had an interchangeable quality
about them which suggested to a casual observer that they were of equal meaning and worth, which is to say, meaningless and worthless. The fact that these

responses often came across as having been blithely improvised prevented Wilde from establishing any sort of reference point or guideline whereby those in the courtroom could have judged either the sincerity or the authenticity of his remarks.

Although from his perspective, Wilde was right to have put his faith in his strengths—in his wit, erudition, and linguistic facility—he sometimes exploited his talents in the wrong manner and at inopportune moments. The result was inadvertently to undermine his own cause. Wilde's inappropriate whimsicality was as intellectually amusing to the solidly middle-class court-room audience as his flippant tone and casual disdain for the proceedings were socially and culturally alienating. His efforts to be amusing and entertaining contrasted sharply with the rigorous formality and solemn gravity of the legal proceedings. There were moments, however, when his levity was particularly appreciated by many in the courtroom because it served briefly to ease the accumulated strain and tension that accompanied discussions of the more "unpleasant" aspects of the case. But for all his cleverness and linguistic virtu-osity, it could not have gone unnoticed by those in the Court that Wilde's responses, while attractive in form, were often devoid of meaningful content. Certainly the audience within the courtroom must have recognized hypocrisy when they saw it, no matter how impressively it may have been disguised.[27]

The next set of questions referred to Wilde's own contribution to *The Chameleon*, the "Phrases and Philosophies for the Use of the Young." Some of the axioms quoted by Carson were the following:

> Wickedness is a myth invented by good people to account for the curious
>   attractiveness of others.
> Religions die when they are proved to be true.
> If one tells the truth one is sure, sooner or later, to be found out.
> Pleasure is the only thing one should live for: nothing ages like happiness.
> A truth ceases to be true when more than one person believes in it.
> The condition of perfection is idleness.
> There is something tragic about the enormous number of young men in
>   England who at the present moment are starting life with perfect profiles,
>   and end by adopting some useful profession.

Carson asked Wilde if he thought his axioms were likely to encourage moral-ity among young men. Wilde claimed that his work "never aimed to produce anything less than literature." When asked if he was concerned whether his work had a moral or immoral effect on his readers, Wilde replied that *no* book or work of art ever produced *any* effect on conduct. Probing beneath this state-ment, and subtly referring back to the original libel printed on Queensberry's card, Carson asked Wilde if he merely "posed" at not being concerned about morality or immorality. Wilde said in reply that he did not like the word "pose." Carson pressed him:

> "Pose is a favourite word of your own."
> WILDE: "Is it? I have no pose in the matter. My own work in writing a play or a book is concerned entirely with literature, that is, [with] art. The aim is not to do good or evil, but to try to make a thing which shall have some quality or form of beauty, wit, emotion, and so on."

Wilde played discreetly with the ambiguity of the word "pose," and deployed it rather innocuously to indicate a position, attitude, or world-view, whereas Carson had loaded the term suggestively to imply the adoption of mannerisms or affectations which might enhance or secure a successful impersonation. This line of questioning resulted in an impasse.

Carson turned next to Wilde's novel, *The Picture of Dorian Gray*. He asked whether or not Wilde had revised the story in response to all the criticism that followed its publication in *Lippincott's Monthly Magazine* in July 1890.[28] Wilde replied that he had not, but said that additions had been made. Clarifying the point, Wilde stated that he generally disregarded what was said in the newspapers, and paid attention instead to the only critic whose opinions he valued highly, Walter Pater.[29] Pater had suggested at the time that certain passages were indeed liable to misconstruction, and to address Pater's criticism Wilde had made the additions.

A brief excerpt of Carson's verbal dueling with Wilde on the subject of the novel is worth reproducing in full, if only to provide a sense of the flavor and richness which was typical of their other exchanges as well:

> CARSON: "This in your introduction to *Dorian Gray*: 'There is no such thing as a moral or an immoral book. Books are well written, or badly written.' That expresses your view?"
> WILDE: "My view on art, yes."
> CARSON: "Then, I take it, that no matter how immoral a book may be, if it is well written, it is, in your opinion, a good book?"
> WILDE: "Yes, if it were well written so as to produce a sense of beauty, which is the highest sense of which a human being can be capable. If it were badly written, it would produce a sense of disgust."
> CARSON: "A perverted novel might be a good book?"
> WILDE: "I don't know what you mean by a 'perverted' novel."
> CARSON: "Then I will suggest *Dorian Gray* as open to the interpretation of being such a novel?"
> WILDE: "That could only be to brutes and illiterates. The views of Philistines on art are incalculably stupid."

CARSON: "An illiterate person reading *Dorian Gray* might consider it such a novel?"

WILDE: "The views of illiterates on art are unaccountable. I am concerned only with my view of art. I don't care twopence what other people think of it."

CARSON: "The majority of people would come under your definition of Philistines and illiterates?"

WILDE: "I have found wonderful exceptions."

CARSON: "Do you think that the majority of people live up to the position you are giving us?"

WILDE: "I am afraid they are not cultivated enough."

CARSON: "Not cultivated enough to draw the distinction between a good book and a bad book?"

WILDE: "Certainly not."

CARSON: "The affection and love of the artist of *Dorian Gray* might lead an ordinary individual to believe that it might have a certain tendency?"

WILDE: "I have no knowledge of the views of ordinary individuals."

CARSON: "You did not prevent the ordinary individual from buying your book?"

WILDE: "I have never discouraged him." [Laughter][30]

Carson then read several excerpts from *The Picture of Dorian Gray* and questioned Wilde upon them. After a passage describing the introduction of the artist to Dorian Gray, Wilde was asked if the feeling described therein was a proper or an improper feeling. Wilde said it was the most perfect description possible of what an artist would feel upon meeting a "beautiful personality." Asked if it was a "moral" kind of feeling that one man should have for another, Wilde implied that morality had nothing to do with it. Rather, it expressed a feeling an artist often had toward a "beautiful personality" who enhanced his art and his life. With this statement, Wilde privileged the artist and set him apart from and above the rest of society. Carson probed further:

"Have you ever known the feelings you describe here?"

WILDE: "I have never allowed any personality to dominate my art."

CARSON: "The passage I am quoting says, 'I quite admit that I adored you madly.' Have you ever had that feeling?"

WILDE: "I have never given admiration to any person except myself. [Laughter] The expression was, I regret to say, borrowed from Shakespeare." [Laughter]

It is interesting to compare this version of events from the *Daily Telegraph* to the unexpurgated version given by Hyde in *The Trials of Oscar Wilde*. Hyde's version of the transcript purports to be taken from the original shorthand reports of the trial, and includes the "censored" homoerotic subtext that underlay Carson's questions regarding the contents of *Dorian Gray*. Beginning at the point at which Carson questions Wilde about the feeling of adoring someone madly, Hyde adds the following:

> CARSON: "So far as you are concerned, you have no experience as to its being a natural feeling?"
>
> WILDE: "I think it is perfectly natural for any artist to admire intensely and love a man. It is an incident in the life of almost any artist."
>
> CARSON: "But let us go over it phrase by phrase. 'I quite admit I love you madly.' What do you say to that? Have you ever adored a young man madly?"
>
> WILDE: "No, not madly, I prefer love— that is, a higher form ..."
>
> CARSON: "Never mind about that. Let us keep down to the level we are at now."
>
> WILDE: "I have never given adoration to anybody except myself." [Laughter]
>
> CARSON: "I suppose you think that a very smart thing."
>
> WILDE: "Not at all."
>
> CARSON: "Then you have never had that feeling?"
>
> WILDE: "No. The whole idea was borrowed from Shakespeare, I regret to say— yes, from Shakespeare's sonnets."
>
> CARSON: "I believe you have written an article to show that Shakespeare's sonnets were suggestive of unnatural vice."
>
> WILDE: "On the contrary, I have written an article to show that they are not. I objected to such a perversion being put upon Shakespeare."[31]
>
> CARSON: [repeating] "'I have adored you extravagantly.'"
>
> WILDE: "Do you mean financially?"
>
> CARSON: "Oh, yes, financially! Do you think we are talking about finance here?"
>
> WILDE: "I don't know what you are talking about."
>
> CARSON: "Don't you? Well, I hope I shall make myself very plain before I have done."[32]

Wilde went on to argue that he was not responsible for how other people interpreted the contents of *Dorian Gray*, and maintained his position that books, or persons for that matter, could not significantly influence anybody toward good or evil. Because Dorian's vice remained unspecified throughout the novel, Wilde suggested that whatever vices people detected in Dorian reflected the reader's own vices and not the author's.[33]

Inconsistent with his ruling that permitted Wilde to be examined on his views of "The Priest and the Acolyte"—a piece he had not authored—Justice Collins ruled that Carson could *not* ask Wilde's views on the morality of Joris Karl Huysmans' novel, *A Rebours*, which had been referenced in *The Picture of Dorian Gray*. Carson then passed from Wilde's published writings to the remaining pieces of "literary" evidence against Wilde, which were the allegedly compromising letters written by Wilde to Lord Alfred Douglas retrieved from Clibborn. Carson asked first about the aforementioned letter written from the house at Babbacombe, near Torquay, the letter which began with the words, "My own boy." In a telling exchange, Carson asked Wilde if it was an ordinary letter, and after replying in the negative, Wilde said that it was a beautiful letter. "Apart from Art?" asked Carson. Wilde replied, "I cannot answer apart from Art."[34]

At one point during this exchange, Wilde criticized the manner in which Carson read his letter as "unartistic," and this earned him a rebuke from his own counsel. Carson invited Wilde to read the next letter, but he declined. Carson then read the following letter addressed to Lord Alfred Douglas, written from the Savoy Hotel, and dated March 1893:

> Dearest of All Boys, Your letter was delightful, red and yellow wine to me; but I am sad and out of sorts. Bosie, you must not make scenes with me.[35] They kill me, they wreck the loveliness of life. I cannot see you, so Greek and gracious, distorted with passion. I cannot listen to your curved lips saying hideous things to me. I would sooner—[the *Daily Telegraph* here states that Mr. Carson could not decipher the letter[36]]—have you bitter, unjust, hating. I must see you soon. You are the divine thing I want, the thing of grace and beauty; but I don't know how to do it. Shall I come to Salisbury? My bill here is £49 for a week. I have also got a new sitting-room over the Thames. Why are you not here, my dear, my wonderful boy? I fear I must leave; no money, no credit, and a heart of lead. Your own, Oscar[37]

Carson had only one question, which sought to cut Wilde to the quick: "Is that the kind of letter a man writes to another man?" Wilde answered that he did not know and did not care what some men wrote to other men. He defended the letter as a tender expression of his great admiration for Lord Alfred Douglas, clarifying that it was not, like the previous letter, a prose poem. Carson was content to let this matter drop unresolved, for he had much better cards up his sleeve.

Suggestions of Impropriety

With the "literary part" of the case completed, Carson began to pursue a different line of questioning altogether, a line which began to introduce an ominous note into the proceedings. This new line of questioning appeared to surprise Wilde and shake him visibly, even though, as Hyde notes, he gallantly maintained "his brilliant flow of repartee." Carson returned the discussion to the matter of the attempted blackmail by Wood, Allen, and Clibborn that

Sir Edward Clarke had introduced in his examination-in-chief. Wilde admitted he had been acquainted with Wood long before the blackmail attempt. In fact, he remembered, Lord Alfred Douglas had introduced them. They had had supper together, and Wilde had given Wood a present of £2 on this occasion. Asked about their different social positions—Wood had been an unemployed clerk at the time—Wilde claimed that social positions meant nothing to him. When Carson accused Wilde of having given the money in exchange for "immoral relations" with Wood, Wilde denied the allegation vociferously.

Wilde subsequently admitted giving Wood £30, and then an additional £5 the following day, explaining that Wood had initially come to blackmail him, but had broken down and confessed that he could not go through with it. Wood claimed that he was merely a pawn in the whole scheme, and that he had been put up to it by Allen and Clibborn. Wilde said he had felt sorry for Wood, and gave him the money out of pure kindness and compassion. Asked why he had given Allen ten shillings, Wilde said he gave it in order to demonstrate his contempt and indifference to someone he knew to be a notorious blackmailer.

Again emphasizing the age differential between Wilde and his preferred companions, Carson referred to the "youth," Edward Shelley, who had been at the time of his first meeting with Wilde employed by Wilde's publishers, Messrs. Elkin Mathews and John Lane. Wilde became indignant when Carson asked him if he had "become fond of their office boy." Wilde said he had invited Shelley to dinner in a private room at the Albemarle Club, and Carson mused aloud that the twenty-year-old Shelley must have been a real intellectual treat for Wilde.[38] Wilde admitted there was a connecting door that led to a bedroom, and also that he had not stinted his guest on whiskies and soda, but he denied that any improper conduct had occurred between them.[39] Wilde also stated that Shelley had dined at his home with him and his wife, and that he had taken Shelley to the theatre, to an exhibition, and to various clubs and cafés. He admitted to giving Shelley money on three separate occasions, in amounts of £4, £3, and £5. Because Shelley made continual references to his ongoing financial struggles to support his mother, Wilde said that he had wanted to help in any way that he could.

Next, Carson introduced the name of Alphonso Conway, a "lad" of eighteen who sold newspapers at the pier at Worthing. Wilde said that he and Lord Alfred Douglas had befriended Conway, took him sailing, and bought him lunch. Carson accused Wilde of having been seen "kissing him and indulging in familiarities," a charge that Wilde vehemently denied. When Carson produced an expensive and extravagant silver-mounted walking-stick which Wilde had given to Conway as a present, those in the courtroom were audibly shocked.[40] Asked if he had been fond of the boy, Wilde replied, "Naturally, he had been my companion for six weeks." Wilde also admitted to having outfitted Conway in a brand new blue serge suit and a straw hat with a band of red and blue in order to take him on an overnight trip to Brighton. Wilde explained that the clothes were not meant to make Conway appear as an equal, but were given instead as a reward for having been such a pleasant companion. Wilde recalled that the trip to the seashore had also been intended as a reward, but was unable to remember whether or not their bedrooms interconnected by a "green baize door." At this point, Carson's cross-examination was interrupted as the Court rose for the day. Lord Queensberry was liberated on his own recognizance of £500.

The next morning, Thursday, April 4, 1895, Wilde was recalled to the witness-box, and Carson resumed his cross-examination. Carson began by questioning him about his relations with Alfred Taylor, an acquaintance with whom Wilde admitted he was still on friendly, but not "intimate," terms. Carson was most interested in eliciting information about Taylor's rooms at 13, Little College St., in London. He emphasized the elaborate furnishings, the tasteful decor, and the fact that the curtains were always drawn, even in the middle of the day. Carson hinted that Taylor's heavily perfumed rooms were too "pretty" for a bachelor, and implied that their luxuriousness smacked of a certain "effeminacy." The double set of curtains which never seemed to open suggested that what went on in those rooms required concealing. Wilde was asked if he knew that Taylor kept a lady's costume in his rooms, and he said that he had never actually seen Taylor in fancy dress. Asked if he knew of Taylor's notorious reputation as a procurer of young boys for older men, he said that he did not. Wilde also denied knowing that Taylor had been under surveillance by the police.

He stated that Taylor had introduced him to "six, seven, or eight" young men, all between the ages of twenty and twenty-two.[41] He subsequently said that he later became "intimate" with "about five" of these young men. When Wilde freely admitted that he enjoyed the society of young men, Carson then probed into the nature of this "society," trying to discover what interests Wilde might have shared with the young men. The young men in question were invariably unemployed and from the working classes. They were neither educated, intellectual, literary, nor artistic. Wilde admitted giving all of them money and presents, yet stated adamantly that he had never received anything in return. Startled by this apparent saintliness, Carson asked Wilde what pleasure he received by entertaining grooms and coachmen. He replied that he enjoyed the company of those who were "young, bright, happy, careless, and free. I do not like the sensible [or] the old."[42]

Wilde was asked specifically about his past relations with Charles Parker, an unemployed valet whom he had met through Alfred Taylor. Wilde had generously and lavishly entertained Parker on several occasions in private rooms at some of the finest restaurants and clubs in London. Wilde denied that any improprieties had ever taken place between them. Pressed again by Carson to account for his uncommon attraction to these young men, Wilde reiterated that he recognized no social distinctions and stated simply that he preferred the company of those much younger than himself, especially those who were "idle and carefree." Carson, and probably the rest of the Court as well, were no doubt able to read between the lines, interpreting "idle and carefree," as "hungry, financially desperate, and available." To the great amusement of the Court, Wilde declared that he would much rather spend half-an-hour with a street Arab "than be—well, cross-examined in Court."

Despite all the aspersions that had been cast on Wilde's character, and despite Carson's attempts to insinuate a "business" connection between the activities of Wilde and Alfred Taylor, to this point in the case the defense had failed to present any really damning evidence against Wilde. Naming names was one thing, but ultimately everything reported thus far was nothing more than hearsay evidence. Certainly the Court's suspicions had been raised, but much more was needed. The charge of libel against Queensberry would have been sustained without corroborating testimony from independent witnesses. In a surprise move which stunned everyone in the courtroom, Carson announced that he had such independent witnesses. Carson declared that Charles Parker was present in the building and ready to testify against Wilde. This bombshell reverberated throughout the courtroom and pandemonium temporarily reigned. It was difficult for those in the audience to believe that anyone would step forward voluntarily and incriminate himself in order to implicate Wilde. Certainly Wilde himself seemed to be relying on this fact. However, unbeknownst to Wilde, a deal had apparently been cut between the witness and the authorities.[43]

Carson's announcement instantly transformed the whole tenor of the case. Despite the fact that he himself was not on trial, Wilde's position suddenly appeared very precarious. Carson then began to increase the pressure. In addition to the names of Alfred Wood, Charles Parker, Edward Shelley, and Alfonso Conway, Carson introduced the names of Freddy Atkins, Ernest Scarfe, and Sidney Mavor into the proceedings. Atkins had been a nineteen-year-old bookmaker's tout when he had met Wilde through Maurice Schwabe and Alfred Taylor. Another un-literary, charming, "idle kind of a fellow," Atkins was taken in late 1892 by Wilde on a short trip to Paris, ostensibly to serve as his "secretary." They stayed at a hotel with communicating bedroom doors, and Atkins had his hair curled at Wilde's insistence. Wilde further admitted to being in correspondence with Atkins up to the current year.

Ernest Scarfe had been introduced to Wilde in 1893 by Taylor.[44] Scarfe, a twenty-year-old unemployed clerk, had previously met Douglas at a skating rink.[45] Wilde admitted dining with Scarfe in private rooms at several fashionable establishments, and presenting him with a silver cigarette case. Wilde did not recall having given Scarfe any money. Wilde first met Sidney Mavor in September 1892. Wilde initially denied giving Mavor a silver cigarette case, but after Carson produced the bill of sale, Wilde reluctantly admitted the gift. Mavor had dined with Wilde at the Albemarle Club, and then spent the night in Wilde's rooms despite residing only a short distance away. Asked to explain this strange situation, Wilde said that he had asked Mavor to stay for companionship, and that it had no doubt been a real treat and an amusement for Mavor to have spent the night at such a nice hotel.

The last name brought up by Carson was that of Walter Grainger, who had been just sixteen years old when Wilde met him. Grainger had worked as a servant at a house in the High Street, Oxford where Lord Alfred Douglas had rooms, and had waited on Douglas and Wilde several times at table. Carson asked Wilde if he had ever kissed Grainger, and Wilde made a regrettable slip. Wilde said, "Oh, dear no! He was a peculiarly plain boy. He was unfortunately, extremely ugly. I pitied him for it." Carson exploited the implications of Wilde's response and, through a relentless grilling, was able to shatter Wilde's heretofore remarkable self-restraint. According to Hyde, Carson's interrogation on the point of Grainger's ugliness moved Wilde to the verge of tears.

CARSON: "Was [his ugliness] the reason you did not kiss him?"

WILDE: [angrily] "Oh, Mr. Carson, you are pertinently insolent."

CARSON: "Did you say that in support of your statement that you never kissed him?"

WILDE: [verging on tears] "No, it is such a childish question."

CARSON: "Did you put that forward as a reason why you never kissed the boy?"

WILDE: "Not at all."

CARSON: "Why, sir, did you mention that this boy was extremely ugly?"

WILDE: "For this reason. If I were asked why I did not kiss a door-mat, I should
say because I do not like to kiss door-mats.[46] I do not know why I
mentioned that he was ugly, except that I was stung by the insolent
question you put to me and the way you have insulted me throughout this
hearing. Am I to be cross-examined because I do not like it? It is ridiculous
to imagine that any such thing could have happened in the circumstances."

CARSON: "Then why did you mention his ugliness, I ask you?"

WILDE: "Perhaps you insulted me by an insulting question."

CARSON: "Was that the reason why you should say the boy was ugly?" [Wilde
was here reduced to inarticulate mumbling, and as Hyde says, tried
pathetically to collect his thoughts.]

CARSON: [stridently] "Why? Why? Why did you add that?"

WILDE: [blurting] "You sting me and insult me and try to unnerve me—and at
times one says things flippantly when one ought to speak more seriously. I
admit it."[47]

CARSON: "Then you mentioned his ugliness flippantly? That is what you wish to convey now?"

WILDE: "Oh, do not say that I wish to convey anything. I have given you my answer."

CARSON: "But is that it? That it was a flippant answer?"

WILDE: "Yes, certainly, it was a flippant answer."

This exchange represented both the dramatic climax and the endpoint of Carson's cross-examination. Heretofore an endless fount of cleverness and brilliant repartee, Wilde had been reduced to silence. After several more rather pointless questions, Carson gathered up his papers and sat down, leaving Wilde to sigh with relief. Wilde's counsel, Sir Edward Clarke, then began the difficult task of repairing the damage wrought by Carson. Clarke had been left with few options, however, and was forced to read into evidence the contents of Queensberry's insulting letters to Wilde. These letters also betrayed Queensberry's tremendous antipathy toward several members of his own family. Clarke had not wanted to introduce fresh evidence into the case because it would allow Carson the right to cross-examine upon it, but given his client's position, it was unavoidable.

Clarke re-examined all the literary evidence in the case, as well as the testimony referring to Taylor and the various young men that comprised Taylor's dubious circle, and tried to put a positive spin on it. Clarke's questions to Wilde were of a much gentler nature, and these questions gave Wilde the opportunity to correct and clarify his previous responses. Wilde denied that improprieties occurred with any of the young men, and claimed he had no reason to suspect that any of them had been "immoral" or "disreputable" persons. He maintained that all his actions vis-a-vis the young men in question had been inspired by the noblest motives of charity and kindness. After Wilde had answered several more innocuous questions put to him by the foreman of the jury, Clarke announced the conclusion of the prosecution's case. This struck the Court as a great surprise as well, for everyone seemed to expect that Lord Alfred Douglas, and perhaps even Alfred Taylor, would have been called upon to defend their good names and to testify on Wilde's behalf.[48] The fact that no one at all was called to corroborate Wilde's damaged testimony was taken as a very bad sign indeed by those inside the courtroom. When Wilde was ten minutes late in returning to the courtroom from lunch, speculation was rife that he had bolted for the Continent.[49]

After lunch, Carson's opening speech for the defense made it clear that his client adhered to all the charges he had put forth against Wilde. Moreover, Carson stressed the fact that Queensberry's actions were justified by the nobility of his motivation, which was to save his son, "a young man on the threshold of life," from the corrupting influence of one of the most immoral characters in London. According to Carson, Wilde had been proved to have been associating with disreputable young men who were not his coequals in either age or station. Alfred Taylor, the alleged procurer of "young boys," was described as the "pivot of the case," and characterized as Wilde's "right-hand man." Publicly, Carson interpreted the fact that Clarke called no one to corroborate Wilde's testimony as evidence that there was no one who *could* corroborate Wilde's testimony. This, of course, boldly suggested that Wilde had been lying all along.

Carson pointed to the contradictory positions adopted by Wilde in the witness-box. With respect to his literary works, Wilde presented himself as an elite artist, and argued that his expressions had to be understood intellectually and within the proper aesthetic context. This attitude appeared to contrast sharply with Wilde's alleged behavior with the aforementioned youths, whom he claimed to have befriended out of the egalitarian goodness of his heart. Carson's announcement that Alfred Wood was also present in Court brought another gasp of amazement from the crowd. Wood was prepared to testify that Wilde's treatment of him had been neither noble nor egalitarian. Carson said that Wood's evidence would explain the mystery of the sums of money paid by Wilde for the letters he had written to Lord Alfred Douglas. He had not quite concluded his speech when the Court rose for the second day. Queensberry was again released on his own recognizance of £500.

On the third morning, Carson resumed the opening speech for the defense. He stated that it would be his distasteful duty to bring before the jury a string of young men to tell their "startlingly similar" tales regarding their associations with Wilde.[50] In the middle of Carson's speculations on why Wilde had been tolerated in London for as long as he had been, however, Sir Edward Clarke interrupted Carson and asked Justice Collins for permission to interpose a statement. Alluding to a terrible anxiety over their proposed course of action, Clarke said that the prosecution had failed to prove their case regarding the literary dimension of the proceedings, and admitted that Wilde's letters and literary works could indeed be interpreted in the way that Queensberry and the defense had interpreted them. Noting that there was little likelihood of obtaining a verdict favorable to his client, and more importantly, wanting to avoid at all costs a parade of witnesses which might inflict further damage upon their case and cause irreparable harm to Wilde, Clarke decided to withdraw the prosecution.

Clarke attempted to limit the verdict to "not guilty having reference to the word 'posing.'" Carson was happy to acquiesce to Clarke's motion, but demanded that the record should indicate that the defendant had succeeded in his entire plea of justification. Justice Collins concurred, and confirmed that Queensberry's plea of justification had indeed been proved, and that the publication had been for the public benefit. Wilde had already left the building by a side door when the reading of the verdict led to a "loud burst of applause from the public gallery." Justice Collins was said to have penned a short note to Carson, commending his cross-examination and congratulating him on avoiding "most of the filth."[51]

At the close of the proceedings, a flurry of messages crossed London. Charles Russell, Lord Queensberry's solicitor, immediately sent a note to Hamilton Cuffe, "the Director of Prosecutions, the Treasury, Whitehall." The note read:

> Dear Sir—In order that there may be no miscarriage of justice, I think it is my duty at once to send you a copy of all our witnesses' statements, together with a copy of the shorthand notes of the trial. Yours faithfully, Charles Russell.

Queensberry sent the following message to Wilde:

> If the country allows you to leave, all the better for the country; but, if you take my son with you, I will follow you wherever you go and shoot you.

For his own part, Wilde wrote a letter to the *Evening News*, explaining his refusal to ask Lord Alfred Douglas to testify on his behalf, and once again casting his behavior in altruistic terms:

> To the Editor, It would have been impossible for me to have proved my case without putting Lord Alfred Douglas in the witness-box against his father. Lord Alfred Douglas was extremely anxious to go into the box, but I would not let him do so. Rather than put him in so painful a position, I determined to retire from the case, and to bear on my own shoulders whatever ignominy and shame might result from my prosecuting Lord Queensberry.[52]

Meanwhile, in the Director of Public Prosecutions' office in the Treasury building in Whitehall, the decision was made to apply for a warrant for Wilde's arrest. At about three-thirty in the afternoon of April 5, Detective-Inspector Brockwell of Scotland Yard appeared before Sir John Bridge, the Bow Street magistrate, to apply for a warrant. The *Daily Telegraph* reported that Justice Bridge met privately with Detective Brockwell, two youths whose names figured prominently in the case, and two of Queensberry's counsels, Mr. C.F. Gill and Mr. Charles Russell, and later issued the warrant. After the meeting a warrant was issued for Wilde's arrest on the charge of committing "acts of gross indecency." Hyde suggests that the very humane Justice Bridge did not grant the warrant immediately, but rather that "the magistrate was careful to inquire the time of the boat-train's departure...and to have fixed the time of the application for a quarter of an hour later."[53] At any rate, Wilde had not fled, and instead had sequestered himself in the Cadogan Hotel, where he sat smoking cigarettes and drinking "glass after glass of hock and seltzer" in an effort to calm himself. Wilde was arrested by two policemen at approximately half past six and taken to the Police Court at Bow Street. A consummate host even in an hour of tremendous despair, Wilde was most courteous and gave the officers the least possible trouble. Not far away, at the St. James Theatre, where *The Importance of Being Earnest* was being performed, Wilde's name was quietly being removed from the advertisements and the playbills.

Queensberry, Rosebery, and the Outcome of the Trials

Immediately after Wilde's first criminal trial ended on the afternoon of Thursday, May 2, 1895, Edward Clarke's initial application for bail for Wilde was rejected by Justice Charles. But after a special appeal by Charles Mathews and Travers Humphreys, Clarke's co-counsels, to Baron Pollock, a judge of the High Court, it was determined that bail could not be denied in cases of misdemeanor by virtue of a statute of Charles II.[54] Bail was finally set at the amount of £5,000, which took several days for Wilde and his friends to raise.

On Monday, May 6, the *Star* printed a short paragraph reporting that the Marquess of Queensberry paid an unexpected visit to Holloway Gaol on Saturday evening (May 4) where the two prisoners, Wilde and Taylor, were awaiting the decision of the Treasury regarding a new trial. The object of Queensberry's visit was unknown, but it was reported that he had had an interview with the chief prison officials. H.M. Hyde notes that news was leaked by the Treasury to the effect that the new prosecution against Wilde would be led by Sir Frank Lockwood, the Solicitor-General. The prosecution's enlistment of the Solicitor-General gave a clear signal that the Crown was now making every effort to secure a conviction against Wilde. Hyde reports a conversation between Edward Carson, the advocate who had defended Queensberry at the first trial, and Sir Frank Lockwood, in which Carson asked Lockwood why the Crown would not let up on Wilde, arguing that he had been punished enough. Lockwood reportedly responded:

> I would, but we cannot: we dare not; it would at once be said, both in England and abroad that owing to the names mentioned in Queensberry's letters we were forced to abandon it.[55]

In a letter written shortly after Wilde's conviction, Alfred Douglas claimed that the government's prosecution was motivated by pressure from a cabal of morally righteous members of Parliament—"maniacs of virtue," as he referred to them—who threatened to expose the homosexuality of "certain members of the government," thus (potentially) precipitating a crippling scandal which might cost the Liberal Party the next general election:

> I want to ask Mr. Asquith, then Home Secretary and an old friend of Oscar Wilde, if on a certain occasion he was not informed by Lord Rosebery that unless a second trial was instituted and Mr. Wilde convicted, the Liberal Party would be out of power...the fact is that the Liberal Party contained a large number of men whom I have already called the salt of the earth [i.e., homosexuals].[56] The mock moralists threatened a series of legal actions against members of the government which would have produced a scandal without precedent. If Oscar Wilde was found guilty and punished, there would be an end of the matter. Thus it became necessary to obtain a verdict of guilty at any price. Oscar Wilde's conviction was one of the last acts of the discredited Liberal Party....[57]

It has also been surmised that the pressure on the Crown to convict Wilde at all costs came from Queensberry. Both of Wilde's major biographers, H. Montgomery Hyde and Richard Ellmann, intimate that Queensberry possessed some sort of evidence implicating persons high in the government, and in particular, Lord Rosebery, the Prime Minister. The evidence itself, of unknown form and content, was suspected of containing information confirming a "homosexual" link between Rosebery and Queensberry's eldest son, Francis Archibald Douglas, Viscount Drumlanrig.[58] Drumlanrig, who had served as private secretary to Lord Rosebery, then Foreign Minister, was killed in a mysterious shooting accident on October 18, 1894. Although the death was officially listed as "accidental," suicide was suspected. It was believed by persons in a position to know that Drumlanrig had been threatened with exposure over his alleged affair with Rosebery and had elected instead to take his own life in order to avoid implicating him.[59] Ellmann reports that Queensberry had long been suspicious of Rosebery's influence on his favorite and most successful son (also his heir), and was furious with him because of it.[60]

In a letter written to his first wife's father, Alfred Montgomery, shortly after Drumlanrig's death, Queensberry vented some of his spleen at Rosebery and alluded to his possession of evidence against him:

> Now that the first flush of this catastrophe and grief is passed, I write to tell you that it is a judgement on the whole lot of you. Montgomerys, The Snob Queers like Rosebery & certainly Christian hypocrite Gladstone the whole lot of you/Set my son up against me indeed and make bad blood between us, may it devil on your own heads that he has gone to his rest and the quarrel not made up between him and myself. It's a gruesome message: If you and his Mother did not set up this business with that cur and Jew friend [?] Liar Rosebery as I always thought—At any rate she [Lady Queensberry] acquiesced in it, which is just as

bad. What fools you all look, trying to ride me out of the course and trim the sails and the poor Boy comes to this untimely end. I smell a Tragedy behind all this and have already *got Wind* of a more *startling one*. If it was what I am led to believe, I of all people could and would have helped him, had he come to me with a confidence, but that was all stopped by you people—we had not met or spoken frankly for more than a year and a half. I am on the right track to find out what happened. *Cherchez la femme*, when these things happen. I have already heard something that quite accounts *for it all*. Queensberry.[61]

Queensberry included his addressee as one of those deserving his contempt. H.M. Hyde theorizes that Queensberry suspected Montgomery of being homosexual probably because he was a patron of the arts and a close personal friend of the Prince of Wales, later Edward VII.[62]

Ellmann and Hyde both suggest that the shock of Drumlanrig's death, exacerbated by Queensberry's belief that his son had died in order to avert a homosexual scandal, contributed significantly to his resolve to terminate his son Alfred's relationship with Wilde, at whatever cost.[63] It was shortly after Drumlanrig's death that Queensberry became Wilde's *bête noire*, relentlessly pursuing and persecuting him, hounding him at every turn throughout the entire ordeal of the three trials, and after. It was Queensberry who tried to disrupt the opening-night performance of *The Importance of Being Earnest*. It was Queensberry's insulting card at the Albemarle Club, accusing Wilde of "posing as a somdomite [sic]," which prompted Wilde to initiate the ill-conceived libel suit against him. It was Queensberry, aided by information provided by two actors with grudges against Wilde, Charles Brookfield and Charles Hawtrey, who hired the detectives who uncovered the damning connection between Wilde and Taylor.[64] It was Queensberry who apparently paid each of the witnesses against Wilde £5 per week from the beginning of Wilde's prosecution of Queensberry until Wilde's own conviction.[65] It was Queensberry who, after Wilde had been granted bail following the second trial, hired a small gang of thugs to follow him and prevent him from securing admittance to any hotel in London.[66] And even after Wilde's release from Reading Gaol after serving two years hard labor, it was Queensberry who hired a detective to follow him to France in order to prevent, if possible, a reunion between him and Douglas.[67]

Ellmann claims that it was Queensberry's letters which were read into evidence in the first (libel) trial, introducing the names of Rosebery and Gladstone into the case, that made it impossible for the government to dismiss the case against Wilde.[68] I believe Ellmann is correct in arguing that Queensberry was at the center of the government's "plot" against Wilde, but not for the reasons that he provides. The letter introducing the names of Rosebery and Gladstone into evidence had nothing to do with Queensberry's accusations against Wilde, but rather with Queensberry's anger over a perceived "Rosebery-Gladstone-Royal insult handed to [him] through [his] other son [Drumlanrig]."[69] In his opening statement for Queensberry's defense, Edward Carson was very clear on this point:

> It was clear now that the letters were before the Court and jury, that if ever there were any impression of that kind [that Rosebery or Gladstone had in any way been linked to Wilde], the letters connected with these distinguished individuals were quite distinct from the allegations as regarded Mr. Wilde; that they related to purely political matters, arising out of the fact that one of Lord Queensberry's sons, Lord Drumlanrig, had been made a member of the House of Lords, of which Lord Queensberry was not a member, and felt aggrieved that such an honour could be conferred upon his son while not given to him; and that was why these names of eminent politicians were introduced.[70]

Queensberry's vendetta against Wilde has never been doubted and is therefore relatively easy to document. However, the evidence asserting Queensberry's influence over Rosebery—which I believe represents the heart of the matter—is much sketchier and more circumstantial in character. Nevertheless, the evidence presented in this section is intended to support speculation that such influence existed and was palpably felt by Rosebery—and, more importantly, that such influence had a deleterious effect on both Rosebery and, through him, on the Liberal Party.

It is clear that whatever leverage Queensberry had against Rosebery was deployed tactically to achieve two different aims. At Wilde's first criminal trial, Queensberry's evidence was used to keep his son Alfred's name completely out of the case.[71] This was one instance in which Wilde's and Queensberry's interests were in complete accord. Both wanted to protect "Bosie" (Lord Alfred Douglas), Queensberry as his father, and Wilde as his friend and lover. Queensberry's leverage was used a second time at the end of the first criminal trial to pressure the government to re-try Wilde and, this time, to obtain a conviction.

Our knowledge of Queensberry's role in the threat of blackmail consists entirely of the allegations and insinuations previously listed. With this known, the question then becomes, how much is documented about Rosebery's role? The honest answer is that there is no paper trail or "smoking gun" linking Rosebery to Queensberry in any way. This much said, there may exist evidence of another sort. Curiously, the period of the Wilde trials and the hypothetical pressure from Queensberry coincides with a "breakdown" in Rosebery's health from late February until the end of May. Historian David Brooks attributes Rosebery's nervous collapse—which manifested itself chiefly as depression and insomnia that lasted for months, and which seriously affected Rosebery's performance of his public duties—to an influenza epidemic which laid Rosebery low on February 24, 1895.[72] Peter Stansky notes the possibility that Rosebery's depression stemmed from the effect of a young nephew's death in mid-January.[73] The insomnia was to keep Rosebery out of action—either absent altogether, or distracted and ineffectual when he was present—for most of the month of March. It also forced him to take an additional three weeks off in May and June to go sailing in order to try to repair his health.[74]

My argument is based on the assumption that Queensberry was somehow putting pressure on Rosebery, exactly how and in what way we cannot be sure, but most likely by threatening public exposure of the alleged incriminating evidence. A direct correlation can be found between Rosebery's health, especially his mental health, and the events surrounding the Wilde trials.[75] It can be argued that it was Queensberry's pressure—assuming for the moment that pressure was indeed applied and that it did, in fact, originate from Queensberry—that severely affected Rosebery and made him ill, and that Rosebery's illness manifested itself in physical and psychological symptoms (disorder of the stomach, nervousness, extreme anxiety, depression, and insomnia). The evidence is hardly overwhelming, but it is plausible enough to warrant consideration.

On February 19, 1895, Rosebery threatened to resign as Prime Minister, claiming insufficient support in the House of Commons.[76] Already by this time, however, Rosebery seems to have been suffering from the severe anxiety and acute insomnia that would haunt him until the end of May. The diary of Sir Edward Hamilton, the Assistant Financial Secretary and close friend and confidant of Rosebery's,[77] provides the best independent documentation of the progression of Rosebery's illness. On March 8, 1895, Hamilton reported seeing Rosebery for the first time in quite a while. He told Hamilton he "attributed his illness, or at any rate his predisposition to becoming ill, to the harassing time he had had in seeing all his colleagues individually, & hinting to them that he must be better supported. ..."[78]

A March 10 entry concerned Wilde:

A case of some disagreeable interest came before Newton, the Police Magistrate yesterday. Queensberry had left an insulting card the other day on Oscar Wilde at his club. O. Wilde now desires to bring an action for libel against that eccentric peer; and the case was committed for trial. Queensberry with some reason objects to the intimacy between one of his sons and Oscar Wilde, and in giving expression to his objections he used some opprobrious epithet which can be more easily grasped than written. Oscar Wilde was of course bound to take notice of the insult, and Queensberry declares that he intends to stand by what he said, no matter how difficult it may be to prove justification.[79]

On March 17, Hamilton expressed concern about Rosebery, who was getting only two hours' sleep a night. A doctor, Sir W. Broadbent, said he had never seen such an acute case of insomnia. Broadbent claimed to have identified the cause of the mischief as "a want of nervous muscular power in the stomach which in consequence fails to fulfill its functions properly."

> He [Broadbent] accounts for this stomachic derangement by Rosebery's being given to take his meals alone and reading while eating, with the result that nervous power has gone from the stomach to the brain.[80]

On Sunday, March 31: "Rosebery had a very bad night last night. He only got about 2 hours sleep."

On April 4 and 5, the Wilde trials figured prominently in Hamilton's diary.

> The Oscar Wilde case is proceeding; and some horrible disclosures are being made. It seems impossible that a British Jury can do other wise than acquit Queensberry of defaming O. Wilde's character by imputing to him the character of "posing as" an unmentionable creature. The net seems to be closing round the brute; though he certainly is a very clever one, and has given utterance to many smart sayings in his cross-examination by Carson who is conducting the case for Queensberry with great skill.[81]

> The Oscar Wilde case came to a somewhat unexpected end this morning. Queensberry's Counsel—Carson—was proceeding to discuss the miscreant's relations with the young men, when Sir E. Clarke intervened, and announced that those who were prosecuting felt that, what with the literature involved in the case and O. Wilde's own admissions, they could not expect a verdict. Accordingly the prosecution was withdrawn and a verdict of "not guilty" given. ...The Public Prosecutor was at once communicated with, and a warrant was granted this afternoon with the result that O.W. was arrested in an Hotel in Sloane Street—(he seems to have been acquainted with innumerable London Hotels)—and taken to Bow Street. He is said to have been aware that the Police have been watching him for some time, and that he took proceedings in the hope that he would win in the action which he brought against so crack-brained a man as Queensberry, and that he would thus stave off Police proceedings.[82]

A letter written by George Wyndham, M.P., to his father within forty-eight hours of Wilde's arrest indicates that other well-placed persons knew that the wheels of government had already been set in motion against Wilde.[83]

On April 12, Hamilton recorded that Rosebery had been thinking about suicide, at least abstractly.

Rosebery seems to have made little or no progress; the last 3 nights have been very bad again; and meanwhile Broadbent does nothing and tries nothing. ... He is certainly more depressed about himself than he was—and no wonder. He says he can quite appreciate the feelings which prompt suicide, when night after night he lies awake.[84]

On April 25, the day before Wilde's criminal trial was to begin, Rosebery was feeling better. "If he sleeps fairly well, he is much less depressed about himself."[85] On May 9, two days after Wilde was released on bail following the jury's inability to agree on a verdict, Hamilton's entry described an assembly the previous night at the National Liberal Club, and

... Rosebery, who having already appeared again in public was bound to show himself, came to a full stop in the middle of his speech. Something put him off & he lost completely the thread of his thoughts. It must have been most painful for those who were present.[86]

From May 13 to 20, Rosebery went yachting to get away from things for a week. On May 21, Hamilton recorded that

The Oscar Wilde & Taylor cases have been brought forward again; & unless there is some cantankerous jury-man a verdict is confidently expected this time. A verdict of guilty would remove what appears to be a wide-felt impression that the Judge & Jury were on the last occasion *got at*, in order to shield others of a higher status in life.[87]

And on May 25:

On our return I met F[rank] Lockwood at the station (Charing Cross). He had just won his case and was very triumphant over it. Oscar Wilde & Taylor have each got 2 years with hard labour. I am more glad than I can say about the verdict; for I never had a shadow of a doubt about the guilt of the two beasts, and there was I am sure a very prevalent suspicion abroad that the Government were trying to hush up the case in order to screen certain people of higher rank in life.[88]

On Tuesday, May 28, immediately after the conclusion of the Wilde case, Hamilton's entry begins, somewhat surprisingly, with "Rosebery seems better." After this date, there is no further mention of Rosebery's ill health. While less than airtight, this evidence certainly suggests, from one viewpoint at least, that the (hypothetical) threat of exposure which had privately haunted and publicly paralyzed Rosebery for the previous three months had been lifted, and that he had received a psychological reprieve.

The entries of May 21 and 25 seem to confirm Lockwood's assertion, quoted in Hyde, earlier, that disinformation had been circulating to the effect that the government had somehow conspired to influence the judge and jury during the first criminal trial, in order to acquit Wilde and thereby protect certain unnamed, but important, persons. These rumors suggested (falsely) that it was Wilde himself who was blackmailing the government with incriminating information about the unnamed but highly placed persons, when it seems clear it was the other way around. If the evidence presented here is to be believed, then what was apparently happening was that the head of government was being blackmailed by a peer of the realm. It was not Wilde's acquittal, but rather his conviction that was the aim of the blackmail. That Hamilton and Lockwood were ignorant of who was being protected, and of who was pulling the strings, is probably not as surprising as it might appear to us at first.

One stray piece of evidence that might suggest Rosebery may have indeed shared Wilde's sexual predilections is contained in a curious letter written on December 30, 1897 by the British Consul to Italy, E. Neville-Rolfe, and sent to Lord Rosebery, who was at that time vacationing at his own private villa near Naples:

> Oscar Wilde calling himself Mr. Sebastian Nothwell [sic] is in a small villa at Posillipo [sic] fully two miles from you. He and Alfred Douglas have definitely parted and Wilde lives a completely secluded life. He came here as Mr. Nothwell for some business and I let him suppose that I did not know him by sight. He looks thoroughly abashed, much like a whipped hound. He has written a volume of poems, but no one in London would publish them and I hear he is printing them at his own expense. I really cannot think he will be any trouble to you, and after all the poor devil must live somewhere.[89]

Whether the information regarding Wilde's whereabouts was solicited by Rosebery or volunteered by Neville-Rolfe we cannot be sure. From either point of view, however, this represents an intriguing communique. Clear knowledge of Wilde's relationship with Douglas is evinced in the letter. One must ask what possible trouble Wilde could have been to Rosebery in Naples? They were both far from England. Wilde had been out of prison for only six months and had chosen to live in exile on the Continent, and Rosebery was out of office, but still a public figure. It seems likely that they would have moved in different social circles, especially since Wilde's public disgrace deprived him of the social cachet he had previously enjoyed.

Interpreted benignly, the letter would suggest that any association with Wilde, no matter how casual, might be misconstrued by the public—Wilde was damaged goods, and any contact between the two would have tainted or contaminated Rosebery. A second interpretation would insinuate the opposite—that any contact between Wilde and Rosebery in Naples might be construed *properly*, indicating that it was possible that Wilde and Rosebery were both in Naples for the same reason: not only to escape the cold English winter, but also to take advantage of the prevalence of many young, willing, beautiful boys. At this time, Naples, along with Algiers and other towns in Algeria, was a popular destination for English "homosexuals" and pederasts.[90] Even though Rosebery and Wilde doubtlessly moved in different social circles, it is possible that they moved in the same sexual circles. Ellmann records that before their devastating break-up, Wilde and Douglas spent "most of their time dawdling about the cafes or the beaches, good-humoredly competing for Neapolitan boys."[91] The chance is that if Rosebery were indeed a "homosexual," he may have been engaged in similar pursuits, and if that were so, it would not have been in his best interest to be seen in the company of Wilde.

If we accept for the moment the possibility of Rosebery's "homosexuality," and advance the hypothesis that Rosebery and Drumlanrig had been lovers, and if we accept the likelihood that Queensberry did indeed possess incriminating evidence regarding Rosebery's relationship with his son, we can then advance an alternative explanation for Rosebery's strange behavior from the period following Drumlanrig's death to the end of the Wilde trials. This explanation would suggest that Drumlanrig's death had severe psychological effects on the Prime Minister. If they had been lovers, Drumlanrig's death would be expected to have elicited great feelings of loss and mourning, and possibly even remorse or guilt if Rosebery had felt himself to be responsible for the accident in one way or another. Secondly, if Queensberry was indeed blackmailing Rosebery, this might account for Rosebery's private anxiety, nervousness, dyspepsia and insomnia, as well as his public dysfunction, all of which seem to have abated, coincidentally enough, immediately after Wilde's conviction. I would further suggest that the anger Queensberry felt toward Rosebery (ostensibly as a "homosexual"), as demonstrated in the letter to Alfred Montgomery, was displaced onto Wilde. Certainly there were several inescapable associations that Rosebery shared with Wilde—an aristocratic bearing, cultured tastes, education, a certain effeminacy. After all, Drumlanrig was dead, and for Queensberry the present and perhaps still preventable danger was that posed by Wilde to his still living other son, Lord Alfred Douglas. Queensberry obviously demonized Wilde, and certainly spared no expense or effort to bring pain and humiliation into his life. In all likelihood, Rosebery may have looked upon Queensberry's persecution of Wilde as an object lesson which foreshadowed his own fate if the government failed to convict Wilde. George Ives, an acquaintance of Wilde's and one architect of the nascent "homosexual cause" in the eighteen-nineties,[92] claimed that Rosebery considered doing something to help Wilde (perhaps, from Ives' point of view, as one "homosexual" helping another) during his initial prosecution of Queensberry for libel, but was warned off by Arthur Balfour, the Chief Secretary, who claimed such interference would be a bad political decision which might cost the Liberals the election.[93]

In the general election of 1895, the Liberals did, of course, suffer the worst defeat of any party since 1832. Historian Peter Stansky has commented that the most powerful influences working against the Liberals in the election were those of "Bible, Beer, and Bad Trade."[94] It is interesting to speculate on the possible effect of the Wilde trials on the outcome of the general election. It is clear from the diary entries of Edward Hamilton that Rosebery's political effectiveness was greatly impeded by his physical and psychological breakdown in the crucial months leading up to the election. In effect, his illness had rendered the government a "rudderless ship." While it is clear that Rosebery's government suffered from a general apathy and internal discord long before the Wilde trials, it may also be supposed that a sharp, healthy, and vigorous Rosebery might have been able to make a difference in many of the local elections, especially those that were very close.[95] If pressure was coming from Queensberry, as I have proposed, then it can be suggested that the Wilde trials indeed affected the outcome of the elections, albeit in an indirect manner.

The second, and more direct, effect of the Wilde trials on the outcome of the general election may have had to do with what Peter Stansky identified as the influence of the "Bible." Although this issue will be examined in greater detail in the final chapter, it might be argued at this point that the public spectacle surrounding the Wilde trials—which dragged on for the better part of three months—caused a moral "backlash" against the Liberal Party. The party, for example, may have been perceived as having departed from its Gladstonian heritage of evangelism and temperance and, for that reason, be considered too permissive in regard to moral matters. Or perhaps a majority of the voting public simply felt that the Liberal Government, under Rosebery's tenure, had not been vigorous enough in its prosecution of Wilde. Thus it is difficult to say whether the voters were merely expressing their dissatisfaction with Rosebery's government in particular, or if in fact the results of the general election signified a "protest" vote against the whole sordid state of affairs, over which the Liberal Party had temporarily, and arbitrarily, presided.

2 WILDE'S CRIMINAL TRIALS

The Anatomy of a Sex Crime: The First Trial

After his arrest, Wilde was immediately transferred from Bow Street to
Holloway Prison. He remained there from April 6 until May 7, when he was
released on bail after the jury's failure to reach a verdict after his first trial.
Wilde was remanded three times before the Police Court, on April 6 and 11,
before finally being committed for trial on April 19. Both Wilde and Alfred
Taylor, who had also been arrested, were repeatedly denied bail on each occasion by the magistrate, Sir John Bridge. Justice Bridge refused to grant bail
because of what he termed the "gravity of the offence," and also because the
prosecution's evidence against Wilde and Taylor appeared to be quite substantial.

The first criminal trial began on Friday, April 26. The courtroom was
densely packed, and the crowd was hard to control. Mr. Justice Arthur Charles
presided. The prosecution was headed by Mr. Charles Gill, along with Mr.
Horace Avory and Mr. Arthur Gill. Wilde was defended again by Sir Edward
Clarke, Mr. Charles Mathews, and Mr. Travers Humphreys. Alfred Taylor was
represented by Mr. J.P. Grain. The *Star* described Wilde's appearance as "hag-
gard," and Taylor's as "effeminate."[1] The indictment contained twenty-five
counts under the Criminal Law Amendment Act. Wilde and Taylor were
jointly charged with committing "acts of gross indecency," a relatively recent
category of misdemeanor which included all forms of sexual intimacy between
men, as well as three counts of conspiracy to commit these acts. Because of the
conspiracy charges, the prosecution had thought it best to try Wilde and Taylor
together.

Justice Charles ruled that the counts of indecency and conspiracy could indeed be joined together lawfully in the same indictment. Although no one knew it at the time, this decision would cause problems for Wilde at the end of the trial. Gill's introduction to the case classified Wilde as the principal, and Taylor as the procurer. The twenty-five counts included nine counts alleging misconduct with the brothers Charles and William Parker; three counts of misconduct with Frederick Atkins; five counts of misconduct with Alfred Wood; two counts of misconduct with unknown boys at the Savoy Hotel; two counts of misconduct with Sidney Mavor; one count of misconduct with Edward Shelley; and three counts of conspiracy with Alfred Taylor. Alfred Taylor was charged with attempting the actual felony (sodomy) with both Charles and William Parker.

In his opening statement, Gill declared that

Taylor was familiar with a number of young men, who were in the habit of giving their bodies, or selling them, to other men for the purpose of sodomy. It appears that there was a number of youths engaged in this abominable traffic, and that one and all of them were known to Taylor, who went about and sought out for them men of means who were willing to pay heavily for the indulgence of their favorite vice. It will be shown that Taylor himself was given to sodomy and that he has himself indulged in these filthy practices with the same youths as he agreed to procure for Wilde.[2]

Gill's interrogation of Parker elicited a "revolting" piece of evidence against Wilde. Charles Parker claimed that "He [Wilde] committed the act of sodomy upon me."[3] Parker said Wilde gave him £2 and told him to come back in a week. As it emerged in the trial testimony, Wilde's characteristic pattern of seduction was to take his companion to dinner or supper, ply him with food and wine and liqueurs, talk a lot about poetry, art, and "the old Roman days," and (after having sex) to give him some money and some sort of gift, usually a silver cigarette case. Wilde looked ill after Parker stated that ...

I was asked by Wilde to imagine that I was a woman and that he was my lover. I had to keep up this illusion. I used to sit on his knees and he used to play with my privates as a man might amuse himself with a girl....He [Wilde] used to require [me] to "[toss] him off"... and he would often do the same to me. ... He suggested two or three times that I [should] permit him to insert "it" in my mouth, but I never allowed that.[4]

In an effort to taint Parker's testimony, Edward Clarke's cross-examination tried to smear Parker's character by describing him as a blackmailer and prostitute.

CLARKE: "You understood the practices you were going to enter upon?"
CHARLES PARKER: "Yes."
CLARKE: "When you allowed yourself to be introduced to Mr. Wilde, you knew
    perfectly well the purpose for which the introduction was made?"
CHARLES PARKER: "Yes."[5]

Unfortunately for Wilde's case, Clarke could not portray Parker as a liar.
William Parker (age twenty-two), Charles Parker's elder brother, testified
that he also knew the purposes for which he had been introduced to Mr.
Wilde.

CLARKE: "Did you know when you went with your brother to the dinner that
    you were to be treated as women, and that you were to have money for it?"
WILLIAM PARKER: "That was what I understood."[6]

When asked about a dinner attended by himself, his brother, Wilde, and
Taylor, William reported that

during the meal Wilde often fed his brother [Charles] off his own fork or out of
his own spoon, and that his brother accepted a preserved cherry from Wilde's
own mouth. "My brother took it into his [mouth], and the trick was repeated
three or four times."[7]

On Saturday, Alfred Wood testified that,

During dinner ... Wilde would put his hand inside my trousers underneath the
table and compelled me to do the same with him. Afterwards, I lay on the sofa
with him ... It was a long time, however, before I would allow him to actually do
the act of indecency. [8]

The fourth witness, Frederick Atkins, recalled that at a dinner at Café
Florence, Wilde had kissed the waiter.[9] Atkins also claimed that Wilde had
invited him to Paris. At one point, Atkins recalled going into Wilde's (adjoin-
ing) bedroom and discovering him in bed with a young man whom he recognized as Maurice Schwabe.[10] Clarke's cross-examination of Atkins was done
again with the express purpose of disparaging the character of Atkins, characterizing him, as Wood and the Parker brothers before him, as a blackmailer and
prostitute. A less impeachable witness, however, Mrs. Mary Applegate, the
housekeeper at a house in Osnaburgh Street where Atkins lodged, confirmed
that "one of the housemaids complained of the state of the sheets on the bed in
which Atkins slept after Wilde's first visit," claiming that "they were stained in
a peculiar way."[11]

The next witness was Sidney Mavor, "a youth of some education and better breeding." Mavor admitted to having slept with Taylor, but denied any misconduct between himself and Wilde.[12] Mavor's testimony surprised and annoyed the prosecution because he apparently retracted the incriminating statement about Wilde he had initially given to the police. H.M. Hyde attributes Mavor's disavowal to the influence of Lord Alfred Douglas, who dissuaded him of placing himself on the same level "with scum like Wood and Parker," and encouraged him to deny his earlier statement, attributing his confession to coercion by the police.[13]

Almost by default, Edward Shelley was the prosecution's star witness because he alone among the key witnesses (Charles and William Parker, Wood, Atkins, Mavor) did not belong to Taylor's coterie. Shelley had met Wilde at a publishing office where he was unhappily employed (underemployed, he felt) as a clerk. An aspiring writer, Shelley was enthralled by Wilde's literary reputation. Wilde gave him encouragement about his writing, plied him with liquor until he was drunk, and attempted unsuccessfully to seduce him. The attempted seduction apparently caused Shelley a great deal of psychological distress, for he recalled that "[he] felt insulted, degraded, and objected vigorously" to Wilde's unwelcome advances.[14]

During the cross-examination, Clarke, aided by Shelley's erratic and nervous manner in the witness-box, was able to portray Shelley as "mentally unstable" on the basis of several "morbid and hysterical" letters he had written to Wilde begging for money (ostensibly because he had quit his job and was desperate for cash). The fact that Shelley had once been arrested for physically assaulting his father (who had protested his acquaintance with Wilde) did not help his testimony. However, Shelley's previous employer, a respectable and trustworthy publisher, claimed that it was common knowledge that Shelley had been involved somehow with Wilde, and this testimony gave credence to at least part of Shelley's story.[15]

On Monday, the third day of the trial, the *Star* observed that three workers from the Savoy Hotel, a masseur, chambermaid, and housekeeper, reported seeing Wilde in bed with a boy in his hotel room and confirmed that Wilde's bed sheets had been "stained in a peculiar way."[16]

LEGAL MATTERS

The conclusion of the Crown's case consisted of the reading into the court record of the transcript of Carson's cross-examination of Wilde during the Queensberry libel trial. The prosecution's intention was further to prejudice the case against Wilde by adding insult to injury, and, to this end, they were successful. The Queensberry libel trial, of course, had ended with the embarrassing collapse of Wilde's case, the acquittal and complete vindication of Lord

Queensberry, and Wilde's subsequent indictment on criminal charges. The rereading of the "wonderful series of Oscarisms which made up a day and a half of cross examination unparalleled in the history of the Old Bailey," in light of the graphic evidence that had just been presented at this trial, especially the testimony of Charles Parker and Alfred Wood, caused Wilde to become visibly uneasy in the witness-box.[17] Wilde's witty paradoxes, which had been delivered with such great panache at the Queensberry trial, fell dreadfully flat upon retelling, their cleverness now tinged with an intolerable irony. The intellectual bravado and impeccable self-control Wilde had demonstrated at the Queensberry trial contrasted sharply with his present paralysis. Before the defense could even begin their presentation, the prosecution moved to drop the conspiracy charges against Wilde. This move caught everyone in the courtroom by surprise and provoked a strong objection by Edward Clarke. Clarke protested that if the three counts of conspiracy had been withdrawn in the first place, the defense would have petitioned to have Taylor and Wilde tried separately. Justice Charles considered the motion without ruling on it, and overruled Clarke's objection without, apparently, feeling the need to explain why. The trial subsequently resumed without further fanfare.

Sir Edward Clarke began Wilde's defense by protesting the prosecution's introduction of the Queensberry trial transcript into the criminal trial, and noted that the latest date at which Wilde was charged with "misconduct"[18] was September 1893, a full eighteen months prior to the current trial. In calling attention to these dates, Clarke alluded to the time lag between the commission of the alleged crimes and their subsequent arraignment, and suggested that such a lengthy time span might have had a deleterious effect on the memories of the witnesses.

Clarke's opening speech to the jury had the effect of constructing an unusual "sanity defense" of Wilde. He began by stating the simple fact that Wilde knew of the catalog of charges against him on March 30, several days before the libel trial against Queensberry was to begin. Clarke then argued that armed with such foreknowledge, if Wilde had indeed been guilty of these crimes, he naturally would have left the country. Clarke's logic suggested that any guilty person would shrink from such an investigation as was presently occurring. Clarke suggested that Wilde's openness, candor, and even his very presence in the courtroom should be perceived as providing incontrovertible proof of his innocence. He pointed out that men guilty of the offences with which Wilde was charged generally suffered from "a species of insanity." Clarke suggested that since, by all appearances at least, Wilde was a sane man—educated, talented, respected, honored—and possessed of a great career and a respectable family, he would have to have been "insane" to be guilty and yet to risk his family and career by facing a public investigation. Therefore, Clarke concluded, if the Court believed Wilde to be sane, then the Court would have to find him innocent as well.[19]

Clarke explained to the Court that Wilde's suit against Queensberry was only withdrawn on advice from counsel (himself, Mr. Mathews, and Mr. Humphreys), and not because Wilde had wanted to quit. At the time, Clarke felt "it was perfectly obvious that the jury would not convict Lord Queensberry (a well-known peer of the realm) of a criminal offence" and therefore that there was no point in continuing.[20] Clarke made it perfectly clear that he himself bore complete responsibility for the present case coming before the court. In the witness-box, Wilde categorically denied all allegations of indecent behavior made against him by Charles Parker, Wood, Atkins, and Shelley. He un-hesitatingly admitted being acquainted with them, but vehemently denied any improprieties.[21] Alfred Taylor was then called to testify, and he also categori-cally denied all charges of gross misconduct. He said he knew what the counsel for the prosecution (Gill) meant when alluding to "the depraved life of certain lads," but denied that he had contributed to this depravity in any way.

Clarke's summation for the defense asked the jury to set aside whatever prejudice they might feel toward the defendants, and toward the nature of the alleged crime, and consider only the evidence that had been presented to them at this trial. He argued that trying the prisoners jointly had constituted a cruel hardship for his case, since each defendant had been charged with different crimes, and the only charge which had linked the defendants together (con-spiracy) had now been dismissed by the prosecution. He stated that the prose-cution's maintenance of conspiracy charges against Wilde and Taylor until late in the case caused his client great embarrassment. He dismissed the frivolous-ness of the prosecution's accusations and the irrelevance of their arguments, and argued that the prosecution's attempt to judge Wilde by books and articles that he had not written was simply unfair. Clarke suggested that the prosecu-tion's key witnesses, and especially Charles Parker, Alfred Wood, and Frederick Atkins, constituted a "tribe" of blackmailers who were bound together by the "cowardice of guilt" and argued that the jury should not convict on the uncor-roborated evidence of men such as these.[22] Moreover, he argued that by clear-ing Wilde, "one of *our* most renowned and accomplished men of letters of today," from this fearful imputation, "[the jury would] clear society of a stain as well."[23]

Mr. Gill had the last word. He pointed out that the verdict of the Queensberry libel trial demonstrated that Queensberry's plea of justification was proved and that the libel had indeed been published for the benefit of the public. In defending the credibility of his own witnesses, Gill argued, "what purpose would these witnesses have in testifying if their stories were not true?" They have each incriminated themselves "of shameful and infamous acts" in order to furnish this testimony.[24] Gill appealed to common sense and claimed that no independent corroboration of the alleged acts was possible because these acts were naturally furtive and secretive. He contended that the stories told by Parker, Wood, and Atkins were similar enough to act as an associative form of corroboration. In addition, Mr. Gill argued that the gifts, dinners, and visits to the hotels should be construed as physical evidence which gave further credence to their stories.[25] Gill's final words evoked a medical model of cultural crisis, and depicted Wilde as an infectious agent which needed to be exorcized from the healthy social body:

> You (the gentlemen of the jury) owe a duty to society, however sorry you may feel yourselves at the moral downfall of an eminent man, to protect society from such scandals by removing from its heart a sore which cannot fail in time to corrupt and taint it all![26]

On May 1, the *Star* reported that, "it is long since any Old Bailey trial has lasted five days, and longer [still] since there has been so much uncertainty as to the issue of a case of equal importance with this." This comment can be seen as an indication of just how complex and confused the central issues in the trial had been, especially to those present in the courtroom.[27]

In his summation, Justice Charles directed an acquittal on charges of conspiracy against both prisoners, and admonished the jury to prevent preconceived opinions from influencing their decision. He also reminded the jury that both defendants were of good education and high intellect. The judge ruled that the verdict of the Queensberry libel trial was in no way binding on the jury in this trial. In regard to the "literary" aspects of the case, Justice Charles instructed the jury to "confuse no man with the characters of the persons he creates," and stated that "The Phrases and Philosophies for the Use of the Young" which prefaced *The Picture of Dorian Gray* might be construed as "cynical, amusing, or silly, but never wicked."[28]

In essence, Judge Charles dismissed the bulk of the evidence from the Queensberry libel trial, considering it as largely irrelevant to the proceedings at hand. Also irrelevant were Wilde's benign interpretations of the two sonnets by Lord Alfred Douglas, "In Praise of Shame" and "The Two Loves," which were alleged by the prosecution to have expressed immoral and unnatural tendencies. His lordship did want the jury to consider the two letters written by Wilde to Douglas, which the prosecution regarded as embodying the most horrible and indecent character. Justice Charles said the evidence of Shelley would also have to stand despite Shelley's "semi-intoxicated" performance in the witnessbox. In the judge's opinion, Shelley's evidence was sufficiently corroborated by his employer, and moreover, Shelley was not tainted with the sorts of offences with which Wood, the Parker brothers, and Atkins were charged.

As to Freddy Atkins' testimony, the judge told the jury to disregard Atkins' trip to Paris in the company of Wilde and the events that transpired there, because they were out of his court's jurisdiction. The relevant charge concerned the alleged agreement between Taylor and Wilde at the Café Florence to get hold of Atkins for immoral purposes. Charles ruled that although Atkins had proved himself to be a most unreliable, untruthful, and unscrupulous witness in regard to other matters in question, his testimony as regards this specific event ought to be accepted by the jury.[29]

Passing to the charges regarding Wilde's alleged misconduct with two unknown boys at the Savoy Hotel in March of 1893—which he termed "the most unpleasant part of an unpleasant case"—Justice Charles dealt with this "repulsive" phase of the case conscientiously and with consummate attention to every "disgusting" detail. Faced with the corroborated testimony of the hotel employees as to the indications on the sheets that "conduct of the grossest kind had been indulged in,"[30] his lordship advanced the possibility of an innocent explanation for the stains (diarrhea). Given the gravity of the alleged affront, Justice Charles found it strange and remarkable that there had been so little attempt at concealment on the part of Wilde, as well as no attempt to publicize it by the hotel staff. The judge left it to the jury to decide if the hotel servants were telling the truth.

The jury also had to decide whether or not Lord Alfred Douglas had introduced Alfred Wood to Wilde for immoral purposes. Evidence against Taylor confirmed that his apartment had been for some time under police surveillance, and that it was a well-known haunt for "Piccadilly young men," such as Wood, Atkins, and Parker. Justice Charles noted that Charles Parker's story had been confirmed by his brother William, who was deemed a reliable witness since no charge of blackmail had been levelled against him. Also confirming Parker's association with Wilde was Mrs. Margery Bancroft, a woman of "good reputation" and a fellow lodger at Parker's apartment in Chelsea. Justice Charles reiterated that Wilde admitted the acquaintance, but denied the "utterly indescribably filthy action" which Parker said had taken place there.

The Star was critical of Justice Charles' summation, reporting that "the summing-up became so overloaded with detail, being practically a repetition of the whole of the evidence which has been given in the case, that it is doubtful whether the effect was not rather to confuse than to elucidate the facts."[31] After noting how important this case was to the public at large, the judge suggested that the social class of the defendants be remembered in their deliberations. Justice Charles reminded the jury that Wilde was "a man of highly intellectual gifts, a person whom people would suppose to be incapable of such acts as are alleged." Taylor also, "though nothing has been said about his abilities, has been well brought up [and] belongs to a class of people in whom it is difficult to imagine such an offence."[32]

The summation concluded, the jury was instructed to consider the evidence and to find the defendants innocent or guilty in regard to four questions: Did Wilde commit indecent acts with Edward Shelley and Alfred Wood and with a person or persons unknown at the Savoy Hotel or with Charles Parker? Did Taylor procure or attempt to procure the commission of these acts? Did Wilde and Taylor together, or either of them individually, attempt to get Atkins to commit indecencies? Did Taylor commit indecent acts with Charles Parker or William Parker?[33] Given the confusion of the case, it was expected by many in the courtroom that the jury would have great difficulty in arriving at a verdict. The jury deliberated three hours and forty-five minutes before they agreed to disagree on three of the four questions. They returned a formal verdict of "not guilty" on the count relating to Atkins, but could reach no consensus on the other three questions. It was decided by mutual consent between Justice Charles and the legal counsels to re-try the case in the next Central Criminal Court Sessions, beginning May 20.

The Trial Redux: Wilde's Second Criminal Trial

In many ways, Wilde's second criminal trial replicated the first, except for the outcome. The same witnesses testified, and no new evidence was presented either against Wilde, or on his behalf. Clarke's defense of Wilde also underwent no serious alterations. In several other respects, however, the two trials contrasted remarkably. In particular, there were three crucial differences which, in the end, can be said to have accounted for Wilde's conviction. The first was the substitution of Sir Frank Lockwood, the Solicitor-General, for Charles Gill. While Gill was a very able prosecutor, Lockwood had a reputation for ruthlessness, and an even more aggressive prosecutorial style. His assignment to the case was a clear signal to all that the Crown was serious about convicting Wilde. The second difference was the replacement of the congenial and impartial Justice Charles with Sir Alfred Wills, a seventy-seven-year-old expert on circumstantial evidence, a scholar in the fields of mathematics and classics, and an accomplished mountaineer, who also happened to share a Tite Street address with his most famous defendant.[34] It became apparent very early on in the case that the alleged crime was particularly abhorrent to Justice Wills, and he was in several instances less than discreet in his support of the prosecution's case. He rather gleefully admitted all the evidence that Justice Charles had disallowed, and his summation of the case virtually commanded the jury to find Wilde guilty. The third major difference between the two trials was that Wilde and Alfred Taylor were tried separately. Even more importantly, however, was the fact that Taylor was tried first. Wilde's trial was held immediately after Taylor had been convicted.

On Monday, May 20, the *Star* reported that it was by special arrangement that Mr. Justice Alfred Wills was appointed to preside over the second trial of Oscar Wilde. The Solicitor-General, Sir Frank Lockwood, Q.C., M.P., Mr. H.

Sutton, Mr. Charles Gill, and Mr. Horace Avory were the prosecutors, and, as in the previous trial, Mr. Edward Clarke, Mr. Charles Mathews, and Mr. Travers Humphreys defended Wilde. Mr. John P. Grain defended Alfred Taylor.[35] The *Star* referred to Lockwood, Gill, and Avory as a most "destructive trio in a Treasury prosecution," whereas Clarke, Mathews, and Humphreys were termed "as powerful a defensive combination as could be desired."[36]

Sir Edward Clarke, believing Taylor had become a liability for Wilde, wanted Wilde and Taylor tried separately. The Solicitor-General apparently concurred with Clarke's assessment of Taylor, for he wanted Wilde and Taylor tried together so they could incriminate each other as they had in the previous trial. Justice Wills, however, had already made up his mind on this matter and decided it would be best for all concerned if the two prisoners were tried separately. Lockwood argued that Taylor should be tried first, but Clarke protested, claiming—rightly, as it turned out—that a negative verdict against Taylor would unduly prejudice the jury against Wilde. Ignoring Clarke's protests, Wills ruled that Taylor would be tried first. Then Wills refused Clarke's further request to postpone Wilde's trial until the next criminal sessions in order to let some time pass between Taylor's trial and Wilde's. Wilde was then released on the same bail as before, and Alfred Taylor's trial began at once.

The testimony in the second trial was as lurid as in the first. Highlights of the first day included Charles Parker's testimony that "Taylor kept him in his rooms for a whole week, during which time they rarely went out," and that Taylor called him "Darling" and referred to him as his "little wife." Taylor told Parker he would never want for cash, and that he (Taylor) "would introduce me to men prepared to pay for that kind of thing." Evidence of indecent acts with men other than Wilde was given by Parker as well.[37] William Parker corroborated his brother's evidence about the introduction to Wilde, and his (Wilde's) selection of "Charlie" as "the boy for me." Alfred Wood confirmed that he had been introduced to Wilde at Taylor's "snuggery" at Little College Street by a third person, subsequently revealed to have been Lord Alfred Douglas.

Although Sir Edward Clarke had no *locus standi* before the Court with respect to the case against Taylor, he remained at the solicitor's table and closely watched the proceedings. A great deal of evidence implicating Wilde was presented during Taylor's trial, and this evidence was well publicized in the newspapers. A waiter at the Savoy Hotel testifed to having seen young men in Wilde's private room. Taylor's landlady identified both Charles Parker and Wilde as having visited Taylor. Two telegrams from Wilde to Taylor putting off appointments with young men were found among Taylor's possessions. Finally, a second landlady of Taylor's also reported seeing Wilde at Taylor's lodgings.

The Solicitor-General's examination succeeded in flustering and intimidating the usually calm and self-possessed Alfred Taylor. Lockwood introduced evidence exposing Taylor's relationship with a man named Charles Mason, whom Taylor, dressed as a woman, was alleged to have "married" in a mock ceremony. Also introduced into evidence was a passage in what Lockwood described as an "extraordinary" letter from Mason to Taylor which read in part,

> ... I have not met anyone yet. Come home soon, dear, and let us go out sometimes together. Have very little news. Going to a dance on Monday and to the theatre to night. With much love. Yours always, Charles.[38]

Taylor argued that the meaning of the words depended upon how they were read, while Lockwood claimed that such language of intimacy and endearment between men was a clear and obvious indicator of an improper relationship. Taylor freely admitted sleeping in the same bed as Mason, but denied any "improprieties" took place between them.

The *Star* reported that Mr. Grain believed Taylor had emerged triumphantly from the trying ordeal.[39] Grain thought the jury would acquit the defendant because the key evidence lacked independent corroboration, and because the "lads" themselves were generally considered unreliable witnesses. With the right of the last word, however, Lockwood impressed upon the jury the fact that such acts can never be corroborated because by nature they are performed furtively and in secret. In his scathing final comments, Lockwood denounced Taylor's "unnatural affections," and urged the jury to make an example of him.[40] In his own review of what he certainly believed to be an open-and-shut case against the defendant, Justice Wills left it up to the jury to decide whether or not there was corroboration for the acts of indecency. The jury deliberated only forty-five minutes before returning a verdict of guilty on the charges of committing "acts of gross indecency." It disagreed only as to the charge of Taylor's "procuring" for Wilde. Taylor's sentencing was postponed until after Wilde's trial, which was to begin the next day with a new jury.[41]

On Wednesday, May 22, the *Star* began its coverage of Wilde's trial by noting how unusual it was for anyone to make three appearances at the Old Bailey during three consecutive sessions and before three different judges. The bad news for Wilde was that his co-defendant at the previous trial had just been convicted of an "abominable" crime, and that virtually everyone in London knew about it, including, presumably, the members of his own jury.[42] The good news was that his own charges had been modified and reduced. The conspiracy charge had been dropped, and the new indictment contained only eight counts, down from twenty-five at the first trial. These alleged that Wilde unlawfully committed indecent acts with Parker (four counts), Wood (one count), certain persons unknown at the Savoy Hotel (two counts), and Shelley (one count). A new jury, "a dozen potent, grave, and reverend signors," had been empanelled that morning. In the dock,

Wilde was described as looking ill—"anxiously gnawing at his fingers and nervously playing with his gloves."[43]

Lockwood began the case by reversing the order of witnesses in the previous trial and putting first in the witness-box Edward Shelley, the only witness "untainted" by association with Taylor, and whose evidence would be corroborated by his employers. Shelley's testimony was much the same as it had been at the previous trial. The main difference between Gill's and Lockwood's handling of Shelley's testimony was that whereas Gill had been concerned with eliciting detailed descriptions of the "indecent acts" themselves, Lockwood chose instead to emphasize the fact that great effort was made to commit the acts in secret, and then later to conceal them. During Lockwood's examination of Shelley, Queensberry entered the courtroom and was allowed to take a seat at the end of the judicial booth. No doubt the irony of this act was not lost on Wilde, for Queensberry's place near the judge has to be interpreted as an actual and symbolic representation of his tremendous influence over the outcome of the case.

Clarke's cross-examination of Shelley in the second trial, as in the first, attempted to portray the witness as mentally unbalanced, with similar success. The testimony of the next witness, Alfred Wood, again raised the question of the nature of the relationship between Wilde and Douglas, and their mutual connection with Taylor. The *Star* reported that the Solicitor-General was beginning to inquire about the terms of Wilde's relationship with Douglas, but someone, presumably Justice Wills, objected to this line of questioning, claiming that it had been forbidden ground all through the trials.[44] It can be assumed that Queensberry's power was felt in this instance as well.

On Wednesday, May 22, the carnival atmosphere surrounding the Wilde trial was enhanced by a sideshow involving the Marquess of Queensberry and another of his sons, Percy, Lord Douglas of Hawick (Alfred's elder brother), both of whom were arraigned on charges of assaulting each other on the streets in Piccadilly. Before the magistrate, Lord Douglas accused his father of repeatedly sending obscene letters to his wife and refusing to desist, and argued that a physical confrontation was his final recourse.[45] Queensberry claimed the assault was unprovoked, although he surely must have felt betrayed by Percy's role in securing Wilde's bail. The case was quickly dismissed by the magistrate, who released both parties on their own sureties of £500 and the promise to keep the peace for six months.

On Thursday, May 23, the *Star* reported that the case had reached a dull stage, because all the accomplices in the alleged acts of indecency had testified the day before.[46] The evidence presented this day concerned the reputed incidents at the Savoy Hotel, in which the alleged accomplices were unknown. Clarke managed to discredit the chambermaid's testimony because she usually wore eyeglasses but for some reason she had not worn them the morning she was supposed to have seen a boy in Wilde's bed.

Clarke's strategy with the hotel witnesses was to point out the length of time that had transpired between the alleged incident and the present trial, a period of two years, to cast doubt upon their recall of details, and to elicit discrepancies in their testimony. This tactic worked with some, but the testimony of others remained unshaken.

Lockwood's reading into evidence of the transcript of the Queensberry libel trial rapidly cleared the courtroom, for this was certainly old news to everyone who had been following the case. The Solicitor-General had promised to confine his reading to the passages which referred specifically to Wood, Shelley, Parker, and Taylor, but he also managed to introduce into evidence those passages which concerned the verbal sparring between Wilde and Carson about Wilde's correspondence with Alfred Douglas. This presentation concluded the case for the prosecution, and Edward Clarke rose to begin Wilde's defense.

On the basis of the evidence that had been presented, Clarke argued that the prosecution had no case because there was no independent corroboration of the evidence. Justice Wills, as an expert on circumstantial evidence, refuted Clarke's assertion and ruled instead that the condition of the hotel rooms themselves furnished sufficient corroborative evidence to warrant the charge of misconduct. The fact that a man of Wilde's position was found in bed with a boy was deemed by Wills so utterly unusual that very little additional evidence was needed to send the case to the jury. Wills also found the chambermaid's evidence sufficiently corroborated. Justice Wills left it to the jury to decide whether or not Wood's testimony was corroborated. In a move that surprised both the Court and the defense, Lockwood withdrew the complaint regarding Shelley on the grounds that there had been too many contradictions in his testimony. This action greatly pleased Wilde and Clarke, for it was generally believed that because Shelley was untainted by implications of blackmail, his evidence constituted the strongest part of the prosecution's case.[47]

Before calling on Wilde to testify on his own behalf, Clarke, in a fine speech, admonished Lockwood not to use his power of the last word to take unfair advantage of the case. He urged Lockwood to remember that his interest in this case was as a public servant and not as a private citizen, and therefore his duty was not to obtain a conviction by any means necessary, but rather to present the facts of the case as clearly and impartially as possible.[48] In the witness-box for the third time, Wilde denied once again any and all acts of impropriety. In his cross-examination, Lockwood then reintroduced the "art and morality" debate from the Queensberry libel trial. In his interpretation of Wilde's two letters to Douglas, Lockwood emphasized the indecency of Wilde's fantastic, extravagant language. He probed delicately into Wilde's relationship with Lord Alfred Douglas, and forced him to repeat aloud the charge made against him by Lord Queensberry: "posing as a sodomite."

Lockwood stressed the importance of Wilde's abandonment of his prosecution of Queensberry, and suggested that this withdrawal constituted an admission of guilt—a suggestion which Wilde did his best to refute. When Lockwood pressed him about his relationship with Taylor, Wilde stated that the knowledge that boys habitually shared Taylor's bed was not shocking to him in the least. When asked about his frequent association with social inferiors, Wilde responded that he "had no sense at all of social differences," and that he was "enormously fond of praise and admiration," no matter what the source. He said it pleased him greatly to be made much of by his social inferiors.[49] Nothing new was elicited about Wilde's relationship with Parker, and Wilde equivocated about the stained bed linen at the Savoy Hotel. He argued hypothetically that if indeed the stains were there, "they were not caused by the way the prosecution has most filthily suggested."[50]

In his final statement on Wilde's behalf, Sir Edward Clarke began with praise for Lockwood's fairness in cross-examining Wilde. Clarke's argument asserting Wilde's innocence was essentially the same as that advanced in the previous trial, minus the "sanity defense." Clarke argued simply that the directness and eloquence of Wilde's responses, along with his willingness to answer any and all questions put to him, must—despite appearances to the contrary—stand as evidence of Wilde's good character, and should be interpreted as evidence of his innocence as well. "Good character," in turn, was implicitly equated with civic virtue, "manliness" and adherence to normative heterosexual patterns of behavior and desire. Clarke contrasted Wilde's integrity and respectability with the tainted character of those who had given evidence against him. Strangely enough, Clarke's ultimate appeal was to posterity. He ended his impassioned closing speech by damning the Press and waxing lyrical about Wilde's literary reputation and its promise of future contributions to the greater glory of Britain:

> If on examination of this evidence you see that it is your duty to say that this charge has not been proved, I am sure you will be glad that that brilliant promise which has been clouded by these accusations, that light of reputation which was nearly quenched in the torrents of prejudice which a few weeks ago were sweeping through—I will not say our courts, but through at all events our Press—you will be glad that your verdict has saved that reputation from absolute ruin, and has left him a distinguished man of letters, a brilliant Irishman, to live among us a life of honour and repute, and to give, in the maturity of his genius, gifts to our literature of which we have only the promise in his brilliant past. [Cheers][51]

The fourth, and last, day of testimony took place in a less crowded and less oppressive courtroom than the previous day, when Wilde's cross-examination attracted the sensation-seekers. The *Star* noted that the present trial was the second important case in which Lockwood was brought in especially to exert his special power of "the last word."[52] Lockwood's influence had been effective in the first, a murder trial, and the defendant was found guilty and subsequently hanged. The final day was marked by several sharp exchanges of temper between Clarke and Lockwood. Clarke criticized Lockwood for providing "rhetorical descriptions" of what had never been proved in evidence, especially pertaining to Lockwood's assertion that there existed an intimate friendship between Wilde and Taylor. Lockwood argued speciously that Taylor and Wilde called each other by their Christian names, and that no greater proof of intimacy could ever be required. Lockwood then attempted to draw parallels equating Wilde's behavior and character with the behavior and character of Taylor, who had just been convicted. He argued that however great Wilde's literary reputation and future potential might be, it was certainly irrelevant to the proceedings at hand, and thus ought to carry no weight with the jury. Lockwood suggested that the jury should treat both men (Wilde and Taylor) "equally," in the double sense of that term.

Referring to the letters from Wilde to Douglas containing expressions of affection and endearment between men, Lockwood adamantly stated that "this sort of thing" was not appreciated in Britain. He argued that the letters could be interpreted in only one way, which was at a level "somewhat lower than the beasts." The Solicitor-General rejected Clarke's argument that the most serious issue in the case concerned the attempted blackmail of Wilde by Wood. Lockwood maintained instead that

> ... the genesis of the blackmailer is the man who has committed these acts of indecency with him, and the genesis of the man who commits these foul acts is the man who is willing to pay for their commission. Were it not for men who were willing to pay for the vice, there would be no blackmail.[53]

Lockwood reasoned that Parker and Wood had nothing to gain by giving evidence, and much to lose. He also claimed that the workers from the Savoy Hotel had no reason to lie, and therefore that they ought to be believed.[54]

If anything, Justice Wills' summing-up of the case was even more prejudiced, self-righteous, and arrogant than Lockwood's.[55] In one final bit of irony, the last day of the trial, Saturday, May 25, was the Queen's birthday as well, and thus the air was full of patriotic fervor as Wilde was being denounced by Justice Wills.[56] The judge's first comment to the jury was to disregard Wilde's social position, his education, and his literary accomplishments. Wills maintained that the decision in favor of Queensberry in the libel trial *would have been reached* even if the prosecution had not withdrawn, and hence that it *was already proven* that Wilde had "posed" as a sodomite.[57] The judge expressed the opinion that the prosecution in the previous trial of Wilde had botched the case by introducing the conspiracy charges and thus confusing both the issues and the jury in the process. When a member of the jury questioned the extent of Lord Alfred Douglas' involvement in the case, Justice Wills equivocated and dissembled in a very judicial manner, and in that way managed successfully to evade the issue altogether.[58] Wills also avoided discussing the literary merit of Wilde's letters to Douglas, but based on their content, he decreed that Queensberry was right to have taken the course of action he did in order to protect his son from Wilde's "poisonous" influence.

Wills left it up to the jury to determine whether Wilde's relationship with Parker was innocent or not, but made it a point to express his belief in the aphorism that "a man must be judged by the company he keeps." His Lordship also expressed the opinion that he could think of no valid economic reason to explain why two men as wealthy as Taylor and Wilde would ever have to share their bed with other men. The judge lamented the fact there was no medical evidence to corroborate the testimony of the Savoy Hotel employees.[59] The jury was finally instructed that the "question they must answer was whether there was evidence of guilt or suspicion only."[60]

On Monday, the *Star* reported that the end of the trial was a tragic surprise, and noted how unusual it was that so many of the most sensational Old Bailey trials terminated on a Saturday afternoon.[61] The *Star* commented on the fairness of the summing-up, which had seemed to minimize the evidence of crime, while "condemning the pose [and] the dalliance with filth." The newspaper reported that the opinion inside the courtroom was that there would be a second disagreement, and that this time Wilde would be permitted to go free. It was not to be, however, as Wilde was found guilty of the seven remaining counts, the count concerning Shelley having been previously dismissed.[62] At the reading of the verdict, Wilde's face was reported to have resembled that of a corpse, and there was a great commotion as cries of "Shame" and murmurs of approval filled the courtroom.

Taylor was immediately brought into the courtroom from a holding cell, and stood together with Wilde for the sentencing. Justice Wills' relatively colorless summation had not prepared the courtroom for the scathing denunciation that accompanied the sentencing. He stated,

Oscar Wilde and Alfred Taylor, it has never been my lot to try a case of this kind before which has been so bad. One has to put a stern constraint upon oneself to prevent oneself from describing in language I ought not to use the sentiments which must arise in the breast of every man who has a spark of decent feeling in him, and who has heard of details of these two terrible trials. That the jury have arrived at a correct verdict I cannot persuade myself to entertain the shadow of a doubt, and I hope that at all events those who sometimes imagine that a judge is half-hearted in the cause of decency and morality because he takes care that no prejudice shall enter into a case may see that that is consistent at least with a stern sense of indignation at the horrible crimes which have been brought home to both of you. People who can do these things must be deaf to every sense of decency which can influence conduct. [It is the worst case I have ever tried.][63] That you, Taylor, kept a kind of male brothel, it is impossible to doubt, and that you, Wilde, have been the centre of a circle of extensive corruption among young men of the most hideous kind it is equally impossible to doubt. I shall, under the circumstances, be expected to pass the severest sentence that the law allows. In my judgment, it is utterly inadequate for such cases. The sentence upon each of you is imprisonment with hard labour for two years.[64]

The *Star*'s representation of the final moment in the trial is full of pathos and irony, contrasting as it does the private drama of the defendants with the casual indifference of the public:

Those nearest the dock say [Wilde] cried "May I not speak, my lord?" but the only words generally audible were two deeply articulated words, astonishing in such a connection, the words "Shame! shame!" which came from the back of the public gallery, and were instantly drowned in the ushers' strident cries of "Silence! silence!" Taylor was already leaving the dock with the light cat-like tread habitual to him, but Wilde seemed to have lost control of his limbs. When at last he turned away, between two warders, he trailed his feet like a man smitten with paralysis, and descended with obvious difficulty the steps leading to the cells. Already the voices of the newsboys could be heard crying "Wilde Verdict" in the sunny street, and the facile cheers of the ever-virtuous British crowd had been audible throughout the judge's address. The Old Bailey was filled with a Saturday afternoon crowd, which applauded and made jokes upon the result indifferently.[65]

3 THE RECEPTION OF THE TRIALS IN THE PRESS

To this point in my treatment of the trials, I have simply tried to provide a sense of what transpired within the courtroom and to highlight some of the factors that doubtlessly influenced their outcome. In this chapter I will explore certain aspects of the press coverage and examine in some detail the reception of the press reports by select members of the reading public. As with any trial, those present inside the courtroom were treated to a much fuller appreciation of the intricacies of the case than those who merely read about it in the newspapers. Those privileged few were able to hear the unedited, unexpurgated testimony of the witnesses and to view the proceedings first-hand. They were able to observe the whisperings and the machinations of the counsels and the judges, and permitted to study the body language, actions, and non-verbal communications of all the participants. In comparison, those outside the courtroom were at a distinct disadvantage. They could only experience the trial one-dimensionally as a text that was edited, censored, and presented for public consumption in a pre-digested form. This monumental difference in perspective resulted in perceptions of the case that were often poles apart. For example, whereas those who followed Wilde's second criminal trial in most metropolitan daily newspapers were led to believe that a guilty verdict was a foregone conclusion, the general sentiment of those inside the courtroom appeared to be that the jury would again disagree and that Wilde would be acquitted.[1]

The "public response" (which represents, of course, the sum of many individual responses) to such important public events as the Wilde trials is important for historians to examine because it provides a way of coming to grips with the complex processes through which a society constructs and authenticates "meaning." The variations within the spectrum of responses to press reports provide insight into how and why the public "meaning" produced by the press reports was accepted or resisted by certain individuals. While a complete picture of the public response to the Wilde trials is impossible to obtain, a limited picture is possible to present. Although I would hesitate to argue that a limited picture of the public response to the trials is representative of the views of English society, or even the views of those within the metropolis of London, this glimpse does provide us with an indication of what opinions the newspaper editors saw fit to print—for whatever didactic, moralistic, or mercenary motives—and this in itself gives us an idea of how the parameters, issues, and terms of the public debate were set by the "institution" of the Press, and how, in a larger sense, these parameters, issues, and terms reflected the dominant cultural attitudes of the times.

A limited sense of the public reaction to the trials can be obtained by examining the contents of editorials, and the contents of the letters written in response to them, which were published in the correspondence columns of the major London newspapers.[2] In 1895, the correspondence column itself was a relatively recent innovation within the world of print journalism. As John Stokes suggests, the mid-nineties was "a time when the correspondence column was widely offered as providing the ideal structure for democratic debate, a newspaper forum which would allow individuals to express themselves in a manner entirely appropriate to modern conditions."[3] Along with the "byeline, the headlines, the enquiries [investigative pieces], the pictures, and the interviews," the correspondence column was one of the devices developed by the "New Journalists" of the eighteen-eighties and eighteen-nineties to humanize the Press, to broaden its appeal, and to involve its readers.[4] All these innovations represented concessions to the economic realities faced by newspaper publishers during the last quarter of the nineteenth century, as well as a dilution of, or a disenchantment with, the liberal ideal of the didactic function of the Press.[5]

In the eighteen-sixties, "most newspapers were still written by and for the middle classes," but in the eighteen-seventies, "readership was beginning to be taken more into account by those who started and ran newspapers" because publishers were becoming increasingly dependent upon advertising revenue to keep afloat financially, and that revenue depended in part upon an accurate assessment of their readership.[6] Newspapers such as *The Times* (of London), for example, occupied a special niche in news reporting, specializing, as it did, in international news and diplomatic and political intelligence. This was what its readership—predominantly upper middle-class professionals and the governing elites of Europe—demanded.[7] *The Times* aside, however, the other major London dailies and Sundays felt a greater responsibility to their shareholders than to the public, and "placed crime second only to war in their hierarchy of selling values." This led one observer to comment wryly that "in times of peace a first class sex murder is the best tonic for a tired sub-editor on a dull evening."[8]

By the time of Wilde's criminal trials, it can be claimed that the "sex scandal" was already well established as a sub-genre within the genre of crime reporting. W.T. Stead, maverick editor of the *Pall Mall Gazette*, had earlier pioneered an exploitative brand of investigative journalism in the service of the more mercenary goals of the "New Journalism" in his 1885 exposé of white slavery and child prostitution, entitled "The Maiden Tribute of Modern Babylon."[9] From a historical perspective, the Wilde trials should be seen as one in a long line of (mostly) sex-related scandals involving important persons that gripped the public imagination in the eighteen-eighties and eighteen-nineties: "the divorce case of [the radical politician] Charles Dilke in 1886; [the unsolved Ripper murders of 1888]; the divorce case of the Irish leader Charles Parnell in 1890; the scandal of the Cleveland Street homosexual brothel, 1889–90, said to involve the eldest son of the heir to the throne; and the Tranby-Croft gambling scandal of 1891, which involved the Prince of Wales himself."[10] Without a doubt scandals such as these, and sex crimes in general, made excellent copy for the newspapers, and often boosted circulation to record levels.[11]

Of course, from a contemporary perspective, most of the major metropolitan penny daily newspapers, which catered to a predominantly middle-class readership, were more or less responsible in their reporting of events.[12] Publishers of these papers generally saw themselves as providing a genuine public service, and claimed that the reporting of crime stories served the general purposes of social control.[13] Other newspapers, however, especially the Sunday papers and the "non-political sensation sheets" such as the *Illustrated Police Budget* and the *Illustrated Police News*, which were aimed primarily at an uneducated working- and lower middle-class audience, were more often guilty of sensationalizing a story. As with their tabloid successors today, the more lurid and disgusting the story, the more newspapers were sold, and their primary function, then as now, was not to stimulate thought, but to amuse and entertain their readership.[14]

It was not surprising that Wilde held the lowest opinion of journalists and their function in society:

> there is much to be said in favour of modern journalism. By giving us the opinions of the uneducated, it keeps us in touch with the ignorance of the community. By carefully chronicling the current events of contemporary life, it shows us of what very little importance such events really are. By invariably discussing the unnecessary, it makes us understand what things are requisite for culture, and what are not. ...[15]

The leading articles of the newspapers, said Wilde, were "full of prejudice, stupidity, cant, and twaddle," and journalism itself was a most degrading profession.[16] For Wilde, the Press represented the tyranny of public opinion over and against the self-realized artistic individual, and symbolized everything that was wrong with England:

> England has done one thing; it has invented and established Public Opinion, which is an attempt to organize the ignorance of the community, and to elevate it to the dignity of physical force.[17]

Wilde's view echoed that of Søren Kierkegaard, who similarly argued that the Press creates the public, and the public lives only through the Press. The levelling power of the public emerges through the Press, but while the Press poses as the organ of the public, in reality it is the powerful voice of a handful of influential individuals.[18] Wilde noted that while the Press, ostensibly representing public opinion, constrained artists and rationed beauty, it paradoxically encouraged and extolled journalists who were purveying the worst sort of trash and ugliness.[19]

Wilde was incensed at the journalistic predisposition to dig into the lives of private citizens and to exploit the pain and suffering of others for the amusement of their readers. He believed instead that "the private lives of men and women should not be told to the public...private life should not be for public consumption."[20] Wilde understood full well that public scandals meant increased circulation for the papers, and that this in turn represented increased revenues and increased power to influence public opinion. He also believed that most journalists, as individuals, were decent human beings who were merely victims of an oppressive and patronizing capitalist economy:

> men of education and cultivation, who really disliked publishing these things, who know it is wrong to do so, and who do it because the unhealthy conditions under which their occupation is carried on oblige them to supply the public with what the public wants, and to compete with other journalists in making that supply as full and satisfying to the gross popular appetite as possible.[21]

Wilde considered it outrageous that "earnest, solemn, thoughtful journalists" were pressed by their employers to drag before the reading public incidents in the private lives of public figures,

> and invite the public to discuss the incident, to exercise authority in the matter, to give their views, and not merely to give their views, but to carry them into action, to dictate to the man upon all other points, to dictate to his party,

to dictate to his country, in fact to make themselves ridiculous, offensive, and harmful.[22]

Ironically, of course, only four years after writing these words in "The Soul of Man Under Socialism," Wilde found himself the unwilling subject of a lengthy journalistic inquisition, and had his own soul laid bare before a rabid and self-righteous public.

In many ways, the editorial reactions to the results of the Queensberry libel trial were amazingly prescient. Across the board, the metropolitan newspapers were unanimous with praise for the Marquess of Queensberry, and critical of Wilde to greater or lesser degrees. For example, the *Illustrated Police News* characterized the trial as "th[e] most gruesome tragedy of the nineteenth century." It was felt that Queensberry's actions during the trial, motivated as they were by his "natural" parental desire to protect his son from the evil influence of Wilde, may have also been undertaken in order to ameliorate his controversial patronage of prize-fighting and perhaps even his cantankerous reputation in the House of Lords.

> ... he is a man, despite his peculiarities, to be admired for the fact that he has had in his public life the courage of his convictions, and thus stands head and shoulders above the majority of hereditary personages of his own rank.[23]

While Queensberry was redeemed in the public eye, Wilde was prematurely mourned. The *Illustrated Police News* waxed nostalgic over the fact that Wilde's distinguished and brilliant career as a poet, novelist, and dramatist now seemed to be over, and lamented the possibility that Wilde, "a man whom a month ago thousands would have been glad to have known, a man who was fawned and cringed to and lionised by many, today stands without a friend in the world."

It seems ironic that the comments of the *Illustrated Police News*, which catered (theoretically) to an uneducated lower-class readership, displayed a greater sensitivity toward Wilde's existential predicament than any of the major dailies. On the other hand, the majority of metropolitan dailies, oriented primarily toward an educated middle-class readership, generally treated Wilde as if he had already been convicted. The *Echo*, for instance, considered Wilde "damned and done for," and suggested that

> ... the best thing for everybody now is to forget all about Oscar Wilde, his perpetual posings, his aesthetical teachings, and his theatrical productions. If not tried himself, let him go into silence, and be heard of no more.[24]

W.T. Stead's *Pall Mall Gazette*, the predominant "Clubland" newspaper,[25] did not want to condemn Wilde before he had been convicted, but still "could not overlook the fact that the jury found a verdict of guilty against him [Wilde] on his own admissions, and before any witnesses were called."[26]

Wilde, and what was described loosely as "his school," were most harshly criticized by the *Daily Telegraph*, the metropolitan daily newspaper with the largest circulation:

> We have had enough, and more than enough of Mr. OSCAR WILDE, who has been the means of inflicting upon public patience during the recent episode as much moral damage of the most offensive and repulsive kind as any single individual could well cause. If the general concern were only with the man himself—his spurious brilliancy, inflated egotism, diseased vanity, cultivated affectation, and shameless disavowal of all morality—the best thing would be to dismiss him and his deeds without another word to the penalty of universal condemnation....[27]

To this point in this rather lengthy editorial, Wilde was admonished as more of a public nuisance than as someone who posed a serious threat to society. The *Daily Telegraph* seized upon the implications contained in the evidence against Wilde and used them as a filter through which to view Wilde's past accomplishments. With perfect hindsight, the *Telegraph* was able to detect a pattern in Wilde's past behavior. The "just verdict" of the trial confirmed the suspicion that Wilde had all along been trying "to establish a cult in our midst," a cult, moreover, that would influence and subvert the nation's youth. "These men," said the *Telegraph*, referring to Wilde and his crowd, "linking a certain real sense of beauty with profligate tastes and profane mockery, have undoubtedly exercised a visible influence upon the generation cursed by their presence."[28] Even worse was that this cult was somehow under the French sphere of influence. Since England and France had been "natural" enemies for centuries, and since it was well known that France had always been a hotbed of vice, permissiveness, and radical ideas, Wilde's "cult" was viewed as unpatriotic if not treacherous, and as necessarily immoral and irreverent as well. The French and pagan roots of this "plague" were explored in depth, and the analogy was drawn: "have we to look further than to the declining population of France; the decay there of religion, reverence, obedience, and legality...?" What was perceived as the present "(im)moral condition of France" was thereby portrayed as an object lesson for England.

The *Daily Telegraph*'s analysis was driven by a heightened moral conviction and an exaggerated sense of outrage at the real or imagined violation that Wilde had perpetrated against an unwitting and vulnerable public; a violation that threatened not only the "family values" of the domestic sphere, but the very fabric of society:

It will be a public benefit, compensating for a great deal that has been painful in the reports of this trial, if the exposure of a chief representative of the immoral school leads to a clearer perception of its tendency and a heartier contempt for its methods....The aestheticism that worships a green carnation or a perfume has lost so much the sense of what is precious in parental and filial relations that we saw in this case a son addressing his father in terms which in ancient days would have involved his death. The superfine Art which admits no moral duty and laughs at the established phrases of right and wrong is the visible enemy of those ties and bonds of society—the natural affections, the domestic joys, the sanctity and sweetness of the home....[29]

Like the *Star*, the *Daily Telegraph* was quick to interpret the meaning of the trial, and to draw the appropriate moral lessons from it. The moral was presented in terms which juxtaposed the productive social values of diligence, industry, sobriety, and duty—values essential to the smooth functioning of a market-driven, capitalist economy and the maintenance of the Empire— with the anti-social cultural values which emphasized play, leisure, hedonistic self-indulgence, and narcissism. In the midst of preaching an intolerance toward deviants of all stripes, the *Telegraph* inadvertently became the first to record Wilde's social demise: eventual failure

A nation prospers and profits by precisely those national qualities which these innovators deride and abjure. It goes swiftly to wreck and decay by precisely that brilliant corruption of which we have just had the exposure and demonstration. All the good literature and the noble art in our own and other countries has been sane, moral, and serious in its object; nor can life be wholesomely lived under guidance of brilliant paradoxes and corrosive epigrams. To those who know how to observe, this man WILDE in the act of his defence condemned himself and his system by his vanity, egotism, artificiality, and distorted perceptions, before the Judge and jury had pronounced upon him the indirect sentence which eliminates him from the society he has disgraced. We shall have purchased the pain and shame of such an exhibition at a price, perhaps, not too high if it lead the youth of our generation, on the one hand, to graver thoughts of duty and propriety, and the public, on the other, to a sterner impatience with those who, under the name of Art, or some other pretence, insidiously poison our stage, our literature, our drama, and the outskirts of our press.[30]

The pronouncement of such grave sentiments was not the prerogative of newspapers alone. The *National Observer*, a weekly political journal, published a leading article viciously attacking Wilde, even going so far as to suggest that Wilde kill himself, thereby sparing society the pain and embarrassment of another trial.

There is not a man or woman in the English-speaking world possessed of the treasure of a wholesome mind who is not under a deep debt of gratitude to the Marquess of Queensberry for destroying the High Priest of the Decadents. The obscene impostor, whose prominence has been a social outrage ever since he transferred from Trinity Dublin to Oxford his vices, his follies, and his vanities, has been exposed, and that thoroughly at last. But to the exposure there must be legal and social sequels. There must be another trial at the Old Bailey, or a coroner's inquest—the latter for choice; and the Decadents, or their hideous conceptions of the meaning of Art, of their worse than Eleusinian mysteries, there must be an absolute end.[31]

Art's celebration of the virtues of decadence and dissolution was simply too much for this writer to bear. Still, it remains a mystery why the writer of the article, knowing, as he pretended to, the truth about Wilde's character, would have thought Wilde capable of an act of "honor" such as suicide.

Given the sensational nature of the Wilde story and its popularity with the reading public, the newspapers seemed to feel obliged constantly to supply their readership with detailed updates regarding the numerous smaller practical matters which arose after the Queensberry libel trial. Beneath a long column announcing the arrests of Wilde and Alfred Taylor, the *Star* printed four separate paragraph-length articles, each with its own headline. Under "Lord Queensberry's Threat" was printed Queensberry's final message to Wilde, which had been sent at the close of the trial, but before the warrant had been issued for his arrest: "If the country allows you to leave, all the better for the country, but if you take my son with you I will follow you wherever you go and shoot you."[32] "About 'The Chameleon'" contained a notice from Messrs. Ward, Perk, and McKay, the publishers of the *Chameleon*, stating that they had stopped the sale of the magazine "directly as they were aware of the contents."[33] "The Family Feud" stated Lord Percy Douglas' position that he "and every member of [his] family, excepting [his] father (Queensberry), disbelieve absolutely and entirely the allegations of the defence."[34] Finally, "Oscar's Plays Still Run" announced that Wilde's plays were produced the previous night as usual (*An Ideal Husband* was being performed at the Haymarket, and *The Importance of Being Earnest* was at the St. James). "At neither place was there any hostile demonstration," although the audiences appeared "much smaller than usual." At the St. James Theatre, it was noted that

... at one or two places slightly discordant remarks were made, especially when reference was made to the town of Worthing [where Wilde's alleged indiscretions with Alphonso Conway took place], but these chiefly came from the gallery and were of a trifling character.[35]

Wilde had been arrested on the evening of April 5, and had been interned in Holloway Gaol awaiting his arraignment and news of whether or not bail would be allowed him.[36] It was still not known at this time whether Wilde would be brought up on felony (sodomy) or misdemeanor (acts of "gross indecency") charges. After three separate hearings before Sir John Bridge, the magistrate at the Bow Street Police Court, it was decided to charge Wilde with the misdemeanor and commit him to trial on April 19. Although he was technically obliged to grant bail since the offence was not a felony, Justice Bridge refused it because of the extreme gravity of the case, stating "there is no worse crime than that with which the prisoners [referring also to Alfred Taylor] are charged."[37]

In the meantime, Lord Queensberry said in an interview with the *Star* that since the trial he had "been overwhelmed with congratulations from all quarters of the globe."[38] The Marquess said,

> You know, I have not much to do with distinguished people, but I had a very nice letter from Lord Claud [sic] Hamilton, and a kind telegram from Mr. Charles Danby, the actor, with "Hearty Congratulations," et cetera. Various clubs have telegraphed also. Here is a message: "Every man in the City is with you. Kill the——!"[39]

Queensberry also said that he was "astounded at the abrupt conclusion [of the trial] and did not think Wilde half so bad a man as he had proved to be." He further noted that his son's (Lord Percy Douglas') statement that the family sided with Wilde was incorrect, for "his brother, Rev. Lord Archibald Douglas had written to the contrary." In a statement that he would later qualify, Queensberry reportedly "expressed his sorrow at the position of the strange apostle of aestheticism."[40]

The *Star* also printed an excerpt from the journal *Truth*, in which its editor, Henry Labouchere, M.P. (and author of section 11 of the Criminal Law Amendment Act, the statute under which Wilde was prosecuted), reflected on Wilde's extremely enjoyable but otherwise warped personality which was driven by what he interpreted as a pathological need for attention:

> I have known Oscar Wilde off and on for years....clever and witty he unquestionably is, but I have always regarded him as somewhat wrong in the head, for his craving after notoriety seemed to me a positive craze. There was nothing he would not do to attract attention...."Insult me, throw mud at me, but only look at me" seemed to be his creed; and such a creed was never acted upon by anyone whose mind was not out of balance. So strange and wondrous is his mind when in an abnormal condition, that it would not surprise me if he were deriving a keen enjoyment from a position which most people, whether really innocent or guilty, would prefer to die rather than occupy.[41]

Labouchere's statement ironically contained a kernel of truth. As a result of the trial, Wilde had certainly received all the notoriety he could possibly desire, and more. Certainly, in a contrary moment, Wilde may have relished the spotlight, for he was doubtlessly the most discussed man in England,[42] but the enjoyment of his celebrity status must have been tempered by the knowledge of just how serious his predicament actually was, and ruined by an increased awareness of the pain, anguish, and humiliation which potentially lay in store for him.[43]

In another series· of developments related to the trial, the Haymarket Theatre decided to terminate its extremely successful run of *An Ideal Husband* on April 13, noting that Wilde's play had been "longer before the public than almost any play now running in London." For inexplicable reasons, the management of the Haymarket transferred the play, "with its present cast," to the Criterion Theatre.[44] The hypocrisy of the theatre managers who removed Wilde's name from their playbills while continuing to perform his plays was roundly condemned by the *Illustrated Police News*.[45] And it was not merely English theatres that were affected by the scandal surrounding Wilde. The *Daily Telegraph* reported that the Lyceum Theatre in New York was planning to discontinue the performance of *An Ideal Husband* the following week. The *Telegraph* included the fact that "Miss Rose Coghlan, who has been playing *A Woman of No Importance* in the Western States, has resolved to omit the play from her repertoire."[46] In an entirely different vein, the Parisian daily, *Le Figaro*, took the opportunity to lampoon the fickleness of the English theatre owners and theatre-going public, and to highlight the differences in the French and British attitudes toward scandals, printing on their front page a fictitious dialogue:

> DIRECTOR: "If I had gone on presenting Oscar Wilde's play, there would not have been a single spectator in my theatre—and all the theatres are in the same situation. That's what I find so wonderful about this country of ours."
> SECRETARY: "It is the only country in which even scandals serve to highlight public morality. Oscar Wilde is not only finished as a gentleman but also as a playwright."
> DIRECTOR: "In France, if such a thing had happened to a dramatist, it would have given his play enormous publicity. Box office receipts would have shot up overnight."[47]

The French reactions were not all so jocular, however, as less than a week later the *Star* reported that a duel was fought (with swords) between two well-known French writers, Jules Huret and Catulle Mendès, after M. Huret made some remarks in the *Petite Chronique des Lettres* which "referred to the amicable relations subsisting between M. Catulle Mendès and Mr. Oscar Wilde."

The *Star* said that M. Mendès took exception to Huret's statements, but it was not clear whether Mendès was defending or repudiating his association with Wilde. It was further noted that "other duels arising out of the same motive are pending."[48]

Speculation was rife at the time, too, that Lord Alfred Douglas would also be charged along with Wilde and Taylor.[49] Such speculation was ill-informed, however, as indicated in this letter from George Wyndham, M.P., to his father:

> ... I ought to tell you that I know on the authority of Arthur Balfour [Conservative M.P., later Prime Minister in 1902], who has been told the case by the lawyers who had all the papers, that Wilde is sure to be condemned, and that the case is in every way a very serious one, involving the systematic ruin of a number of young men. Public feeling is hostile to him, among all classes.
>
> There is no case against Bosie [Douglas], but he has associated himself with Wilde up to the last moment; and is spoken of as having known the witnesses who will be called. Men like Arthur [Balfour] and Lord Houghton, who have spoken to me, speak in kind terms of him; but are unanimous in saying that he had better go abroad for a year or two. ...
>
> But Wilde is, humanly speaking, sure to be imprisoned. I told Bosie so; and he agreed that it was almost certain.
>
> ... Whatever is proved, it is common knowledge in London that there was a sort of secret society around the man Taylor.[50]

The fact that Balfour, a very influential and respected M.P., as well as a major player in the Conservative opposition to Rosebery's government, was at this early date closely following the developing situation surrounding the trial, indicates just how important and potentially explosive the case seemed to many in the highest government circles. The fact that there was apparently no case against Lord Alfred Douglas is perhaps less surprising, as I have indicated earlier, since it was Queensberry who had directed the investigation which had uncovered all the evidence on Wilde. Given that Queensberry's reason for pursuing the attack on Wilde was to protect his son, it is only logical that he would have suppressed any evidence that might have incriminated Lord Alfred.

Wyndham's remark referring to the public hostility toward Wilde confirms other comments to this effect which appeared repeatedly in newspaper accounts throughout the trials.[51] While the palpability of hostile public feeling toward Wilde cannot be denied, neither can it be accurately determined whether such animosity preceded the trial or resulted from it. In a retrospective attempt to explain the psychological dynamics of what Frank Harris described as "an orgy of Philistine rancour" directed at Wilde, William Butler Yeats, a friend and fellow countryman of Wilde's, who was living in London at the time of the trials, recalled that

The rage against Wilde was also complicated by the Britisher's jealousy of art and the artist, which is generally dormant but is called into activity when the artist has got outside his field into publicity of an undesirable kind. This hatred is not due to any action of the artist or eminent man; it is merely the expression of an individual hatred and envy, become collective because circumstances have made it so.[52]

What is most important is that although private opinion seems to have been divided as to whether Wilde was courageous or foolhardy to have pursued the case against Queensberry, and then to have refused to flee the country after the failure of his prosecution, public support for Wilde was virtually non-existent. The sad fact of the matter was that at this most crucial moment of his life, Wilde had been abandoned by virtually all his friends.[53] The social stigma attached to the alleged crime was so severe that it would have been unthinkable for anyone to defend Wilde's lifestyle. To do so would have been to invite the panoptic eye of society to examine one's own life. Efforts to differentiate between the man and his work seemed equally fruitless, which made it virtually impossible for anybody to speak out publicly on his behalf. Any defense of Wilde would necessarily have been construed as implying a defense of Wilde's lifestyle.

One of the very few who dared speak out publicly on his behalf was Robert Buchanan, a well-known gadfly, progressive thinker, poet, playwright, novelist, and "frequent contributor to the *Daily Telegraph*."[54] Courageously, Buchanan became Wilde's foremost public champion between the end of the libel trial and the beginning of the first criminal trial. However, even Buchanan's support was limited and qualified. His public defense of Wilde arose out of a deeply felt respect for the democratic principles of equality before the law, and from an admiration for Wilde's literary contributions to society. Buchanan in no way defended Wilde's alleged behavior. Nevertheless, as the lone voice in Wilde's corner, Buchanan is significant for sparking a spirited debate in the correspondence columns of the *Star*, an exchange of ideas whose main subject was the issue of Wilde's pre-trial conviction by the Press. The main points of Buchanan's argument were set forth in the first of his four letters to the newspaper:

Is it not high time that a little charity, Christian or anti-Christian, were imported into this land of Christian shibboleths and formulas? Most sane men listen on in silence while Press and public condemn to eternal punishment and obloquy a supposed criminal who is not yet tried or proved guilty. ...I for one wish to put on record my protest against the cowardice and cruelty of Englishmen towards one who was, until recently, recognised as a legitimate contributor to our amusement, and who is, when all is said and done, a scholar and a man of letters. He may be all that public opinion avers him to be; indeed, he stands convicted already, out of his own mouth, of the utmost recklessness and folly; but let us bear in mind that his case still remains *sub judice*, that he is not yet legally condemned. Meanwhile, we are asked by the advocates of orthodox sensualism not merely to trample an untried man in the mire, but to expunge from the records of our literature all the writings, which, only yesterday, tickled our humor and beguiled our leisure. ...[55]

This passage can, of course, be read in any number of different ways. Two ways, however, stand out. In the first instance, Buchanan can be seen as generally chastizing the public for their sheepishness and for the shortfall of clear Christian sentiments, especially faith, love, and charity. In the second instance, Buchanan can be seen as criticizing the Press and the government for the obviousness of their bias against Wilde, and as humanistically sympathizing with Wilde as the victim of an unfair trial.

Buchanan closed his letter with these words, "let us ask ourselves, moreover, who are casting these stones, and whether they are those 'without sin amongst us,' or those who are themselves notoriously corrupt."[56] Interestingly, Buchanan's closing remarks struck a nerve with Lord Queensberry. As was his wont, Queensberry responded immediately, shooting from the hip:

> ... I have not the pleasure of Mr. Buchanan's acquaintance, but he seems to address a question to myself in this letter to your paper of 16 April when he says, "Who are casting these stones?" and are they without sin...Is Mr. Buchanan himself without sin? I certainly don't claim to be so myself, though I am compelled to throw the first stone. Whether or not I am justly notoriously corrupt I am willing patiently to wait for the future to decide. ...[57]

This letter prompted a rejoinder from Buchanan who, while reiterating his claim that Wilde should be considered innocent until proven guilty, assured Queensberry that the Press, and not he, had been the target of his ire. Even more importantly, Buchanan introduced a new issue into the debate. Buchanan suggested that Wilde, who was still technically innocent at the time, was being treated by the State as if he had already been convicted, and thus that he was being unnecessarily deprived of his civil rights:

> I should like to ask on what conceivable plea of justice or expediency an accused person, not yet tried and convicted, is subjected to the indignities and inconveniences of a common prison, and denied, while a prisoner, the ordinary comforts to which he has been accustomed when at large? Why should his diet be regulated unduly? Why should he be denied the sedative of the harmless cigarette, more than ever necessary to a smoker in times of great mental anxiety?

Why should not his friends visit him? Why, in short, should he not enjoy, as far as is practicable, all the privileges of an innocent man?[58]

Buchanan's plea on behalf of Wilde's legal rights was echoed in a letter from Lord Alfred Douglas to the editor of the *Star*. Rarely original, Douglas did little but reiterate the basic points of Buchanan's first letter. No doubt the letter was intended to help Wilde, and while Douglas' hyperbole was not outrageous for the time, it is hard to imagine that such a sarcastic diatribe would have done much to enhance Buchanan's thoughtful and carefully reasoned argument:

> When the great British public has made up its great British mind to crush any particular unfortunate whom it holds in its power, it generally succeeds in gaining its object....I feel therefore, that I am taking my life in my hands in daring to raise my voice against the chorus of the pack of those who are now hounding Mr. Oscar Wilde to his ruin; the more so as I feel assured that the public has made up its mind to accept me, as it has accepted everybody and everything connected with this case, at Mr. Carson's valuation. I, of course, am the undutiful son who, in his arrogance and folly, has kicked against his kind and affectionate father....I appeal to interfere and to stay the hand of "Judge Lynch." And I submit that Mr. Oscar Wilde has been tried by the newspapers before he has been tried by a jury, that his case has been almost hopelessly prejudiced in the eyes of the public from whom the jury who must try the case will be drawn, and that he is practically being delivered over bound to the fury of a cowardly and brutal mob. ...[59]

This letter is perhaps more important and interesting for what it reveals about Douglas. The letter reflects Douglas' own narcissistic injury and his own suffering, arising from being deprived of his lover, best friend, and alter ego. He portrayed himself as a victim along with Wilde, and lashed out, on behalf of both of them, at their perceived oppressors, the British public and the Press. That he linked the perceived oppressors in a conspiratorial fashion can probably be attributed to the more or less justifiable paranoia which usually accompanies the choice of a clandestine lifestyle. Psychologically, Douglas' attempt to appear publicly in the guise of Wilde's savior might be seen as an attempt to compensate for possible feelings of inadequacy or helplessness resulting from his inability to alleviate Wilde's situation. From another perspective, it might also be seen as a way of belatedly assuming responsibility in order to assuage possible guilt feelings about his own complicity in Wilde's predicament.[60]

The letters of Buchanan and Douglas apparently drew a number of responses, many of which, for reasons that were never articulated, the *Star* decided not to print.[61] Two that were printed, either because they were seen to have expressed what might be regarded as "representative" views, or else because of their potential to incite further public comment, were signed with the upper-case pseudonyms, COMMON-SENSE and HELVELLYN. The use of pseudonyms in correspondence columns was a Victorian commonplace. John Stokes points out that correspondence columns provided many opportunities for professional writers, and that there is really no way of distinguishing between an ordinary reader and a professional writer, who may have been hired by the newspaper "to whip up heated debate" on a given topic in order to boost circulation.[62]

The *Star's* headline—"Oscar Wilde: Two Views of his Present Position," with the sub-headline, "Has he been Unfairly or Prematurely Judged by Magistrate and Public, or does His Case Illustrate the Need of Prison Reform?" —framed the issues very neatly around the contents of the letters the editors had elected to print. COMMON-SENSE criticized both Douglas and Buchanan for different reasons. COMMON-SENSE attacked Douglas' character and used his reputation as a "scoundrel" as a basis for rejecting the serious points that Douglas had raised on Wilde's behalf. Responding in particular to Douglas' description of the crime with which Wilde had been charged as "comparatively trifling," COMMON-SENSE retorted,

> I apprehend, however, that the majority of decent English folk will fully endorse Sir John Bridge's sentiments as to the gravity of the offence with which Wilde is charged. Be that, however, as it may, it seems to me that Lord Alfred Douglas is the very last man on the face of creation who is entitled to express an opinion on the case whatever. His allegation of unfairness against Sir John Bridge—one of the kindest-hearted and most just magistrates that ever sat on the Bench— will be met by your readers with the disdain it merits.[63]

Whereas Douglas' lack of good character provided suitable grounds for the dismissal of his argument, Buchanan's "position, disinterestedness, and ability" entitled his opinions to "respectful attention" and serious consideration. COMMON-SENSE was most concerned with what Buchanan described as the unduly harsh and unfair treatment Wilde had been subjected to while in prison awaiting his arraignment and trial.

> If he [Buchanan] considers that the régime of our prisons, as regards persons awaiting trial, is unduly severe, he has every right to say so; and for aught I know there may be much to be advanced both from his and other points of view. As a general question it is one that may very properly be discussed, but why it should in any way be attached to the case of Wilde more than to that of any poor wretch who is awaiting "presentation at court" I altogether fail to see. I am not aware that it has been alleged that Wilde has been subjected to different treatment from that accorded to any other individual in precisely similar circumstances. If

there were any such evidence, there might be some grounds for raising the question in connection with this case. ... I daresay Wilde misses his cigarettes, but not one whit more than "Bill Sykes" would his "clay." I confess my sympathies would be rather with the latter; but that, again, is neither here nor there.

Despite his protestations to the contrary, one cannot help thinking that it was precisely his contempt for Wilde's reputed sexual proclivities which incited COMMON-SENSE to prefer to sympathize with Bill Sykes, the "manly" murderer, rather than with Wilde, the effeminate dandy and alleged sodomite. The criticism of Buchanan's advocacy of special treatment for Wilde was certainly valid, as it effectively juxtaposed popular notions of the "natural" equality of all men with the elitist conception of the exceptional status of intellectuals in society. However, COMMON-SENSE's assertion that Buchanan's criticisms of Wilde's treatment in prison were analogous to an indictment of the entire prison system appears almost as hyperbolic as Douglas' paranoid claim that the British public and Press were in conspiratorial collusion against himself and Wilde.

In contrast to COMMON-SENSE, HELVELLYN agreed with Buchanan and Douglas that Wilde was being prejudged by the Press. More interestingly, HELVELLYN compared Wilde's alleged criminal exploitation of young men to the widespread and culturally accepted exploitation of young women by men, and in this way alluded to the deeply ingrained hypocrisy of the entire society, especially on matters of sex.

> ... in sexual errors, as in everything else, the real offence lies, and must always lie, in the sacrificing of another person in any way, for the sake of one's own pleasure or profit; and judged by this standard—which though not always the legal standard is certainly the only true moral standard—the accused is possibly no worse than those in society who condemn him. Certainly it is strange that a society which is continually and habitually sacrificing women to the pleasure of men, should be so eager to cast the first stone—except that it seems to be assumed that women are always man's lawful prey, and any appropriation or sacrifice of them for sex purposes quite pardonable and "natural."[64]

On April 23, the editors of the *Star* noted that they had again received "another large batch of letters on this subject, some of them from Liverpool, Middlesbrough, and other far-off centres, but none expresses views different from those which have been published from other correspondents."[65] The heading of the column—"Oscar Wilde: Mr. Buchanan Pleads for a Brother Artist," and subheading, "And Says That Wilde Has Already Lost Everything That Can Make Life Tolerable—Another Correspondent Holds Different Views of 'Christian Charity'"—summarizes, for the most part, the contents of the letters. Buchanan, responding to the comments by COMMON-SENSE, paradoxically suggested that while he agreed that Wilde's exceptional status as an artist did not necessarily entitle him to any special treatment in prison, his natural sensitivity as an artist precluded him from handling the punishments as well as would a common criminal such as "Bill Sykes." In other words, Buchanan was worried that Wilde, despite his immense physical size, was too delicate and too highly strung to tolerate the rigors of imprisonment, and suggested that if the Court could not provide Wilde with clemency, it should at least provide him with mercy.[66]

Buchanan's next correspondent signed himself, "DIKE." It was DIKE's intention to counter what was described as HELVELLYN's "epistle," and to advance the notion that "Christian charity does not mean weakness and toleration of pagan viciousness." DIKE re-emphasized the seriousness of the alleged crime, and contested the charge of hypocrisy levelled by HELVELLYN. He also took the opportunity further to demonize Wilde on behalf of Christians everywhere. "DIKE" suggested that public outrage could only be mollified by the proverbial "pound of flesh."

> When a man has offended the ears of all decent people, in the most ordinary sense, by openly flaunting the universal and not too exacting code of this world's morals, and by posing as the apostle of corruption, and all that is opposed to civilisation itself, it is not Christian Charity that has anything to do with it— until he has reversed his ways and rendered some satisfaction to an outraged public. The howls of execration, if they have reached "Helvellyn," are a healthy sign; and as to the erasure of a name from playbills, I say emphatically that I wonder why the productions themselves have not been withdrawn. ...[67]

On the same day that a notice announced the sale of Wilde's possessions in order to help with expenses relating to the trial, Buchanan responded vigorously to DIKE's "lying perversions of truth."[68] After characterizing DIKE as an "anonymous coward" and someone who "snaps and gnaws at a fallen man," Buchanan addressed himself to "the only serious statement in 'DIKE's' letter," which interpreted Wilde's abandonment of his prosecution of Queensberry as an admission of guilt. Buchanan argued that by withdrawing in the face of "unexpected evidence" Wilde had only done what was prudent and reasonable, and that DIKE had jumped to conclusions based on evidence whose precise contents and sources had yet to be examined and understood. He further defended Wilde by saying that "two thirds of all Mr. Wilde has written is purely ironical, and it is only because they are now told that the writer is a wicked man that people begin to consider his writings wicked [also]."[69] Although Buchanan may not have been aware of it, his sentiments echoed those expressed by Walter Pater in his review of The Picture of Dorian Gray. Pater suggested that rather than being a work of decadence, Dorian Gray was a "work of the highest morality," since its "whole purpose [was] to point out the effect of selfish indulgence and sensuality in destroying the character of a beautiful human soul." Pater had said that the "story [was] also a vivid, though carefully considered, exposure of the corruption of a soul, with a very plain moral, pushed home, to the effect that vice and crime make people coarse and ugly."[70]

In closing his letter, Buchanan claimed that he had even "heard from the Marquess of Queensberry's own lips that he would gladly, were it possible, set the public an example of sympathy and magnaminity [sic]." This, of course, prompted an immediate rebuttal from Queensberry, never one to let an error go uncorrected, who took "exception to the word sympathy that [was] placed in [his] mouth."

> In my time I have helped to cut up and destroy sharks. I had no sympathy for them, but may have felt sorry and wished to put them out of pain as soon as possible. What I did say was that as Mr. Wilde now seemed to be on his beam ends and utterly down I did feel sorry for his awful position, and that supposing he was convicted of those loathsome charges brought against him that were I the authority that had to mete out to him his punishment, I would treat him with all possible consideration as a sexual pervert of an utterly diseased mind, and not as a sane criminal. If this is sympathy, Mr. Wilde has it from me to that extent.[71]

Appearing on the same page as Queensberry's letter was a curiously obsequious reply to Buchanan from DIKE, who, in essence, claimed that he had been responding to HELVELLYN's letter and not Buchanan's, and therefore that he did not deserve to be the object of Buchanan's scathing remarks. It is difficult to say with what regard opinions expressed in the columns of the *Star* were held by their readership, but in any event, it was DIKE who had the last word on Wilde, and that word was negative.

Wilde's own opinion of how the trial was being perceived by the public was more or less in concert with the sentiments that were being expressed in the newspapers. Recalling his feelings in *De Profundis*, he wrote that

> ... outside a small set in those two cities [London and Oxford], the world looks on you [Douglas] as the good young man who was very nearly tempted into wrong doing by the wicked and immoral artist, but was rescued just in time by his kind and loving father.[72]

Wilde saw the trial as a family quarrel between father and son which should have been contained within the domestic sphere, but which had spilled over instead and was now "being played on a high stage in History, with the whole world as the audience, and [himself] as the prize for the victor in the contemptible contest."[73]

The public debate over Wilde ended as the criminal trial began. Despite the inconclusive results and the need for a retrial, when his first criminal trial was over there seemed little else that could be said about him, or on his behalf. Most of Wilde's secrets had been bared, and his dirty linen aired, all to the general disgust of the British public. Yet, even after five grueling days of the most amazing revelations, the *Morning* could still write that "society feels that a gross public scandal has not yet been probed to its depths; and that a great mass of loathsome evidence must once more be heard in open court."[74] Surely by this the *Morning* was expressing the opinion that the proper conclusion to the trial had not yet been reached. Certainly, the Press's handling of the criminal trial served to raise public expectations that Wilde would be found guilty, and since Wilde's conviction was already, in most minds, a *fait accompli*, it came as a bit of a surprise when the first criminal trial ended in a hung jury.

By the end of the second criminal trial, though, most people had grown tired of having the details of Wilde's private life constantly thrust before them on the pages of their daily newspaper. There was a little suspense regarding the outcome of the second trial given what had happened in the first, and a collective sigh of relief must have escaped when Justice Wills pronounced sentence on Wilde and thus put an end to one of the most difficult and fascinating cases in British legal history. The harsh sentence seemed to satisfy the public's need for retribution, and this, along with the public's loss of interest in the case due to its overexposure in the Press for two long months, reasonably explains the muted public reaction to Wilde's sentencing and imprisonment. While there were no doubt a few, such as Robert Buchanan and most of Wilde's close friends, who privately feared that Wilde would not be able to handle the conditions in prison, the overwhelming general sentiment was that Wilde had simply got what he deserved.

4 THE CULTURAL CLIMATE OF THE TRIALS

Heterosexism and Homophobia as Historical Constructs

The Wilde trials occurred within a prevailing cultural climate which I will describe as "homophobic" and "heterosexist."[1] Within the context of this discussion, "homophobia" will denote an individual intrapsychic phenomenon which describes "irrational" feelings of "fear and hatred" toward other individuals who espouse same-sex desire and/or engage in sexual practices with members of the same gender, which I will hereafter refer to as the practice of "same-sex passion." Homophobic feelings can be expressed by individuals in passive or aggressive ways, and in some cases may not be expressed at all. I will define "heterosexism" as the advocacy, rationalization, and institutionalization of the idea of "compulsory heterosexuality" within a specific group, society, and/or culture. Theoretically, "heterosexism" represents the collective expression of the inarticulate fears and narcissistic rage of homophobic individuals. As such, the term describes the "rationalized" expression of an "irrational" phenomenon. "Heterosexism" functions simultaneously to promote heterosexuality as an "ideology," and to articulate a more or less convincing rationale which justifies the hatred and oppression of individuals who practice "same-sex passion." When seen in the aggregate, these individuals effectively constitute a minority group. Instrumentally, "heterosexism" is "institutionalized" in popular and professional discourses and codified in civil and ecclesiastical laws. In effect, "heterosexism" legitimizes and authorizes the use of various means to restrain and suppress a minority group.

It is with great trepidation that the term "homosexual" is employed in this book, even though it would be infinitely more convenient and doubtless have a greater cultural resonance with audiences in the late twentieth century. However, in the Victorian context, and even in the late-Victorian context, it is both problematic and technically incorrect to invoke the modern term "homo-sexuality" as a synonym for "same-sex passion," or "homosexual" as a syn-onym for an individual who practices same-sex passion, because same-sex passion was understood very differently by Victorian contemporaries, as we will see shortly.[2] While some of the most important objections to the use of the terms "homosexuality" and "homosexual" will be highlighted later in this chapter, readers interested in exploring other reasons will find them thor-oughly documented elsewhere.[3]

In some ways, to characterize a culture as heterosexist is to say almost noth-ing about that culture, for one would be hard-pressed to think of a single culture in the history of this world which would not be categorized, to greater or lesser extents, as homophobic and heterosexist. In other ways, however, the very lack of a single legitimate counter-example suggests the extent to which heterosexist ideas, and to a lesser extent homophobic ideas—as well as the mechanisms of restraint and structures of repression which represent the reification of hetero-sexism[4]—have been ingrained in our consciousness and embedded so deeply within our existing cultures that heterosexist ideas, mechanisms, and structures are simply taken for granted, assumed to exist and to function and to have always existed and functioned. Thus, in effect, they have been completely "naturalized" and "normalized." Although "homophobia," and to a much lesser extent "heterosexism," have received a good deal of attention recently from scholars within departments of English, Critical Theory, Anthropology, Sociology, and Gay/Lesbian Studies, historians as a group have thus far displayed little interest in the subject.[5] This study can be interpreted as one act of redress.

I want to suggest that heterosexism is best understood historically—not as a static, timeless, and universal mass-psychological or sociological phenomenon, but rather as a dynamic and transitive phenomenon which is culturally specific and socially constructed. In claiming this, I am proposing that the historical "condition" of heterosexism mutates and evolves over time, that it necessarily demonstrates different characteristics at different times and in different cul-tures, and that it changes in relation to the prevailing definitions or concep-tions of same-sex passion and those who practice it. Specifically, prior to the Wilde trials public expressions toward men who dressed in women's clothing, who were effeminate in appearance or behavior, or who were suspected of committing sexual acts with others of the same gender were generally charac-terized by the same ambiguity and confusion that accompanied the public's understanding of the nature of male effeminacy, cross-dressing, and same-sex passion between men. While heterosexist structures certainly existed in early modern England, and while homophobic feelings were undoubtedly widely prevalent, by all accounts the public expression of those feelings seems, in most cases, to have been relatively restrained (especially compared to what followed), and tempered by a certain tolerance and even pity, which itself might be attributed to widespread public ignorance about both the act and the actors, as well as by a circumscribed Christian sympathy for the sinner.

By the end of the nineteenth century, however, as a result of a combination of several changes in society, the mildness and tolerance that characterized the lingering traces of the early modern structures of heterosexism were gradually displaced by a much harsher and less forgiving set of attitudes. A primary factor in this virtual "sea change" was the gradual emergence throughout the nineteenth century of a professional discourse which attempted to understand and define the phenomenon of "same-sex passion" according to medical and scientific criteria. It was through a litany of debates, aggregate labelling processes, effects, and resistances within select medical, legal, and scientific circles that the behavior which had been deemed criminal by civil and ecclesiastical courts of law, and which had previously been understood by most people, within traditional ontological parameters and within a Christian moralistic context, as a deficiency of willpower and a lack of self-control (i.e. the sodomite considered as "dissipated, dissolute debauchee," or simply as "sinner"), was being increasingly characterized as representing an alternative ontological reality altogether, that is, a third sex, the "sexual invert," whose inclinations and behavior were biologically determined and manifestly "other." Moreover, the behavior of the "invert" (as "other") was now being described by influential medical professionals in terms of mental illness and psychological disturbance (i.e. in terms of perversion). Over the course of the nineteenth century, the newer images of the "invert" and the "pervert" did not simply displace and replace the older popular views of the "debauchee" and the "sinner." Rather, all these views of the "practitioner of same-sex passion" were gradually conflated in both popular and professional discourses. I will argue within the course of this chapter that this conflation took place after, and as a result of, the Wilde trials. In many ways, this conflation brought greater confusion instead of greater clarity. However, it was precisely the mystery, confusion, and ambiguity that surrounded the newly constructed image of the "practitioner of same-sex passion" that gave rise to new public fears—fears of the unknown, fears of the "other," and fears of the potentially "dangerous." In effect, within and around the related events which constitute the "spectacle" of the Wilde trials, one can see the "public face" of homophobia and the structures of a revitalized, more aggressive, and more intolerant heterosexism emerge for the first time within a thoroughly "modern" context.

I will suggest that the main reason the "new" image of the practitioner of same-sex passion aroused such public fear and animosity was because of the peculiarities which characterized the cultural and intellectual context within which this negative "new" image was received by the public. Two important factors described the peculiar condition of this historical ground. The first was the cultural embeddedness of a composite Spencerian-Darwinian world-view which represented society as a dynamic social "organism," perpetually involved in a life-or-death struggle for survival. On an even broader, world-historical scale, each "social organism," or nation-state, saw itself as competing with other nation-states to control economic markets and the sources of raw materials necessary for the perpetuation of the society and nation-state. The developmental trajectory of the "social organism" was described most frequently by cultural optimists as "progress," and by cultural pessimists in terms of "social decay" and "decadence." There are many reasons to believe that in the last decade of the nineteenth century the cultural pessimists had the stronger voices and the better arguments. The second factor was the cultural impact of widely publicized medico-psychiatric and scientific theories of "degeneration." The idea of "degeneration"[6] was often linked conceptually to the idea of "decadence," and referred broadly to the natural (and viewed fatalistically, the inevitable) process of the physical and mental deterioration of the human species, a view which carried more weight and conveyed a sense of greater urgency when presented, as it often was, in the racial language of the imperial nation-state (i.e. the degeneration of the "English Race"). In addition, the concept of "degeneration" was often used in a moral context to connote a sense of "moral backsliding."

The Wilde trials were unusual in that they provided a single forum and a single frame of reference for all of these otherwise disparate concepts: "decadence," "degeneration," and "same-sex passion." As they emerged in the trial testimony and as they were discussed in the newspaper accounts of the trials, all of Wilde's (alleged) sexual acts and all of Wilde's ideas on art and philosophy were continually framed by the issues of criminality, decadence, degeneration, male effeminacy, and same-sex passion. The constellation of ideas that emerged from the crucible of the trials was thus filtered and interpreted through the prevailing popular cultural and intellectual matrix, which was thoroughly laced and imbued with Spencerian and Darwinian ideas. Within the context of this historical convergence of concerns, the "homophobic" moral panic that followed the Wilde trials can be seen to have represented a host of fears which incorporated the various threats ostensibly posed by a "new," dangerous, and suddenly very visible category of persons (which would gradually be referred to as "homosexuals"[7]) to an "organic" social body that perceived itself as struggling for its own survival in an increasingly hostile and unpredictable world. The effect of the "moral panic" that gripped the nation in 1895 was to cause the heterosexist structures of repression and mechanisms of restraint to be drawn tighter in British society—where they would remain tightly drawn until 1967, when sexual acts between consenting adult males were officially de-criminalized by the Sexual Offences Act.[8]

While this chapter will expand upon and substantiate the thesis I have outlined above, Chapter Five will examine the cultural and intellectual rationales that underlay Wilde's perception of his own actions, and Chapter Six will explore in greater detail the ideologically motivated manipulation and exploitation of the public's moral panic by certain quasi-religious groups, especially those associated with the cause of "social purity."

deteriorate morals
= physically   *cultural + moral decay*

Degeneration and Decadence: Literary and Otherwise

The concepts of degeneration and decadence must be understood within the prevailing cultural and intellectual context, which was thoroughly dominated by a Spencerian world-view. Spencer's philosophy (which was influenced but not determined by Darwinian ideas) conceptualized human societies as living organisms that, like all other living beings, were subject to the natural processes of birth, death, decay, selection, and competition. Spencerian evolutionary metaphors pervaded both the popular and professional discourses of the late-Victorian era.[9] Structurally, Spencerian analogies can be seen somewhat reductively as the grafting of ideas and metaphors derived from recent advances in the biological and natural sciences onto anatomical and organic metaphors of the social body, such as the "body politic" and "the great body of the people," which had long been in the public domain.[10]

Spencer theorized that social organisms developed rationally along biological (Lamarckian as opposed to Darwinian) lines, seeking perfection and fulfillment through the inheriting of acquired good characteristics and the purging of bad characteristics (and "bad" individuals).[11] Spencer's version of an evolutionary process tempered by a rational moralism was much easier for the English public to swallow than Darwin's more disturbing version which viewed Nature as an irrational force. The implications of Darwin's theory reduced life to a meaningless series of random events, and this proposition was, to most people, irreconcilable with a Christian teleology. On Spencer's more palatable view, the social organism was evolving toward ethical perfection, where perfection was defined as the harmonious adaptation to existing environmental (i.e. material and cultural) conditions.[12] T.H. Green, the influential Oxford professor of moral philosophy, even went so far as to describe history itself as the history of moral progress.[13] "Survival of the fittest" (Spencer's phrase, not Darwin's) was seen by Spencer to mean "the survival of the most ethical." This implied that those individuals who could adapt to the dictates of public morality would invariably be happier than those who could not or would not adapt.[14]

Spencer's adherence to the Lamarckian theory of the inheritance of acquired characteristics rather than to Darwin's more ruthless theory of "natural selection" gave him two important advantages, the combination of which serves to explain the considerable public appeal of his own theories of moral

evolutionism. The first was that Lamarckian evolutionary ideas could be reconciled with the idea of a benevolent Christian God which was guiding human
adaptation to an industrializing and modernizing world. The second was
Lamarckism's compatibility with the cultural hegemony of the Protestant-
capitalist values of accumulation, self-help, thrift, industry, and initiative.[15]
Self-improvement (or self-help) ideally culminated, if not in self-perfection,
then at least in production of wealth and the achievement of social position
which could afterwards be passed on to one's heirs. Conversely, competition
for wealth and status was considered a spur to self-development, and ultimately a means of personal salvation.[16] Spencer's moral evolutionism was generally perceived as having successfully reconciled Christian teleology and
moral values with the (antithetical) material values of capitalist accumulation.
Spencer's synthesis thus created a seamless web of cultural values that rationalized and naturalized the existing social and cultural norms and promoted the
idea that moral progress was the natural correlative of material progress.[17] In
this way, the logic of Spencer's philosophic system fits in very nicely with prevailing late Victorian middle-class aspirations and expectations.

As to Britain's place in the world-evolutionary scheme, Jose Harris has
observed that

> the sense of British peculiarity and uniqueness...which had been such a marked
> feature of earlier historical consciousness, did not fade away, but it was at least
> partially replaced by the view that Britain had reached a higher stage on a com-
> mon evolutionary staircase, up which all progressive societies were destined to
> travel.[18]

The "powerful culture of hard-headed, no-nonsense, Anglo-Saxon empiri-
cism" as well as the rhetoric promoting the anachronistic cultural and political
ideals of Periclean Athens and Republican Rome did not fade away either.
Instead, they persisted and thrived in many quarters of political, legal, imperial,
and academic life. In other quarters, these ideas were simply realigned or
reconciled with Spencerian ideas.[19]

The concept of degeneration appeared to derive much of its authority and
power from the structure of scientific explanation. The scientific correlative of
degeneration was the concept of "entropy," which describes the degree to
which the energy of a system ceases to be available (i.e. useful) energy—a concept developed in the mid-nineteenth century by Rudolph Clausius and
William Thomson (later Lord Kelvin), two key figures in the development of
the science of thermodynamics.[20] Historically, "degeneration" was the
metaphor used to characterize what Sander Gilman and J.E. Chamberlin have
described as "the dark side of progress," and what Robert Nye has called "the
irony of progress." As Nye pointed out,

the idea of degeneration had a powerful appeal to British men and women in the period after 1885 ... because it appeared to account for developments in British life ... [which included the perceived increase in] "urban" diseases such as alcoholism, crime, insanity, suicide, and various sexual perversions ... about which there was widespread public concern.[21]

The particular appeal of the idea of degeneration during the last quarter of the nineteenth century can be situated within the discursive confines of the seemingly endless debate between the defenders of progress and their critics. The defenders, perhaps best exemplified by William Ewart Gladstone, typically looked at the beneficiaries of progress, and emphasized the concrete material advances which were seen as resulting primarily from the accumulations of technical innovations and positive social reforms.[22] The critics, exemplified by Alfred Lord Tennyson (in his later years) and the French philosopher Georges Sorel, more often examined the victims of progress, and emphasized instead the physical, psychological, and spiritual costs of the processes of industrialization and modernization.[23] Tennyson spoke of the unfulfilled promises of the reformers of the eighteen-thirties, and suggested that progress existed only in the rhetoric of the politicians. Examining the evidence of the last half century, Tennyson concluded in "Locksley Hall Sixty Years Later" (1886) that the country was full of menace, madness, and lies. He found the concept of equality a sham, and democracy an illusion, because the reality was that demagogues were ruling a sheepish public. Looking at the great civilizations of the past, Tennyson believed that, like them, England's greatness too would be ephemeral. He criticized the upper and middle classes for being largely without honor, dignity, nobility, and ideals. Characterizing the situation in terms that were more ideological, Sorel essentially saw the concept of "progress" as bourgeois dogma which was being used to oppress and enslave the working classes, and hence that "progress" was the ideology of the victors in the struggle for power in society.

If the concept of "degeneration" was often used in the evolutionary sense to describe a regressive social process that could be seen as the antithesis or complement of "progress," it was just as often used in the medical and psychiatric sense to describe a developmental process in individuals that was seen increasingly as "unhealthy." Certain sectors of the scientific community were concerned with understanding and explaining the apparently irrational behavior of individuals who regularly engaged in self-destructive, criminal, and antisocial activities. To that end, throughout the latter half of the nineteenth century men such as Bénédict Augustin Morel, the French medical psychiatrist, Cesare Lombroso, the Italian criminal anthropologist, and Henry Maudsley, the English medical psychiatrist, worked toward isolating, analyzing, and classifying various symptoms of degeneracy.[24]

Morel believed criminal and/or deviant traits resulted initially from environmental factors but could then be passed genetically to the next generation—fatalistically resulting in families of criminals. Lombroso believed that the appearance of criminal and/or deviant traits represented a reversion in the individual to a more primitive state of evolution.[25] Within certain psychiatric circles, Morel's Lamarckian theory of inherited criminal characteristics and Lombroso's theory of criminal atavism were, in practice, applied across the board to explain all types of social deviancy. The chronically sick, the mentally ill, the criminals, the sexually deviant, the politically malcontent, and even the chronically poor were labelled "degenerate" and classified medically as abnormal and anomalous members of the human species. This was bad enough, but the "degenerate" label was used so often in popular discourse in connection with virtually every social evil that an inevitable cross-linkage of negative associations occurred. If a person managed to fall into any one of the above categories, he was often, by association, suspected of fitting them all.

Daniel Pick has argued in a Foucauldian vein that the medico-psychiatric model of degeneration should be understood as an ideological production that was embraced by the various European states for purposes of social control.[26] All of the forces generally perceived as criminal or socially disruptive, whether collective phenomena such as the socialist and feminist movements, or individual acts of subversion, such as Wilde's, which contested the hegemony of the dominant moral values, could be, and were, viewed by many as socially regressive, and labelled "degenerate." In accordance with this view, the epithet "degenerate" was widely assumed to characterize anyone who did not meet or aspire to bourgeois standards and values, or anyone who threatened to subvert the existing (religious, social, political, sexual) status quo in any way, shape, or form.

One of the most capable popularizers of this theory was Max Simon Nordau, whose book *Degeneration* (dedicated to Lombroso) enjoyed a brief vogue in England and throughout Europe during the spring and summer of 1895, just as the Wilde trials were being held.[27] Coincidentally, an entire chapter of his book was devoted to Wilde and other so-called "Decadent" writers.[28] For Nordau, any deviation from an idealized middle-class world-view, whose cardinal virtue was complete submission to the existing status quo, was suspect. Placing complacency and conformity as the highest bourgeois ideals, Nordau defined "degeneracy" as the morbid deviation from an original type. Nordau's central thesis was that those who were far above average were just as dangerous as those who were far below average.[29] In *Degeneration*, Nordau attempted to show that society had just as much to fear from artists and geniuses as from the lowliest cretins, the most dangerous criminals, and the craziest madmen.[30] According to Nordau, artists such as Baudelaire, Ibsen, Kierkegaard, Nietzsche, and Wilde represented social threats precisely

OG focuses on constriction (handwritten annotation)

because they believed that difference could be a positive virtue and that individualism represented an ideal of self-perfection which required both self-mastery and the transcendence of the bourgeois idealization of mediocrity. Whereas Lombroso, Nordau's mentor, had been concerned primarily with classifying characteristics of physical degeneration, Nordau himself was concerned with identifying the characteristics of mental degeneration that were commonly found in creative artists. Nordau identified some of these defining characteristics as "unbounded egoism," "impulsiveness," "moral insanity," "emotionalism," the "inability to adapt to existing circumstances," a "predilection for inane reverie," a "propensity for cloudy, nebulous thought," and the "tendency to surrender to aimless streams of obscure, fugitive ideas and desires."[31]

Wilde's particular impulse was defined by Nordau as "an anti-socialistic, ego-maniacal recklessness and hysterical longing to make a sensation," with its chief aims being the "heckling of the Philistine" and the "irritat[ing of] the majority unnecessarily."[32] Nordau felt that Wilde's penchant for "queer costume" (which was not meant to suggest same-sex passion) represented an effeminate and "pathological aberration of a racial instinct."[33] Whereas Nordau devoted only three pages toward distilling the philosophy contained in Wilde's collected works into a celebration of three decadent leitmotifs, inactivity, immorality (including crime), and art—which was not too far from the mark—he devoted sixteen pages toward the analysis of those concepts with the goal of demonstrating the absurdity, irrationality, or anti-social nature of each. For Nordau, this evidence proved sufficient to confirm Wilde's mental infirmity, moral insanity, and inability to adapt to society.[34]

Nordau, among others,[35] identified Wilde as the most important representative of the English school of Aestheticism. English Aestheticism was viewed in turn as a branch of the "Decadent" movement in French literature and the arts. Wilde was initially drawn to aestheticism through an attraction to the Romantic and mystical poetry of Byron, Keats, Shelley, Wordsworth, and Coleridge; to the darker, proto-decadent works of de Quincey, Poe, and Swinburne; and to the dreamy anachronism depicted in the paintings of the Pre-Raphaelites.[36] His aesthetic consciousness was later developed and refined through intellectual apprenticeships to John Ruskin and Walter Pater at Oxford.[37] His own mature aesthetic theories were honed on the lecture circuit in America, and then "fleshed-out" and polished during several extended visits to Paris where he sought out and was sought out in turn by the most important of the French "Decadent" writers: Maurice Rollinat, Jean Lorrain, Paul Verlaine, Stephane Mallarmé, Paul Bourget, Edmond de Goncourt, and Joris Karl Huysmans.[38] Although there is no question that Wilde admired and was greatly influenced by the ideas and styles of these writers, especially Huysmans,[39] it is important to realize that despite many general thematic parallels, Wilde's mature views on aesthetics differed considerably from those expressed by the French "Decadents," as we will see in the next chapter.

The French Decadents represented less a homogenous school or organized group with an articulated ideology and a specific social or cultural agenda than a loose confederation of poets and artists whose works shared a general interest in, and phenomenological approach to, experiences that were regarded by conventional bourgeois standards as unusual, extreme, morbid, or perverse: diabolism, mysticism, dreams, fantasies, bizarre sexual practices, crime, and drug-induced hallucinations, among others.[40] Conceptions of "decadence" were equally varied. Théophile Gautier defined decadence as an artistic style:

> The style of decadence is nothing else than art arrived at that extreme point of maturity produced by those civilizations which are growing old with their oblique suns—a style that is ingenious, complicated, learned, full of shades of meaning and research, always pushing further the limits of language, borrowing from all the technical vocabularies, taking colours from all palettes, notes from all keyboards, forcing itself to express in thought that which is most ineffable, and in form the vaguest and most fleeting contours; listening, that it may translate them, to the subtle confidences of the neuropath, to the avowals of ageing and depraved passion, and to the singular hallucinations of the fixed idea verging on madness. This style of decadence is the last effort of the Word, called upon to express everything, and pushed to the utmost extremity....[41]

Paul Verlaine saw contemporary society in a state of decay which resembled the decay of previous civilized societies: "The decadence is Sardanapalus lighting the fire in the midst of his women, it is Seneca declaiming poetry as he opens his veins, it is Petronius masking his agony with flowers."[42] Gérard de Nerval, on the other hand, defined decadence as an ambivalent, solipsistic, and escapist attitude which was a function of present historical conditions.

> Our period was a mixture of activity, hesitation and idleness; of brilliant Utopias, philosophical or religious aspirations, vague enthusiasms...boredom, discord, and uncertain hopes. Ambition was not of our age...and the greedy race for position and honors drove us away from spheres of political activity. There remained to us only the poet's ivory tower where we mounted ever higher to isolate ourselves from the crowd. In those high altitudes we breathed at last the pure air of solitude; we drank forgetfulness in the golden cup of legend; we were drunk with poetry and love.[43]

Paul Bourget, after Wilde the pre-eminent theoretician of decadence, offered a model of decadence based on Spencerian notions of the social organism, in which society was seen as an organic system, and the individual as a "cell" within that social system. Bourget argued that "decadence denoted a state of society which produced too great a number of individuals unfit for the labours of common life," and a condition in which those unemployed individual cells refused to subordinate their cellular energy to the total systemic energy of the social organism. The willful independence of the individual cells constituted for Bourget the condition of social anarchy and represented the beginnings of the "decadence of the whole."[44]

Implicit in Bourget's theory was the idea that a healthy social organism was one that was able to take care of all its individual "parts." For Bourget, therefore, it was not the artists but contemporary society that was unhealthy and "decadent," or decaying, because the social system failed to provide for all of its constituent members. If society was neglecting its responsibility toward its members, Bourget suggested, then those abandoned individuals ought not to feel any responsibility toward society. But whereas Bourget sided with the individual and regarded dissent as a sign of health and vitality, Nordau privileged the systemic whole over the individual part, and concluded that Bourget's analysis simply demonstrated that "ego-mania makes the degenerates necessarily anarchists, i.e. enemies of all institutions which they do not understand, and to which they cannot adapt themselves."[45] For Nordau, the societal neglect of the individual neither constituted abandonment nor conferred upon the individual any special rights of self-determination. The fact that certain individuals took it upon themselves to abdicate their social responsibility, in effect "seceding" from society, was merely indicative of mental instability, and hence of "degeneracy."

Art historian Jean Pierrot has argued that the decadent aesthetic should be seen generally as constituting an historically specific response to a world and society that were incompatible with the personal ideals and values of the Decadents. Pierrot sees the French Decadents reacting to

> ... a somewhat pessimistic conception of human existence, seen as subject to the pitiless necessities of a physical, physiological, and social determinism that holds man in thrall to the laws of heredity, the species to those of evolution, and the exceptional individual to the law of the majority decreed by democracy. Religious faith has ceased to be anything other than a nostalgic memory; love is merely an unconscious subjection to an instinct aimed solely at the survival of the species. Nature, far from being the attentive and responsive witness conceived by romantics, is an unfeeling and pitiless mechanism.[46]

Pierrot identified two main sources for the cultural pessimism of the French: the first was the lingering national psychological trauma, the feelings of anxiety, dislocation, fragmentation, humiliation, and national inferiority that stemmed from the French defeat at the hands of Prussia in 1870–71.[47] The second source was the dominant and pervasive influence of the pessimistic philosophy of Schopenhauer, which was in vogue in France from the late eighteen-eighties.[48] Schopenhauer posited a spiritual crisis in modern life which grew out of a centuries-long erosion of faith in Christianity,[49] suggesting that with the historical demise of the absolute goal of eternal salvation, life had become a meaningless process with neither *telos*—the goal or endpoint—nor the criteria for evaluating it.[50]

I would broaden Pierrot's thesis by suggesting that on a much more general level, the psycho-historical circumstances to which the Decadents (among others) were responding can be described as encompassing the cumulative psychic effects resulting from long-term systemic changes in European society. These were more than just the long-term effects of war and the increasing inability of the traditional organized religions to compete with the addictive new "religion" of consumerism for the possession of the existential modern soul. The Decadents were also responding, if only subconsciously and indirectly, to the psychic effects resulting from major shifts in the geo-political positions of the European powers: to the unsettling effects of secret diplomacy, ever-changing alliances, the competition for colonies, the steady drain of Empire on the domestic economy, and the waning of popular support for imperial ventures.[51] Domestically, they were responding to all manner of social, political, and cultural upheavals and the accompanying psychic dislocations: the diaspora of the impoverished "residuum" as a result of the planned demolition of urban slum areas;[52] the devaluation and relativization of morality, and other effects of the decline of organized religions and the spread of a materialistic ethos; the loss or attrition of traditional values and local customs, and the increased blandness and uniformity of life; the ongoing forces and effects of industrialization and urbanization; the problems caused by the growing expansion of the electorate and the concomitant politicization of the masses; the pressures resulting from the competition between the established social and political ideologies and the challenges to customary ways of life posed by the new ideologies of mass democracy, socialism, and feminism; the stresses resulting from the challenges represented by new technologies; and the strains resulting from dealing with the contingencies and vicissitudes of an increasingly complex everyday life. In short, the Decadents were responding to a discrete set of historical circumstances, some liberating and others oppressive, that recent social critics have described variously as the effects of modernization, the "experience of modernity," and the onset of the "postmodern condition."[53]

Viewed collectively, the Decadents reacted ambivalently to the disruptive and fragmenting forces of modernity. On the one hand they rejected modernity and "repudiated everything that constituted the ideological foundation of contemporary society: progress, science, democracy, universal suffrage, and the spread of education."[54] As neo-Romantics, many of the Decadents lamented the passing of the (mythical) historical moment when artists were admired for their talent, respected for their accomplishments, and envied for their status as god-like creators. They looked with disdain upon a populace that confused popularity with greatness, and cursed the market-driven mechanisms that controlled the contemporary art-world and dictated what the artist had to produce in order to survive. On the other hand, they lauded the new social freedoms made possible by the decay of old social restrictions, and embraced the novelty, excitement, and possibilities for self-exploration offered by the modern city and the new technologies. They were also keen to exploit, to a greater or lesser extent, the relativization of moral values which had accompanied the relativization of aesthetic values. Since consistency was a virtue that was no longer prized, the various challenges of modern life could be embraced or ignored on a whim.

Paul Bourget suggested that the proper response to the current state of chaos, confusion, and uncertainty in society was to adopt an attitude of "skepticism," which he saw as assuming two basic forms, dilettantism and cosmopolitanism.[55] Dilettantism explained the artist's refusal or incapacity to take up any definitive moral or intellectual positions (what Wilde characterized as the "antinomian" stance), and cosmopolitanism justified the artist's lack of ties to (or commonality with) the community, and rationalized his inability (or unwillingness) to integrate himself within the community. Bourget in some ways anticipated the later Freud of *Civilization and Its Discontents* by suggesting that the prevailing current of cultural pessimism arose from an awareness of the fundamental disharmony between the reality of the world and man's desires, "a disharmony that the advances of civilization can only aggravate."[56] Freud's pessimistic conclusion—that because civilization was inimical to unrestrained instinctual gratification, personal happiness was an unattainable goal—would have been unacceptable to Wilde, Bourget, and many of the other Decadents. They would have argued instead that civilization and the "common good," such as it was, was simply not worth the sacrifice of one's personal happiness.[57]

The ambiguity and ambivalence of the decadent response to the complex set of historical conditions was perhaps best exemplified by Wilde, who, through lots of hard work, made it appear as if he glided effortlessly through each and every moment. Wilde often elected to withdraw from the world at his leisure, to repudiate his social obligations whenever convenient, to flee from the boredom and banality of everyday life whenever possible, and to retreat instead into a secret, solipsistic universe. There, unsullied, he was in an artificial paradise of his own design where his imagination could run freely and where his will was unchallenged. Seen in this way, the decadent aesthetic represented a specific way of ordering and compartmentalizing the world and one's experience of it.

In another sense, the decadent aesthetic, especially as Wilde embodied it, represented a desire to avoid, or transcend, the increasingly intolerable "schizophrenic" conditions of reality in the modern world. Fredric Jameson's view of social schizophrenia is based on Lacan's conception of schizophrenia as a language disorder, where a schizophrenic condition results from a breakdown of the relationship between signifiers. In Jameson's formulation, the schizophrenic experience of reality "is an experience of isolated, disconnected, discontinuous material signifiers which fail to link up into a coherent sequence." Daniel Bell points to a similar fundamental fault, or schizophrenic "rupture," between the societal values of work as described by Weber, and the hedonistic and individualistic values of popular culture.[58] From a psychoanalytic perspective, Wilde's embodiment of the decadent aesthetic served a healing and restorative purpose. Intellectually, the aesthetic provided the rationale which justified and enhanced the physical and emotional pleasures he experienced in his own private world of art and sex. The memory of the complete enjoyment and total satisfaction he encountered in this private world in turn dulled the pain, countered the tedium, and otherwise sustained him psychologically when he was forced to function within the parameters of the aesthetically imperfect, and often intolerable, "real" world. His ability thus to find solace, pleasure, and intellectual and emotional satisfaction was instrumental in replenishing his creative energies and in maintaining the "health" and integrity of his "self," and further compensated for the stupidity and mediocrity he had to endure in the public sphere.[59]

It was ironic that Wilde was primarily responsible for popularizing the ideas and themes of the French Decadents in England, for these same ideas came back to haunt him during the trials. Wilde's critical essays, especially "The Critic as Artist" and "The Decay of Lying"—the contents of which we will explore in greater detail in the following chapter—"pushed the postulates of the decadent aesthetic to their logical extreme" and were thus instrumental in establishing him as the "prime theoretician of French decadence."[60] Wilde's novel, The Picture of Dorian Gray, considered "the benchmark of Decadence in England," borrowed heavily from Joris Karl Huysmans' novel A Rebours.[61] The Picture of Dorian Gray (1890) was coincidentally published in the immediate wake of the "Cleveland Street affair," a highly publicized homosexual scandal involving a member of the Prince of Wales' household, "which nearly grew to the proportions of a Victorian Watergate, [and involved] cover-up charges against the prime minister, Lord Salisbury, and his government."[62] Wilde's literary treatment in The Picture of Dorian Gray of sin and corruption, and of vice and crime, the whole of which was underlain by a sub-text which suggested (but did not explicitly articulate) homoerotic longings and activities, had the notoriety of creating a major literary sensation and sparking a heated public debate on art and morality that was waged for months afterwards in the press.

Wilde's clever and impassioned arguments in defense of the ideas and sentiments expressed in his novel—which he repeated almost verbatim in his trial
testimony—contributed significantly toward linking in the public mind the
notions of decadence, sin, corruption, crime, immorality, and same-sex passion.

Sexual Inversion, Effeminacy, Homosexuality, and Homophobia

In his recent study of the "complexities and internal tensions" of Victorian
"styles of masculinity," James Eli Adams argues that "the dichotomy of hetero-
and homosexuality that emerges from late Victorian discourse has often distorted earlier Victorian constructions of 'manliness' by being unreflectively
read back on them."[63] In many ways, this same notion can be seen to be operating in many otherwise excellent critical studies of Wilde and Victorian same-
sex passion which have appeared in the past decade or two, many of which have
superimposed onto Victorian practitioners of same-sex passion twentieth-
century constructions of the "homosexual." This has resulted in a distortion of
the ways in which and the terms by which same-sex passion is discussed in the
Victorian context. The present study is the beneficiary of a relatively recent
series of brilliant and insightful studies beginning with Eve Sedgwick, and
including Alan Sinfield, Judith Butler, and James Eli Adams. Collectively, these
studies have immeasurably aided and "improved" discussions of Victorian sexual deviance by historicizing the terminology we use to discuss same-sex passion and by focusing on gender as a category of analysis. In this section, I will
present a version of the history of same-sex passion in England which attempts
to synthesize what I feel are the best and the most relevant of these recent conceptual breakthroughs. My aims are twofold: to show how and why culturally
embedded heterosexist structures of repression and mechanisms of restraint
influenced the Court's and the public's understanding of Wilde's deviance; and
to show how and why the Wilde trials radically transformed popular and professional attitudes toward practitioners of same-sex passion.

It is possible to document the more important changes in public and professional attitudes toward practitioners of same-sex passion—considered in
terms of both gender deviance and sexual deviance—at least as far back as the
early sixteenth century. Heterosexuality can be said to have been compelled
and mandated by English civil law since 1533, when an official decree by Henry
VIII superseded ecclesiastical law and brought the offence of sodomy (or bug-
gery) under the jurisdiction of civil authorities.[64] Legally, the act of sodomy
remained a capital offence until 1861 (although the death penalty was not
applied after the 1830s). Prior to the second half of the nineteenth century,
however, the legal classification of the act of sodomy was vague, and the epithet

"sodomite" was often used broadly to describe anyone who engaged in various forms of non-reproductive sex (with either men or women).[65] Historians of same-sex passion have generally agreed in describing the boundaries between sex and gender as much more relaxed and fluid in early modern England than they were during the Victorian era. In his study of "homosexuality" in Renaissance England, Alan Bray has argued that the term "sodomite" did not automatically denote either the practices of same-sex passion or an "effeminate" appearance or manner. Instead, the sodomite was typically represented in terms which indicated a certain deficiency of moral fiber and an inability to control one's impulses: terms such as "disreputable," "indolent," "extravagant," "libertine," and "debauched." Transvestism was also considered a vice in its own right and was not thereby construed as a sign of same-sex passion.[66]

The fluidity of sex and gender boundaries that Bray describes seems to have persisted well into the seventeenth century. Randolph Trumbach has argued that despite the threat of capital punishment, "it was acceptable in late-seventeenth century England for adult males to have sexual relations with women and with male adolescents—neither of whom threatened their status as adult male."[67] Trumbach claims that this casually ambivalent attitude toward sex changed and became obsolete around 1700. Alan Sinfield suggests that in the early eighteenth century a theoretical "sea change" took place regarding the way in which sexual identities were generally perceived. The change was "towards a situation where the masculine/feminine binary structure was much more clear-cut and much more important." Whereas early modern models tended to view women as incomplete men, eighteenth-century models viewed men and women more or less as complementary polar opposites rather than as different by degrees. The rigidity of these new categories prevented easy slippage back and forth, so thereafter a person tended to be seen as either male or female, with appropriate and corresponding social and cultural expectations regarding gender roles and sexual preferences attached.[68] The enforcement of these new sexual and gender boundaries by social, cultural, and legal means effectively marginalized those men who continued ambivalent and/or same-sex practices and drove them underground, in effect creating a subculture of sexual and gendered deviance.[69]

Although the gender roles and sexual possibilities for working-class men continued to retain some of the early modern fluidity throughout the nineteenth century, social and cultural expectations regarding appropriate gender roles and sexual preferences for middle-class men and women were becoming more rigidly drawn by the late eighteenth century.[70] Leonore Davidoff and Catherine Hall have shown that middle-class references to "homosexuality" were few and far between during the late eighteenth and early nineteenth centuries, but when such references were made, "sexual acts between men were regarded with outraged horror."[71] By the mid-nineteenth century, the prevailing middle-class norm of "manliness" was identified with "honest, straightforward speech and action, shorn of any hint of subtlety or equivoca-tion," and tempered by a "muscular aestheticism" whose correlative virtues included honesty, vigor, asceticism, virility, loyalty, industry, piety, candid-ness, and earnestness.[72] Aristocratic men were (if they wished to be—and they often did) largely exempt from this middle-class conception of manliness and also from the correlative social and cultural boundaries which delimited gen-der roles and proscribed sexual acts. In great part this was because they pos-sessed the requisite wealth and power to command privacy and, if necessary, to circumvent the law.

In the mid-nineteenth century, certain individuals within the medical, legal, and scientific communities demonstrated an interest in describing and under-standing the confusing phenomenon of same-sex passion. Jeffrey Weeks has suggested that during the second half of the nineteenth century legal views on "homosexuality" were re-evaluated and reclassified according to the most cur-rent medical and scientific opinions on the subject, a process Weeks has termed "the medicalization of homosexuality."[73] Examples of the most currently avail-able professional opinions on the phenomenon that was referred to as "sexual inversion" include those of Richard von Krafft-Ebing, the German neurologist; Karl Heinrich Ulrichs, the German lawyer; and Cesare Lombroso, the Italian criminal anthropologist whose theories on degeneration we have already encountered.

In *Psychopathia Sexualis*, Krafft-Ebing classified "sexual inversion" as a form of insanity, a disease which affected the nervous system. He believed that "inversion" was inherited rather than learned, but that such a tendency could be aggravated by early habits of self-abuse. Interestingly, though, Krafft-Ebing's critique of "inverts" was predominantly concerned with the outward appearances of inverts and with gendered aspects of identity rather than with the performance of specific sexual acts. Krafft-Ebing focused primarily on traits of effeminacy in men, which he saw manifested as tendencies for cross-dressing and propensities for adopting feminine roles.[74]

Karl Heinrich Ulrichs felt the phenomenon of sexual inversion could be best explained by physiology, and to that end, developed an elaborate taxonomy which attempted to categorize the various forms of "sexual inversion":

The normal man he calls *Dioning*, the abnormal man *Urning*. Among *Urnings*, those who prefer effeminate males are christened by the name of *Mannling*; those who prefer powerful and masculine adults receive the name of *Weibling*; the *Urning* who cares for adolescents is styled a *Zwichen-Urning*; Men who seemed to be indifferently attracted by both sexes, he calls *Uranodioninge*. A genuine *Dioning*, who, from lack of women, or under the influence of special circumstances, consorts with persons of his own sex, is denominated *Uraniaster*.

A genuine *Urning*, who has put restraint upon his inborn impulse, who has forced himself to cohabit with women, or has perhaps contracted marriage, is said to be *Virilisirt*—a virilized *Urning*.[75]

In contrast to Krafft-Ebing, the basis of Ulrichs' classification was sexual object choice instead of gender confusion. Like Krafft-Ebing, Havelock Ellis, Magnus Hirschfeld, and others, Ulrichs put forth a congenital theory to explain the transmission of sexual difference.[76]

The Italian criminal anthropologist, Cesare Lombroso, went even further than Krafft-Ebing and Ulrichs and explicitly linked the concept of "sexual inversion" with his concept of degeneration. Whereas Krafft-Ebing drew a distinction between the vicious and the perverse, in which the vicious was criminal, and the perverse was pathological, Lombroso erased this distinction, and categorized sexual inversion as both vicious *and* perverse, as both criminal *and* pathological. More specifically, Lombroso saw sexual inversion as a symptom of criminal predilection, as a type of "moral insanity," and as an atavistic trait signalling a regressive evolutionary tendency, and thus as a symptom of physical degeneracy. This view led Lombroso to recommend that all criminals, including "inverts," be imprisoned and forbidden to procreate.[77]

Jeffrey Weeks argues that these professional efforts at categorizing and classifying the practitioners of same-sex passion effectively marked a "transition from notions of sin to concepts of sickness or mental illness."[78] Weeks suggests that as a result of the "medicalization" of the concept of the "homosexual," "sexual inverts" were less frequently regarded by civil authorities, as they had been for centuries, as weak-willed sinners who succumbed to irresistible impulses to commit what were generally condemned as "unnatural" and "unspeakable" acts. Instead, due to the "progressive" and "positivistic" efforts of medical, scientific, and legal professionals, "inverts" were afterwards regarded by civil authorities with ever-increasing suspicion and alarm as genetic anomalies.

Weeks' theorization of a major shift in the late nineteenth-century bureaucratic and professional attitudes towards "inverts" is inspired and shaped by the theories of Michel Foucault. Foucault's structural interpretation of this major shift argues that the "old" image of the "sodomite," along with the "old" images of the criminal and the lunatic, which generally attributed causality to the agency of the individual, had been undergoing substantial alterations since the early nineteenth century. The "new" images of the "homosexual," as well as the "new" images of the criminal and the lunatic, which now attributed causality to "nature" or heredity, were constructed, legitimized, and reified by the collective authority of the medical and scientific communities.[79] Foucault has described this historical moment very dramatically in what has now come to be regarded (wrongly, I will argue) as a classic statement whereas:

the sodomite had been [regarded as] a temporary aberration, the homosexual was now [regarded as] a [separate] species....The nineteenth-century homosexual became a personage, a past, a case history, and a childhood, in addition to being a type of life, a life form, and a morphology, with an indiscreet anatomy and possibly a mysterious physiology.[80]

In Foucault's reading of the history of same-sex passion, the "sodomite" represents a step on the developmental curve to the "homosexual," and the identity of the "sodomite" is determined more or less exclusively by the performance of the sodomitical act. Gendered aspects of the "sodomitical type" of person are, if not neglected altogether, then totally subordinated to sexual aspects. According to Foucault and Weeks, in the last quarter (or even last half) of the nineteenth century, "sexual inversion" signified less an alternative behavioral choice than a discrete ontological condition which was probably inherited and possibly contagious. Thus, as Foucault conceptualized it, the "modern" concept of the "homosexual," as defined in the professional discourse of Lombroso, Krafft-Ebing and Ulrichs, represents a clear epistemological break with the early modern concept of the "sodomite."

Weeks (explicitly) and Foucault (implicitly) suggest that the medical efforts to understand and explain "homosexuality" in the second half of the nineteenth century resulted in the strengthening of old censures and the construction of new censures against homosexuals.[81] The older notions of sin were not replaced wholesale by the new scientific views, but were instead conflated with and incorporated into the new scientific conceptualizations of sickness and disease. The old moral censures against "homosexuality" received validation from the new "scientific" concepts of "homosexuals" and "homosexuality," while the new scientific censures against "homosexuals" and "homosexuality" were moralized by the old notions of sin "against God and Nature." Thus, in effect, traditional religious notions of sin suddenly carried the stamp of medical approval, and the medical concepts of insanity and sickness were demonized and pathologized by religious notions of sin, corruption, and damnation.[82] Although the speed with which the newly pathologized medical/scientific conceptions of "inversion" were assimilated into popular culture must be seriously questioned, the eventual hegemony of these concepts in the twentieth century has been seen by some, such as Foucault, as a testament to the increased public respect for the professional status and authority of the physicians and scientists.[83]

According to Weeks, the legal and legislative effect of the "medicalization of homosexuality" was to broaden the scope of the existing laws so that virtually every form of male "homosexual" behavior was prohibited. Whereas before 1885, "the only legislation which directly affected homosexual behaviour was that referring to sodomy," as a result of section 11 of the 1885 Criminal Law

Amendment Act, any act of "gross indecency" between men was considered a misdemeanor and punishable by law.[84] As Weeks implies, the "central point" is that whereas before 1885 the law was aimed exclusively at prohibiting and preventing certain sexual *acts*, after 1885 the law appeared to be aimed at persecuting "a certain type of *person*," the male homosexual, who was defined as the type of person likely to commit "acts against nature."[85]

It is at this point that Weeks' narrative seems somewhat over-determined by Foucault's structuralist reading of the history of same-sex passion. As a result, Weeks' description of this pivotal moment in the history of homosexuality in England becomes somewhat inconsistent and mechanistic. In different places within his larger narrative on the history of sexuality in England, Weeks presents information which is at odds with his own theory of the legal construction of the "homosexual" in the 1885 Criminal Law Amendment Act. By Weeks' own account,

> as late as 1871, concepts of homosexuality were extremely underdeveloped both in the Metropolitan Police and in high medical and legal circles, suggesting an absence of any clear notion of a homosexual category or of any social awareness of what a homosexual identity might consist of.[86]

It is, I think, very difficult to reconcile the London Metropolitan Police's lack of a concept of "homosexuality" in 1871 (presumably the one municipal agency that would have had the *most* knowledge of the behavior of those men who practiced same-sex passion) with Weeks' contention that by 1885, section 11 of the Criminal Law Amendment Act was aimed specifically at "a certain type of person" who seemed likely to commit "acts against nature." Weeks' suggestion that a clear conception of this "certain type of person"—"the homosexual"— could have been developed, disseminated, understood, legislated for, and instituted within such a short space of time (fourteen years) seems particularly dubious, especially considering the contentious nature of Parliamentary politics, the relatively slow and sometimes glacial pace at which even mandated changes took hold in governmental agencies at both the national and municipal levels, and the great difficulty most Victorians had in discussing any form of sexuality at all.

For as Jeffrey Weeks also points out, throughout the nineteenth century, and even into the early decades of the twentieth century, English publishers resisted publishing books which discussed sexuality (even heterosexuality), and large sections of the English public resisted reading them.[87] Accordingly, public discussions of a subject as taboo as "homosexuality" were virtually unthinkable. Writers like John Addington Symonds and Havelock Ellis who produced serious scholarly works which speculated on the nature of the phenomenon of "sexual inversion" were not only unable to find publishers, but they also had to worry about the possibility of prosecution. Havelock Ellis' book, *Sexual Inversion,*

> was labelled "lewd and obscene" in a[n English] court of law in 1897 and Ellis refused to publish further volumes of *Studies in the Psychology of Sex* in English until the 1930s, and when Krafft-Ebing's *Psychopathia Sexualis* was translated into English in the 1890s, translators discreetly rendered potentially offensive passages into Latin.[88]

J.A. Symonds' *Studies in Sexual Inversion* had to be published privately, even as late as 1928.[89] Although the widespread public, private and governmental efforts to control, proscribe, and prohibit discussions of all forms of sexuality in the last decades of the nineteenth century certainly provides evidence of the existence, viability, and effectiveness of heterosexist repressive structures and mechanisms of restraint, such evidence does not lead us necessarily to conclude that the laws were aimed specifically at discrete "types" of sexual beings, as Foucault and Weeks would have us believe.

John Marshall offers an alternative reading of this important historical moment in the "social construction" of "the [English] homosexual" which more closely fits the evidence provided by the various discourses that emerge from the Wilde trials.[90] While the broader outline of Marshall's history generally follows that of Weeks, Marshall's narrative diverges in two crucial respects. First, Marshall disputes Weeks' chronology regarding the medical/legal definition of the "homosexual"; and secondly, in a related point, Marshall challenges Weeks' theory about the intent of the Labouchere Amendment (section 11 of the 1885 Criminal Law Amendment Act which prohibits "acts of gross indecency between men"). Marshall disputes Weeks' contention that the medical/legal concept of the "homosexual" emerged historically with the Criminal Law Amendment Act of 1885, and provides convincing evidence to suggest that a clear concept was lacking well into the twentieth century.[91] Moreover, Marshall argues that it was not until the nineteen-forties and even nineteen-fifties that medicalized accounts of the pathological "pervert" tended to replace the older, essentialist concepts of the "invert."[92] Marshall suggests instead that what persisted in the public mind in the interim was a vague "distinction between 'real' homosexuality, or inversion, [an essentialist position] and pseudo-homosexuality, or perversion [a moral position]."[93] Marshall argues most convincingly that the Labouchere Amendment was consistent with the general drive against sexual decadence (broadly construed) and did not presuppose the existence of a special type of person:

> Labouchere was concerned with indecent assaults involving males, which at that time had to be committed on persons under 13 years of age to be punishable. His

clause was designed to make any assault of this kind punishable whatever the age of the assailant. However, the actual amendment referred rather vaguely to "acts of gross indecency," and it was this undefined offence that was to be so widely interpreted in the years that followed. Apparently Labouchere did not intend his clause to penalize "grossly indecent" acts which involved the consent of both parties.[94]

Marshall's interpretation is echoed by H. Montgomery Hyde. Hyde states that sometime after the passage of the Criminal Law Amendment Act Labouchere admitted that he had gotten the idea for his clause from the French penal code, which suggests that

> he [Labouchere] must have had in mind primarily the corruption of youth, since the French code did not penalize homosexual acts between consenting adults in private ... but it did protect children and juveniles against sexual inter-ference.[95]

In Marshall's account, late-Victorian attitudes toward practitioners of same-sex passion are much more consistent with early modern attitudes in that the "sodomite" seems to be viewed primarily as constituting a moral dilemma, not only for the individual himself but also for society. What we do not get from Marshall's reading is the sense that sodomitical urges represent the bio-logical imperatives of an aberrant, anomalous species. While the sodomitical act is certainly condemned and criminalized, the crime itself is *still* represented within the context of moral laxity, and as a function of a personal lack of self-control and a dissolute, debauched lifestyle—that is, as a combination of agency and environment. In light of this evidence, Foucault's claim—that "the nineteenth-century homosexual became a personage, a past, a case history, and a childhood, in addition to being a type of life, a life form, and a morphology, with an indiscreet anatomy and possibly a mysterious physiology"—does not ring true. If we accept Marshall's argument, then both the substance and the timing of Foucault's theory of the "epistemological break" between the concept of the "sodomite" and the concept of the "homosexual" have to be re-evalu-ated. The evidence provided by the Wilde trials suggests that if an "epistemo-logical break" did indeed occur, it did not occur *before* the trials took place.

I would argue that Foucault's theory of the "epistemological break" between the "sodomite" and the "homosexual" and Weeks' theory of the "medicaliza-tion of homosexuality" err fundamentally, in that they superimpose a some-what rigidly conceived late twentieth-century (structuralist) model of the "homosexual" (which conceptualizes deviance almost exclusively in sexual terms) onto what was still in the late-Victorian period a very fluid and ambigu-ous construct that tended to conflate gendered and sexual forms of deviance.

The more precise "scientific" term "sexual invert," which one would expect to see in the Court records and the newspaper accounts of the Wilde trials, if the term or the concept was indeed available and current in popular or professional circles as Weeks and Foucault assert, never appears. Instead, Wilde's deviancy was consistently described in moral and social terms (as a failure to fulfill his moral "duty" or "obligation" to society), and his sexual transgressions were still perceived largely in gendered terms—as a violation of the culturally mandated "manly" modes of behavior. With very few exceptions, the concepts that were most often invoked (or alluded to euphemistically) to describe Wilde's behavior and manner were "indecent," "immoral," "corrupt," "decadent," and "effeminate."[96]

Prior to the Wilde trials, "effeminacy" in men did not necessarily signal a predilection or an inclination toward the practice of same-sex passion but rather a behavioral tendency toward the frequent and obvious display of emotions, and a preference for spending time in the company of women instead of men. During the Victorian era, "effeminacy" traditionally referred to "a male person or institution weakened by luxury or inactivity," and was identified with so-called "feminine" virtues: fastidiousness about appearance and manner, secrecy, subtlety, subterfuge, and equivocation. Conversely, "manliness," as we have already seen, was identified most closely with "straightforward, frank, unhesitating action and utterance" and thus with openness, consistency and truth.[97]

Alan Sinfield has argued that, within the Victorian context, there was a distinct class basis for "manliness." Theoretically, working-class men had difficulty in asserting "manly" virtues in the public sphere because they lacked self-determination in the workplace. This logic assumes a "natural" association between masculinity, the ownership of property, and the ability to command authority. In this sense, "manliness" was equated with the ability to control and manipulate one's environment, specifically the external environment.[98] The private or domestic sphere was commonly described as the women's "domain" and as the primary locus of consumption, and as such it was distinctly identified with the "feminine."[99] Recent writers such as Sinfield, Adams, and Sedgwick have described "manliness" as a particularly middle-class attribute. Collectively, they have suggested that it was through the embodiment of the stereotypical Protestant/capitalist virtues of industry, productivity and acquisitiveness in the public sphere that the "typical" middle-class male succeeded in differentiating himself symbolically from the indolent aristocratic male who inherited everything he owned, who was exempt from many laws, who did not have to work, and who could command a degree of privacy that was beyond the means of all but the wealthiest middle-class men. Within these parameters, "manliness" represented a distinctive and distinguishing attribute that could only be acquired through hard work in the public sphere and therefore was not

something that one inherited simply by virtue of one's gender. Hence, in accordance with this view, the aristocracy as a class has been mapped as "effeminate"
because they were seen generally as consumers rather than as producers, as
leisured and even lazy rather than as industrious workers, as secretive and
equivocating rather than as straightforward and earnest, and as fastidious,
indulgent, morally lax and over-refined rather than as common-sensical, dis-
ciplined, ascetic and vital.[100] Within the late-Victorian context then, the link
between "effeminacy" and the aristocracy invoked a nexus of associations
which contained the ideas and imagined effects of indolence, dissoluteness,
luxury, extravagance, connoisseurship, internationalism, high religion, and an
interest in Catholic Europe—all values and virtues which in the popular imagination distinguished the aristocracy from the vigorous, productive, and motivated middle classes.[101]

Sinfield argues that prior to the trials, and despite obvious perceptions of
effeminacy, Wilde was exonerated from suspicions of same-sex practices
because his identifications, aspirations, and affectations associated him in the
public mind with the leisured upper classes. In a parallel argument, Sinfield
suggests that the association between the art-world, aesthetics, and same-sex
practices before the Wilde trials was also very ambiguous. Artists were generally regarded as "lady-killers" perhaps, and as narcissistic, but not necessarily
as homoerotic. After the trials, however, Sinfield implies that the association
between art and homoeroticism was firmly cemented.[102] While one can certainly think of many exceptions to Sinfield's paradigm of the "homoerotic
artist," there are also many turn-of-the-century artists and writers who do fit
that particular mold, Wilde most prominently. In any case, Sinfield's analysis
establishes some very strong impressionistic links between the concepts of
"effeminacy," the aristocracy, artists and the art-world, all of which came
together and were reified and embodied in the public persona of Wilde.
Sinfield asserts, quite rightly, I think, that same-sex passion and practices did
not become part of this constellation until *after* the trials, when "the image of
the queer cohered at the moment when the leisured, effeminate, aesthetic
dandy was discovered in same-sex practices, underwritten by money, with
lower-class boys."[103] Before the trials, the sexuality of effeminate men was "naturally" assumed to be heterosexual, and was secondary in importance; after the
trials, effeminacy in men—as exemplified now by Wilde—invariably signalled
the potential and even the probability of same-sex preference.[104] Whereas
before the trials effeminacy in men was more a function of class and general
dissoluteness and less a function of same-sex practices, after the trials, effeminacy in men became a clear function of same-sex practices, and less a function
of class and general dissoluteness.[105]

With all this said, how then does one begin to measure the historical significance of the Wilde trials vis-à-vis the history of same-sex passion in Britain?

Jeffrey Weeks contends that "the downfall of Oscar Wilde was a most significant event for it created a public image for the 'homosexual,' a term by now
coming into use, and a terrifying moral tale of the dangers that trailed closely
behind deviant behaviour."[106] Weeks' implication is that the trials constituted
a sort of forced and humiliating public "outing," and that Wilde indeed ought
to be seen, as he is by some today, as the first celebrity "poster boy" and martyr for what would later become (in the nineteen-sixties and nineteen-seven-
ties) the "gay liberation movement." In mapping the Wilde trials onto a
teleology of liberation whose present-day manifestations include the late twentieth-century ideologies of "gay rights" and "gay pride," Weeks intimates that
this new public image of the "uncloseted" but still "medicalized" homosexual
(i.e. "liberated" by the truth, but still unfairly stigmatized by the public) should
be seen, issues of intentionality aside, first as a radical political statement, and
second, as a positive and necessary step toward eventual social justice and
possible acceptance by the dominant heterosexist culture.

In contrast to Weeks, Marshall suggests that Wilde was prosecuted primarily because of the general immorality of his behavior and not because Wilde
resembled the special and exclusive "type" of the "homosexual." Marshall
argues that "the public image being presented by [the Wilde trials] was not one
of 'homosexual man' but rather a much more generalized account of moral
decline, unregulated male lust and contagious social disease."[107] Marshall's
position in many ways replicates and reinforces the arguments made at the
time by Victorian feminists. From the viewpoint of many of the feminists in the
"social purity" movement, for example, it was "unbridled male lust and male
privilege," in addition to sexual and class exploitation, that were the most
important issues.[108]

Eve Sedgwick, with a slightly different political spin, sees an entirely different set of issues at stake in the trials:

> the middle-class oriented but ideologically "democratic" virilizing, classicizing,
> idealistic, self-styled political version of male homosexuality which [Edward
> Carpenter and John Addington Symonds] in their tendentiously different ways
> embodied and sought to publicize and legitimate, seems with the protracted
> public enactment of the [Wilde] trials to have lost its consensus and its
> moment.[109]

In effect, Sedgwick argues from the perspective of culturally available models
of "homosexuality" that the "modern" and "masculine" model of male homosexuality promoted by Symonds and Carpenter—which she describes as a
viable alternative to the Wildean model—lost both its impetus and its historical moment because of the hysteria and moral panic caused by the Wilde trials,
and that what endured instead in the public memory was the one-dimensional

"effeminate" model of male homosexuality represented by Wilde. Sedgwick suggests that a crucial effect of the trials was that the nascent Carpenterian model of male homosexuality arrived stillborn on the world-historical scene, to the disadvantage of (presumably) a significant percentage of English homosexuals who had been searching for a more acceptable and more respectable public image. Sedgwick thus implies that the Wilde trials represent both an unfortunate case of bad timing and a missed opportunity for Victorian "homosexuals."

Alan Sinfield's limited and understated conclusion that the Wilde trials ought to be seen as a watershed in the way in which the public perceived "effeminate" behavior in males is perhaps the conclusion that is most compatible with the historical "facts" of the present case. After the trials, Sinfield argues, the concept of male effeminacy would forever be linked in the public mind, not only with same-sex passion, but with a constellation of other associations that include "leisure, idleness, immorality, luxury, insouciance, decadence, and aestheticism"—all terms which were inexorably linked with Wilde as well.[110]

If we can agree with Jeffrey Weeks that the trials were significant for contributing to the creation of a new public image for the "homosexual," we must qualify his conclusion by stating that this new image was in no way a "better" image.[111] If the trials did indeed constitute a major labelling event for homosexual men, as Weeks suggests, then it was a labelling event of the worst possible kind.[112] As Havelock Ellis commented, the trials may have contributed mainly to raising consciousness among homosexuals throughout Europe, and thereby to the beginnings of the formation of a positive and political identity among male "homosexuals"; but it must also be stated that the results of the trials made it clear just *how* hostile society really was toward same-sex practitioners, and just *how* difficult it would be for same-sex advocates to transform public opinion on the subject.[113] While socialists in Germany could afford to be publicly vocal in support of efforts to promote an understanding and tolerance of "homosexuality," in effect trying to link the causes of social and sexual liberation, those (few) socialists in Britain who were privately sympathetic and in positions of influence were forced to remain publicly silent for fear of alienating their own constituency.[114]

I believe the true importance of the trials has to be seen on both real and symbolic levels. Symbolically, they were significant for raising the specter of "homophobia," and for arousing and promoting in the public a (very real) fear of the "new" image of the "homosexual" that emerged from them, an image which effectively fused into an identifiable and recognizable constellation the concepts of male effeminacy, immorality, same-sex passion, decadence, degeneration, criminality, and aestheticism. On both real and symbolic levels, they were even more significant for revealing, reasserting and strengthening the heterosexist structures of repression and the mechanisms of restraint that were already present in English society, if in a somewhat muted form.

In Lacanian terms, the "symbolic order" is defined as

the ideal and universal set of cultural laws that govern kinship and signification and, within the terms of psychoanalytic structuralism, govern the production of sexual difference in accordance with an idealized "paternal law."[115]

The "paternal law" that Lacan hypothesizes is, in effect, the central organizing principle of all cultures. The "law" creates linguistic structures of meaning and signs which in turn limit and determine how we define meaningful experience. The symbolic order is necessarily "masculine" and "paternal" because men have historically been the ones to hold power, especially in Western societies. Therefore, it is men who have generally defined the categories of meaningful experience, had the power to institutionalize them within society and culture, and had the opportunities to support them with rationalist discourses. It is an obvious truism to state that men and women alike must grow up and live within these cultural and discursive constraints.

Judith Butler has argued that within the "symbolic orders" of traditional paternal and patriarchal cultures, an inarticulate "taboo against homosexuality must precede the heterosexual incest taboo; [and that] the taboo against homosexuality in effect creates the heterosexual predisposition" through which the Oedipal conflict becomes possible.[116] According to a Freudian/Lacanian paradigm, the original infantile inclination toward polymorphous perversity, which obviously includes homoerotic desires, is repressed during the Oedipal conflict, and those desires are then channelled exclusively onto heterosexual lines, in accordance with the hegemonic paternalistic values of the dominant culture. Stated somewhat more reductively, the repression of polymorphous and homoerotic impulses in infants and children has the long-term effect in cultures of reproducing a clearly artificial, yet universally "normalized" condition of heterosexuality.[117]

Butler differs from most thinkers today in her approach to the philosophical problem of identity in that she destabilizes and problematizes notions of identity that have previously dominated Western thought. Fundamentally, Butler believes that our identities owe much more to appearances and to the perception of appearances by others than to traditional Hegelian or Romantic notions of identity, which rely on the subject/object dichotomy and which emphasize notions of "substance" and "will," and an "agency" which stems from them. Butler suggests instead that our identities are continually in the process of being "constructed" by ourselves and also by others, inasmuch as other people interpret our identities within the paradigms and through the "signs" that are currently available within any given culture or society. The various aspects of our self that comprise our identity are constituted "performatively," which is to say that over time our identity is constituted through the cumulative effect of the combination of repeated actions, practices and locutionary acts that we execute or "perform."[118] For Butler, identity is defined as "a signifying practice," and her emphasis on "performativity" is meant to highlight the "artificial" nature of our identities. Through the "performative" repetition of actions, practices, and speech we have the possibility of creating, reformulating, and even subverting our own identities. Within Butler's model, the body is theorized as the "site" of cultural inscription, and the sexual and gendered aspects of a person's identity are viewed as the products of the discursive practices of a given society and culture.[119] Butler defines "gender" as "the repeated stylization of the body, a set of repeated acts within a highly rigid regulatory frame that congeal over time to produce the appearance of substance, of a natural sort of being."[120] In other words, gender itself is imagined as an "act," a "role" that one plays, and as a "performance" that conveys the illusion of reality.

With respect to the Wilde trials, Butler's rethinking of gender in accordance with performative criteria and within the parameters of a Lacanian "symbolic order" is important because it permits the possibility of an interpretation of the trials which transcends the relatively narrow bounds of the "history of homosexuality" in England, the field which has heretofore constituted the traditional framework for interpreting the trials. Within the "history of homosexuality"— a field which has been greatly over-determined by notions of sexual deviance— notions of gender deviance and its effects have been largely overlooked. The philosophical ideas of Butler, in conjunction with the work of Sedgwick, Sinfield, and Adams, fundamentally address the issue of gender deviance, and further permit the events and effects of the Wilde trials to be mapped onto the much larger cultural field of "heterosexism" within Victorian England. Within this larger interpretive framework, we can represent the trials as a "performative" event in which Wilde's identity was effectively constituted and evaluated. Wilde's locutionary acts within the courtroom, in conjunction with the evidence provided by his written works, and the further evidence of his sexual practices as they were revealed in the testimony of witnesses, all served to "construct" Wilde's identity in a public way. This "performatively constituted" identity was then interpreted by both the Court and the public according to the culturally available "labels" and other modes of signification, which were themselves influenced and conditioned by the prevailing "heterosexist" values. The result was to emphasize Wilde's transgression of culturally mandated gender roles. Certainly Wilde's sexual transgressions were significant, but they were significant primarily as the legal pretext under which his transgressions of gender could be addressed and punished. The significance of the public "performance" of gender, as Butler intimates, is to maintain gender within a binary frame which privileges heterosexuality and "manly" males.[121] Symbolically then, an effeminate man such as Wilde could not be seen as holding or having power and wielding influence in Victorian England (or anywhere else, for that matter), for that would have been construed as "women" having, holding, or wielding power, a thought which would have upset the entire phallogocentric applecart.

If "heterosexism" is "a mechanism for regulating the behavior of the many by the specific oppression of a few,"[122] then it is surely, from a Spencerian-Darwinian viewpoint at least, a "mechanism" of "cultural defense" that was prompted by perceived threats to the stability and integrity of the social "organism."[123] Although this mass-psychological metaphor is admittedly ungainly, it is useful for making the point that such a defensive response on the part of a society and culture was "compulsively" and even "unconsciously" directed toward the suppression of "internal excitations" which threatened to disrupt the heterosexist equilibrium of the whole.[124] In transgressing the pre-scribed boundaries of "compulsory" heterosexuality, male effeminacy and same-sex practices were seen to threaten the integrity of the family unit and the distinct separation of gendered spheres of responsibility.[125] On both real and symbolic levels, the strong and stable family unit was claimed to be of vital importance to national, and even imperial, security. Thus, the importance of Wilde's transgressions was that, besides being represented as an offence "against God" and "against nature," they were also represented in ideological and political terms which stressed their potential to subvert the prevailing social and geo-political orders. And in his "performatively" constituted role as a "corrupter of youth," Wilde was seen as posing a very real threat to posterity as well.

Although he himself was not blind to certain aspects of the public symbol-ism of his fall, he never really believed in his heart of hearts that what he had done was wrong. While in prison, Wilde saw himself fated to be seen by pos-terity as a martyr—like a hero in a Greek tragedy—and in that regard, as a vic-tim of a conspiracy of larger and uncontrollable forces. However, he felt his enduring martyrdom would be to his Art, and not to his sexuality.[126] His mem-oir, De Profundis, can in many ways be seen as a profound and melancholic meditation on his failed aesthetic life. In some respects, his aesthetic repre-sented an ideal which he was not able completely to realize or fulfill. Surely within that aesthetic life, and prior to the trials, his same-sex practices sus-tained him, occupied his thoughts, and even inspired him, but in De Profundis he downplayed and even dismissed his sexual activities as irrelevant to what he saw as his primary role as a creator of art.[127] Although the trials served to define Wilde—to contemporaries and posterity alike—in terms of "effeminacy" and the practice of same-sex passion, his life up until that point had been defined, publicly at any rate, through his artistic creations and through his aesthetic philosophy. As I will try to show in the next chapter, it was Wilde's aesthetic philosophy that established the general parameters within which his practices of same-sex passion developed, and that dictated many of the forms in which he expressed himself and his sexuality.

5 THE PATHOLOGY OF PLEASURE AND THE ESCHATOLOGY OF IMMANENCE

Theorizing Wilde's Identity and Desire

Wilde's Ontological Aesthetic of Dissent

The key to understanding Wilde's identity (as he himself conceived it), and the world-view that emerged from it, can be found in an offhanded remark during the Queensberry libel trial as he was being cross-examined by Mr. Carson on the "peculiar" nature of one of the letters he had written to Lord Alfred Douglas:

> CARSON: "Was it an ordinary letter?"
> WILDE: "Certainly not. ... It was a beautiful letter."
> CARSON: "Apart from Art?"
> WILDE: "I cannot answer any questions apart from Art[!]."[1]

Within the context of the first trial, Wilde's casual remark that he could not answer "apart from Art" provided Carson with the opportunity of demonstrating just how peripheral art really was in a materialistic society that valued function and utility over everything else. For Carson, art could be decorative, entertaining, and perhaps even edifying, but never any more than that, and the producers of art were suspect in more ways than one. Certainly from Carson's viewpoint, and by extension from the viewpoint of the middle-class "Philistines"[2] whom Carson represented (figuratively, if not literally), the status of the artist was at best marginal, often shading toward the liminal, and at worst verging on the criminal.[3]

I want to suggest that within Wilde's claim that he could not answer "apart from Art" are contained the parameters for a discussion of his aesthetic, and the essence of that aesthetic as well. Since the aesthetic context of Wilde's remarks before the Court—and perhaps more importantly, the aesthetic context of Wilde's sexuality—have never before been developed in any systematic way, it will be a primary goal of this chapter to do so.

I will be concerned primarily with analyzing the substantive and performative aspects of Wilde's identity and with describing the ways in which his identity was informed and shaped by his personal aesthetic. I will be less concerned with constructing a genealogy of Wilde's aesthetic than with elucidating the point to which it had evolved by 1895. Within the larger scope of this treatise, this chapter represents an effort to understand Wilde and his actions on his own terms, and from the viewpoint of the philosophy which justified them.

I want to characterize Wilde's aesthetic as "ontological" in nature. That is, Wilde's aesthetic was fundamentally an aesthetic of "being." In a formal sense, aesthetics is concerned primarily with the evaluation and critique of the appearance and content of a work of art. In Truth and Method, Hans-Georg Gadamer has suggested that from a hermeneutical perspective, an object of art can be seen to represent a separate world that is complete and perfect in and of itself. As a self-contained and self-referential universe, the art object is seen to possess its own logic, morality, economy, history, and so on.[4] What I refer to as "ontological aesthetics" represents the application of formal aesthetic concepts and criteria to the experience and perception of one's self and one's life. In this way, "ontological aesthetics" represents the evaluation of one's self and one's actions in accordance with specifically selected aesthetic criteria. In short, one's self and one's life constitute "artistic works in progress" and are evaluated as such.

Like the work of art, the self is regarded as a perfect self-contained world which has its own logic, morality, economy, and history. The individual's "ontological aesthetic" thus represents the particular world-view, or combination of world-views, that results from the unique existential combination of "the self and its circumstances."[5] In this sense, it is invariably subjective, constructed, contingent, and ephemeral. More importantly, an "ontological aesthetic" is necessarily a product of desire or will which is then cultivated and nurtured. As Nietzsche described it, such an aesthetic of being emanated from the individual's unique self, and thus represented a will to transform or remake the self and the world in accordance with one's own ideas or criteria.[6]

In essence, Wilde's "ontological aesthetic" consisted of three basic elements: first, the core was a philosophy or world-view which Wilde defined as "antinomian." In De Profundis, Wilde wrote, "I am a born antinomian. I am one of those who are made for exceptions, not for laws."[7] Wilde's usage of the term was at once vague and complex, and denoted much more than just a rejection of socially established morality. Secondly, his "antinomianism" was accompanied by a style, attitude, or sensibility which can be identified as "camp." One of the primary attributes of "camp" is a desire to subvert the existing status quo. Thirdly, his "antinomianism" was imbued with a corresponding ethos of hedonism, which exalts the self-indulgent pursuit of pleasure as the primary goal of life. Within Wilde's "ontological aesthetic," hedonism represented the ethical correlative of the "antinomian" world-view and the "camp" sensibility. Together, the three elements complemented and reinforced one another, often giving the (correct) impression of a self in wholehearted concert with itself— that is, of a unified, consistent, and coherent self. Ironically, it was precisely this impression of consistency and coherency that Wilde did his best to undermine during the course of the trials.

In a Christian theological context, an "antinomian" is one who believes that faith alone, and not necessarily obedience to existing moral laws, is necessary for salvation. However, Wilde's usage of the term "antinomian" was a bit more eclectic than that and was, moreover, entirely secular in orientation. He substituted a complete and utter faith in oneself for faith in God and replaced the redemptive goal of eternal salvation with the more immediate and worldly goals of pleasure and material success. It was probably not by coincidence that he elected to retain the idea of disobedience to existing moral laws. I see his "antinomianism" as having been based on his sense of his own narcissistic "exceptionalism" and, indeed, his "superiority," in terms of talent, creativity, and intellect.

There are many ways of evaluating Wilde's "narcissism" from a psychoanalytic perspective. Generally, however, these many different opinions fall into one of two schools of thought: "narcissism" is felt to be either "healthy" and desirable, or "unhealthy" and undesirable. In Freud's usage, "narcissism" is fundamentally unhealthy and undesirable, and, more significantly, hints at the "pathological" and the "perverse." Besides signalling a more or less excessive degree of self-love and self-absorption—traits which are considered undesirable in a social sense precisely because they privilege the existence and demands of the person's "subjective" inner world over and above the existence and demands of the external "objective" reality—Freud's initial conception of "narcissism" also possessed connotations of auto-erotism and "homosexuality."[8] More recently, however, psychoanalysts such as Heinz Kohut have come to see "narcissism" in a much more positive light, and represent it as an indicator of mental health and high self-esteem, and hence as an essential component of a stable, cohesive and well-integrated self.[9] In the case of Wilde, I find Kohut's view to be more persuasive and applicable.

In essence, Wilde's "antinomianism" signified a militant, elitist and egotistical form of radical individualism which justified the flouting of existing civil and moral laws by "exceptional" individuals. As Wilde understood it, "antinomian" was synonymous with "artist," and the artist's main purpose in life was twofold. Publicly, the artist's purpose was to create beautiful things as a protest against an "ugly" world, and to use the gift of expression to speak out against social injustice on behalf of the inarticulate or voiceless masses. In "The Soul of Man Under Socialism," Wilde alluded to the natural affinities between the artist and the criminal, and hence to their natural "alliance" in the eyes of the public. He viewed art and crime as two of the most intense modes of individualism known to man. He interpreted them as fundamental protests against the prevailing conditions of this world: the former against the ignorance, mediocrity, and lack of taste which defined the Philistine hegemony, and the latter against the material inequality within society.[10] He also envisioned the modern artist in the Romantic sense as an iconoclastic and libertarian Prometheus, whose acts of self-discovery and self-liberation were performed altruistically in the interests of the freedom of all humanity. He suggested that as compensation for such selfless acts of public service, artists ought to be exempt from the rules and regulations which governed the "ordinary" person.[11]

Even more importantly, however, in a private sense the artist's purpose was to "create" himself. Whatever else the artist produced was secondary to the molding and shaping of the self in accordance with the professed aesthetic ideals of the artist. Everything and everybody one encountered in life could assist in this task of self-creation, and for that reason, no one could ever be discounted or dismissed. In Wilde's case, this tendency manifested itself through his consistent kindness to and decent treatment of those young men whom contemporaries would have regarded as his social and cultural inferiors. Insofar as one can speak of a Nietzschean "will to power" with respect to Wilde, that "will to power" would represent a conscious desire to know oneself completely and to realize one's full potential as a human being. In this sense, Wilde's "antinomianism" is best understood as a material and metaphysical expression of his "will to power" over himself and the external world.[12]

The existential figure of the artist thus represented for Wilde an entirely different ontological problematic altogether. Whereas for Freud, a contemporary, it was the external world that was "real" and the subjective life of the individual that was largely irrelevant, for Wilde it was just the opposite. Freud believed mental health consisted of accepting reality and the constraints of civilization. Wilde, on the other hand, believed sanity meant "being true to oneself" and acting consistently with one's beliefs.[13] The present condition of English society, Wilde suggested, was that of "artificially arrested growth, or of disease, or death."[14] Despite this, Wilde believed that English society was slowly evolving toward a more pluralistic and caring state which would eventually be more tolerant of the "individualism" of its citizens. While recognizing that individualism was a disturbing and disintegrating force in society, Wilde argued that such a force was necessary to combat the "monotony of type, slavery of custom, tyranny of habit, and the reduction of man to the level of a machine."[15]

Contrary to the prevailing view, Wilde believed that a condition of chronic dissatisfaction with the status quo represented a sign of health in individuals, and by extension, a sign of health in society. Correspondingly, the "will to rebel" was considered a public virtue since it almost always led to change and improvement in society.

As Susan Sontag develops it in her classic essay, the "camp" attitude is based not on the inversion, but on the subversion of value, especially as value relates to the "absolute" standards of "high" culture: truth, beauty, and seriousness.[16] The "camp" sensibility essentially strikes a playful and ambivalent pose toward the established aesthetic canon, allows for multiple frames of reference, and relativizes truth, beauty, and seriousness. At one point, Sontag defines "camp" as "the consistently aesthetic experience of the world" which represents a "victory of 'style' over 'content,' 'aesthetics' over 'morality,' and of irony over tragedy."[17] The subversive attitude was so deeply ingrained in Wilde that he was virtually unable to refrain from mocking almost everything that was meant to be taken seriously in society. Ironically, even the solemn proceedings in his own criminal trials proved to be an irresistible target for his subversive instincts, and the final result was self-destruction.

More recently, film critic Jack Babuscio has written about the idea of "camp" and its relation to what he terms the "gay sensibility."[18] Like Sontag, Babuscio identifies irony as one of the four basic features of "camp," along with aestheticism, theatricality and humor. Babuscio sees irony, defined broadly as "any highly incongruous contrast between an individual or thing and its context or association," as the proper subject matter of "camp." At the heart of this incongruity he sees the "idea of gayness as a moral deviation."[19] Babuscio's views on "camp aestheticism" are straightforward and generally follow Wilde's (and Sontag's) lead. Babuscio suggests that aestheticism represents "an intense mode of individualism and a form of spirited protest against an inflexible moralistic society." As a practical tendency, "camp" represents a performative way of expressing identity that employs style and fashion as masks which simultaneously reveal and conceal what is underneath.

The theatrical aspects of "camp" emphasize role-playing within the larger world-views of "life-as-theatre" and "world-as-stage." Interestingly, Babuscio explains that individuals with "camp sensibilities" tend to appreciate the "intensity" and "uniqueness" which the actor brings to the role being played, rather than merely identifying with what the "character" represents.[20] Humor is seen serving a threefold function: as the ability to appreciate the comic elements within irony; as a subversive strategy toward dealing with a hostile environment; and therapeutically, as a way of dealing with personal bitterness and sadness. Paradoxically, Babuscio also notes that "camp" is a very serious undertaking, in that those who "camp" have to feel earnestly that they are right and morally justified in subverting and making fun of the hegemonic heterosexist culture.[21]

In a different context, Matei Calinescu has theorized "camp" in relation to the condition of "modernity." For Calinescu, "camp" superficially resembles "kitsch," which is defined as the celebration of the "aesthetically inadequate": that is, those things that would normally be considered as trash, junk, of poor quality, mediocre, sentimental, pompous, or overstated. More precisely, "camp" represents the appropriation of "kitsch" by elements of the artistic avant-garde for ironically disruptive purposes.[22] Indeed, the "camp" sensibility "cultivates bad taste—usually the bad taste of yesterday—as a form of superior refinement."[23] Moreover, within the Freudo-Marxist context of Max Horkheimer and Theodor Adorno's critique of popular culture and the modern entertainment industry, Calinescu argues that "kitsch" represents a mode of consumption (of objects and images) that is particularly characteristic of the acquisitive middle classes, and hence that it represents a uniquely modern and self-indulgent form of hedonism that is fundamentally compensatory in nature.[24] Thus, in order to compensate for working so hard and producing so much, the modern person tends to "waste" or "squander" one's leisure time by playing hard and consuming excessively (and even "decadently"), in order to forget the more unpleasant and functional aspects of one's present reality.

Certainly this "modern" tendency to work hard, to play hard and to consume "decadently" was visible in Wilde's extravagant spending habits, his lavish dinners, his excessive drinking, and his frequent "consumption" of the bodies of young men. Beyond the obvious, however, Wilde's understanding of hedonism possessed a philosophical dimension as well. As Wilde understood it in a classical Greek sense, the goal and impetus of hedonism was the pursuit and realization of one's essence.[25] In Aristotelian terms, the essence was conceptualized as "the highest unrealized potential." The concept of "hedonism" therefore represented much more to Wilde than just the mindless pursuit of sensuous pleasure; rather, pleasure, both physical and intellectual, along with pain, were considered as possible modes of perfection. Intellectual pleasure was certainly considered superior to physical pleasure, but even physical pleasure was considered a worthwhile temporary goal as long as one refrained from becoming a slave to one's passions. In turn, the world itself was seen as the locus of objects of possible enjoyment. The better to accommodate and enjoy this range of potential objects, Wilde's "ontological aesthetic" manifested itself instrumentally through an ambivalent and relativistic morality, which was conveniently adaptable to all circumstances, and which permitted the widest possible range of behavior in any given situation.

To this point, I have tried to sketch in the broad outlines of what I have characterized as Wilde's "ontological aesthetic." In what follows, I will be exploring some of the specific ways in which Wilde's antinomian philosophy, "camp" sensibility, and hedonistic ethos were expressed through his behavior, particularly as that behavior was represented within the trial testimony. During the

Queensberry libel trial especially, Wilde spent a great deal of time trying to explain and justify his philosophy and the more innocuous aspects of his "lifestyle" to an often hostile court. Wilde could not afford to admit that the crimes for which he had been charged were perfectly consistent with the lifestyle and attitudes he had advocated in his published works, because the truth would have convicted him. Ironically, it was the defense under Carson (and later the prosecution under Gill and Lockwood) that was compelled to point out the similarities between Wilde's aesthetic philosophy and his alleged lifestyle and activities.

The first section of this chapter will be concerned with analyzing those aspects of Wilde's aesthetic that emerged as problematic issues within the "literary part" of the Queensberry libel trial. In effect, the extensive discussion of Wilde's literary works during the Queensberry libel trial (and for weeks afterwards in the press) constituted a wide-ranging public debate over the ability of art to influence public morality. The corruption of public morality in turn became a central aspect of the criminal charges against Wilde. Since the transcript of the Queensberry trial was read into the record of both subsequent criminal trials, the substance of the "art and morality" debate effectively provided the philosophical context within which the prosecution's portrait of Wilde's sexual activities was later situated. The second section of this chapter will analyze those aspects of Wilde's aesthetic that emerged in the context of the Court's representations of his sexuality.

Decadence as Fashion: The "Literary Part" of the Case

The following passage is excerpted from the Queensberry libel trial and contains a "question and response" between Carson and Wilde on the subject of the moral content of Wilde's "Phrases and Philosophies for the Use of the Young."

> CARSON: "Listen, sir. Here is one of the 'Phrases and Philosophies for the Use of the Young': 'Wickedness is a myth invented by good people to account for the curious attractiveness of others.' You think that true?"
> WILDE: "I rarely think that anything I write is true."
> CARSON: "Did you say rarely?"
> WILDE: "I said rarely. I might have said never; not true in the sense of correspondence with actual facts."
> CARSON: "'Religions die when they are proved to be true.' Is that true?"
> WILDE: "Yes, I hold that. It is a suggestion towards a philosophy of absorption of religions by science, but it is too big a question to go into now."

CARSON: "Do you think that was a safe axiom to put forward for the use of the young?"

WILDE: "It was a most stimulating thought." [Laughter]

CARSON: "'If one tells the truth one is sure, sooner or later, to be found out.'"

WILDE: "That is a pleasing paradox, but I do not set very high store on it as an axiom."

CARSON: "Is it for the good of the young?"

WILDE: "Anything is good that stimulates thought at whatever age."

CARSON: "Whether moral or immoral?"

WILDE: "There is no such thing as morality or immorality in thought. There is immoral emotion."

CARSON: "'Pleasure is the only thing one should live for; nothing ages like happiness'?"

WILDE: "I think that the realization of oneself is the prime aim of life, and to realize oneself through pleasure is finer than to do so through pain. I am on that point entirely on the side of the ancients."

CARSON: "'A truth ceases to be true when more than one person believes in it'?"

WILDE: "Perfectly. That would be my metaphysical definition of truth; something so personal that the same truth could never be appreciated by two minds."

CARSON: "'The condition of perfection is idleness'?"

WILDE: "Oh yes, I think so. Half of it is true. The life of contemplation is the highest life, and so recognized by the philosopher."

CARSON: "'There is something tragic about the enormous number of young men in England who at the present moment are starting life with perfect profiles, and end by adopting some useful profession'? Is that philosophy for the young?"

WILDE: "I should think that the young would have enough sense of humor."

CARSON: "What would anybody say would be the effect of 'Phrases and Philosophies' taken in connection with such an article as 'The Priest and the Acolyte'?"

WILDE: "Undoubtedly it was the idea that might be formed that made me object so strongly to the story. I saw at once that maxims that were mere nonsense, paradoxical, or anything you like—several of them have appeared in my plays—might be read in conjunction with it."[26]

In a nutshell, this passage contains many of the substantive issues that were addressed within the trial. The general discussion of Wilde's views on art and literature—which others have referred to as the "Art and Morality" debate[27]—was dominated by Carson's attempt to prove—and Wilde's attempts to resist—the notion that a direct correspondence existed between the moral content of a work of art and the character of the artist who produced it. Within this central problematic of the relation between art and morality are contained several equally important and related issues. These issues include: first, the related series of ontological problems involving the question of the artist's identity and appropriate social role, the concomitant problem of "posing," and its relation to questions of "sincerity" and "authenticity"; second, the central problem of the relationship between the character of the artwork and the character of the artist; third, the epistemological question of the ability of a work of art to influence others; and fourth, the legal issue of the corruption of youth. In what follows I will look more closely at Wilde's responses to Carson's questions and explore the traces of the "antinomian" substrate—largely derived from his own critical works—which informed them.

At one point during this lively exchange, Wilde stated that "the realization of oneself is the prime aim of life." At another point in the testimony, Carson asked Wilde if any well-written book, no matter how immoral it was, could be considered a good book. Wilde replied,

> If it were well written it would produce a sense of duty, which is the highest feeling a man is capable of....No work of art ever puts forward views of any kind. Views belong to people who are not artists.[28]

At first glance, Wilde's response seems to have inadvertently conflated the seemingly antithetical notions of beauty and duty. The confusion is eased, however, when one realizes that the sense of duty Wilde referred to was the "aesthetic" duty of being true to oneself. Wilde was the first to update the Delphic maxim, "Know thyself," to "Be thyself," thus modifying it to correlate with the conditions of the modern world and his own aesthetic.[29] Wilde attributes the origin of this aesthetic to Christ, and describes "Be thyself" as the essence of Christ's message.

In "The Soul of Man Under Socialism," Wilde suggested that "the real men ... the poets, the philosophers, the men of science and culture ... were the men who had realized themselves" and whose lives were thus "actualized" and fully conscious. The cultivation and full development of the life force within the individual represented for Wilde the highest possible mode of perfection.[30] Life, for him as for Nietzsche, "[was] only a means to something; it is the expression of forms of the growth of power."[31] Wilde's conception of "Life" is related closely to Nietzsche's, in that Life represents a positive force which unifies the disparate forms and forces within the universe. Like Nietzsche, Wilde emphasized Life as process more than product.[32]

For him and Nietzsche alike, art was synonymous with individualism, and as an intense mode of individualism, art represented a disintegrating and disturbing force within society.[33] In *The Will to Power*, Nietzsche echoed Wilde's general view of art as the countermovement to the "decadent" forms of religion, morality, and philosophy which he considered "anti-life."[34] The nihilistic impulse within art was considered positive, critical, and beneficial, not for the artist alone, but for everyone. Moreover, the tension between the artist and society was mirrored symbolically within the self of the artist, manifesting itself as a constant struggle between creative and destructive forces for possession of the artist's soul.[35] The disruptive function of art was seen as expressing a reaction to the monotony of life in an impersonal, mechanistic society, as well as a critique of the mindless conformity to traditions, customs, and habits. In addition, art acted as a spur to the processes of social levelling. Paradoxically, perhaps, the nihilism implicit within the function of art, as described by Wilde, can be seen as representing a therapeutic antidote to the even more destructive nihilism that he saw as implicit in utilitarianism and the Protestant work ethic. Within these signal values of a hegemonic industrial capitalism, the social idealization of competition leads to an ethos of "winning at all costs." Since only a few can ever win (leaving all the rest as losers), the long-term effect of this ethos has been social fragmentation, atomism, alienation, and anomie.[36]

In "The Critic as Artist," Wilde described art as "a way of improving a deficient life, by giving it elegance, form, and permanence." This suggests that everything that matters in life is ephemeral: love, passion, beauty, food, joy ... all of which seem to arrive in haphazard fashion. Arguing logically from this point, Wilde observed that "Life is a failure from an artistic point of view"—because one can never repeat the same emotion twice, and perfect moments can never be planned. In a related statement, Wilde claimed that "Art is a refuge from life"—life in this case meaning the practical, useful organization of life by society—a refuge where one can pursue the contemplative life with its goal of not doing, but being, and not just being, but becoming, reaching our potential—which is described in Aristotelian terms as the *Bios Theoretikos*, or theoretical life. In this regard, art's function transcends the therapeutic and leads one on a process of self-discovery. Moreover, Wilde suggested, "the [real] mission of the aesthetic movement is to lure people to contemplate, and not to lead them to create."[37] Creation without contemplation was to be avoided at all costs as a pointless activity.

Wilde's statement that "[strong] views belong to people who are not artists" suggests that a true artist is necessarily ambivalent, ambiguous, and inconsistent.[38] His comment linking poets, philosophers, artists, and scientists to the concept of "real men" suggests a radical revaluation of the prevailing attitudes toward power. "Real men" were no longer just the "doers" of the world, they were the "thinkers" as well. To Wilde's way of thinking, cultural and intellectual "capital" was infinitely more valuable to posterity than social or economic capital. From a social standpoint, the concept of power was traditionally linked to notions of position, wealth, and status. In contrast, Wilde's concept of power was most closely tied to an Emersonian notion of self-reliance,[39] in which power is represented as an attribute of the self-realized and proactive individual. Such individuals are—especially within the contemporary context of a "schizophrenic" or "atomistic" society[40]—self-confident enough to feel comfortably at home amidst the chaos, strong enough to do without the usual guides, signposts, and reference points of others, and able instead to design and follow their own path through life.

Wilde's concept of the intrepid artist engaging with life and keeping reality at bay resonated deeply with what Georg Simmel would in the following decade characterize as the modern "social type" of the "adventurer."[41] Simmel observed particular affinities between the artist's and the adventurer's modes of experiencing the world: both the artist and the adventurer were detached from society and its concerns; art and adventure have a similar way of compressing time and concentrating experience, allowing it to be more deeply felt; the adventurer, like the artist, was often a "stranger": near, yet remote; similar, yet different; involved, yet indifferent.[42] Moreover, both were beyond life, as art represented an imagined reality, and adventure represented the experience of an "other" reality which was clearly delineated from life, as in a "lived dream."[43] In transcending the grossly mundane, the truly adventurous and artistic lives are given up to the meaninglessness of chance. This "surrender to serendipity" necessitates the dropping of defenses and reservations, and requires an openness to the new, and a trust in fate that derives ultimately from a faith in oneself.[44] When Wilde states that "the condition of perfection is idleness," he suggests that idleness is the necessary precondition for art or adventure.[45] As intimated in the preceding chapter within the context of aristocratic privilege, idleness implies the possession of leisure time, and leisure time implicitly contains within it the possibility of doing anything you desire. "Doing exactly what you want to do at any given moment" constitutes yet another definition of the artist (and the aristocracy).

At one point in their exchange, Carson accused Wilde of "posing" as someone who was indifferent to issues of morality or immorality, and further asserted that "posing" was a favorite word of Wilde's. For his part, Wilde denied both of Carson's allegations, flippantly joking that "he had no pose in the matter."[46] Wilde was in this instance merely toying with Carson by playing with the ambiguous meaning of the word, but within the larger context of the trial, the question was that of trying to decide exactly who Wilde was trying to skewer and caricature from the witness-box: the "antinomian" artist, or the respectable middle-class *bourgeois*? In any case, the notion of "posing" cannot be lightly dismissed, for not only did it play a significant role within the trial, but it represented a key concept within Wilde's aesthetic as well.

Wilde developed the concept of posing within his critical works as a particularly artistic mode of conveying and apprehending the truth. In "The Critic as Artist," Wilde commented on the truths of masks, noting that "man is least himself when he talks in his own person. Give him a mask and he will tell you the truth."[47] In "The Truth of Masks," he developed the idea that although masks are worn to disguise, they often revealed more than they hid. He wrote

> ... in aesthetic criticism, attitude is everything. For in art there is no such thing as a universal truth. A Truth in art is that whose contradictory is also true. Just as it is only in art-criticism, and through it, that we can apprehend the Platonic theory of ideas, so it is only in art-criticism, and through it, that we can realize Hegel's system of contraries. The truths of metaphysics are the truths of masks.[48]

The cryptic last line suggested that absolute Truth was not of this world, and conversely, that the truths of this world were contingent and unreliable. If that was the case, Wilde argued (in a vein that anticipates the postmodern position of Baudrillard, for instance), then one might as well lie as tell the truth. And if a lie was no different from the truth, it followed that meaning became fluid and arbitrary, and the distinction between art and reality could be blurred at will. His statement, "A truth in art is that whose contradictory is also true," anticipates the generic postmodern position which dismisses the possibility of a single, monolithic, absolute "Truth" in favor of the simultaneous existence of multiple and equally valorized "truths" which can be randomly embraced or rejected according to the subjective criteria of the day.

In "The Decay of Lying," Wilde used the "art" of lying as the basis for his entire aesthetic. He argued that consistency was an over-valued trait in society, and a virtue of the "dullard, doctrinaire, and tedious." He distinguished between politicians who misrepresent, and liars who fabricate, and singled out lawyers and sophists as the best liars of all. Wilde suggested that it served a therapeutic purpose within the aesthetic in that lying served to ease guilt, circumvent reality, and avoid confrontation. As Nietzsche put it, "we possess art lest we perish of the truth."[49] The real world was described as "too depressing to write about," and in order to compensate for the disappointment of a dismal reality, the liar's aim was to "charm, delight, and give pleasure," and ultimately to distract from the dreary prison-house of realism. Moreover, Wilde felt that without lying there would be no civilization.[50] Wilde's statement that "the artist's mistake [was] an overreliance on life [as truth]" even hints at the quietistic philosophy of Schopenhauer, which invokes traces of the Hindu concept of *maya* and suggests that the world itself is a dream, or an illusion.

Wilde explicitly linked art and lying, stating that "Art has never once told us the truth."[51] In other words, the business of art is to tell lies. Lying, defined as the "telling of beautiful untrue things," was considered the artistic mode of expression *par excellence*.[52] Thus the object of art for Wilde was "not simple truth, but complex beauty." Moreover, "Art never expresse[d] anything but itself." The reason for this was that art's frame of reference was not the world, but rather other works of art. In other words, Wilde suggested—again antici-pating the postmodern position of contemporary theorists such as Baudrillard, Derrida, Jameson and Lyotard—lies, fictions, truths, and beauty could only be interpreted within the relativistic context of all the other lies, fictions, truths, and beauty that comprised our world. Everything then becomes equally mean-ingful, or meaningless, as one is able to assign meaning and bestow value at will.[53] Again echoing Schopenhauer, the world according to Wilde was revalu-ated and perceived as a product of one's subjective "will and idea." On one hand, the objective world was meaningful and important as a locus of material consumption and a source of subject matter, fame, and money, while on the other hand, the world was "aesthetically inadequate" and therefore meaning-less. Alternating between those two positions was simply a matter of conveni-ence, as evinced by Wilde's performance in the witness-box.

Within the aesthetic of lying, "posing" emerged as a logically inconsistent mode of being-in-the-world. Playing roles, and pretending to be what one is not, or in Wilde's case, arbitrarily emphasizing one aspect of his complex per-sonality over another, was just such a performative mode. It was a mode of being, moreover, that was implicitly self-contradictory. On one hand, it repre-sented the playful ethos which valorized uselessness and worthlessness.[54] On the other hand, "posing" could serve a base utilitarian function, as it did for Wilde in the witness-box. By pretending to be someone other than who he was—a credible law-abiding middle-class citizen—Wilde hoped to achieve his ulterior motive: to sway the Court and secure Queensberry's conviction. From the witness-box, Wilde's testimony parodied middle-class outrage at the accu-sations against him, and did not resist the idea of self-caricature if it would prompt a laugh and garner the audience's support.

Georg Simmel discussed posing as an aspect of the philosophy of fashion, which conceived the individual as "the vessel of social contents which are put on and taken off."[55] In a world in which appearance is often confused with truth and reality, fashion permits posing. Posing through fashion can be described as a mode of lying through one's appearance in an effort to stave off or avoid reality. The symbolic function of fashion is to represent a particular spirit or attitude which, according to Simmel, can never be accepted because of its transience. Adherence to the arbitrary dictates of fashion thus represents a celebration of the ephemeral present, and a continuous subversion of tradi-tions and customs.[56]

Following Wilde's logic of the truth of contradictories, if fashion can serve symbolic purposes, then symbols can serve fashionable purposes. Wilde's attempts to play to the Court for laughs, to appear outrageous, and to mouth the more obvious "decadent" platitudes might be seen from this perspective as part of a more calculated effort to "perform" the "fashion" of decadence in order to fulfill the audience's expectations vis-à-vis his flamboyance and theatricality. Many in the courtroom had come expecting a show, and Wilde was not one to disappoint an audience, even if it wasn't paying. Wilde had never been regarded by contemporaries as a deep thinker in any case, and he would have been content for that impression to remain intact. His decadent "pose," which accentuated his glittery, polished surface, at once disguised the underlying subtlety, depth, and complexity of his operational intelligence and deflected attention away from the real motives that lay behind the actions that were being questioned.

Art and Morality

When Wilde said that "anything is good that stimulates thought...whether it [is] moral or immoral," he was stating his belief that aesthetics and ethics occupied totally separate spheres of reality.[57] Wilde's position on the issue of the moral responsibility of the artist had been a matter of public record long before the trial, and the trial simply gave him the opportunity to articulate his theories in person before another audience.

In July of 1890, Wilde had written a letter to the editors of the *Scots Observer* in response to an anonymous review of *The Picture of Dorian Gray*, which had just appeared in *Lippincott's Monthly Magazine*. The reviewer found the story occupied "with matters fitted for the Criminal Investigation Department" and criticized it for appealing primarily to the prurient interests of "outlawed noblemen and perverted telegraph boys."[58] Wilde accused the reviewer of confusing the artist with his subject matter:

> One stands remote from one's subject-matter. One creates it, and one contemplates it. The further away the subject-matter is, the more freely the artist can work. Your reviewer suggests that I do not make it sufficiently clear whether I prefer virtue to wickedness or wickedness to virtue. An artist, sir, has no ethical sympathies at all. Virtue and wickedness are to him simply what the colours on his palette are to the painter.[59]

In this passage, Wilde described ethics instrumentally as a tool to be used and manipulated in order to create desired effects. In a letter to the editors of the *St. James's Gazette* in response to another negative review of *The Picture of Dorian Gray*, he said that "the function of the artist is to invent, not to chronicle ... the supreme pleasure in literature is to realize the non-existent."[60] In this sentence, he contrasted the often unsatisfying "realism" of life with the potential perfection of art. Reality was an uncontrollable, imperfect realm which was plagued by limitations, and where action always implied compromise. Conversely, the "ideal" realm of art represented a free space in which potential was unlimited and where perfection was therefore attainable. Moreover, Wilde argued, art valued those human traits that interfered with the social values of productivity and efficiency: quality of thought, depth of feeling, and degree of sensitivity.[61]

In his critical works, Wilde stated his preference for Aristotle over Plato on matters of aesthetics, because whereas Plato treated art from a moral point of view in terms of its importance to culture and its effect on the development of character, Aristotle treated art from a purely aesthetic standpoint and concerned himself with determining the relationship of Truth to Beauty.[62] In "The Critic as Artist," Wilde appropriated the Darwinian concept of the evolutionary or developmental continuum and used it metaphorically to suggest that aesthetics represents a higher, more evolved, form of ethics:

> Aesthetics are higher than ethics. Aesthetics ... are to Ethics in the sphere of conscious civilization, what, in the sphere of the external world, sexual is to natural selection. Ethics, like natural selection, make existence possible. Aesthetics, like sexual selection, make life lovely and wonderful, fill it with new forms, and give it progress, and variety and change. And when we reach the true culture that is our aim, we attain to that perfection of which the saints have dreamed, the perfection of those to whom sin is impossible, not because they make the renunciations of the ascetic, but because they can do everything they wish without hurt to the soul, and can wish for nothing that can do the soul harm, the soul being an entity so divine that it is able to transform into elements of a richer experience, or a finer susceptibility, or a newer mode of thought, acts or passions that with the common would be commonplace, or with the uneducated ignoble, or with the shameful vile.[63]

In this passage, Wilde associated ethics with the tedium of necessity and survival, and with law, order, safety, and security. Ethics arose out of necessity from the public realm and was forced upon the individual whether the individual liked it or not. On the other hand, Wilde associated aesthetics with pleasure, fun, passion, and excitement. In contrast to ethics, aesthetics was a very private matter that was cultivated and shaped by choice and desire. Wilde felt that personal growth and development were possible only through the stimulation provided by an "ontological aesthetic." Ethics, especially as it was represented in Christian beliefs and codified in civil laws, was viewed as a rigid, static system that limited the individual's personal growth by stifling the imagination and discouraging experimentation. The most crucial difference for Wilde between aesthetics and ethics was their respective positions with regard to sex and sexuality. From an aesthetic viewpoint, sexual acts were viewed and appreciated as beautiful, wondrous, rapturous events, and sexual pleasure was described almost wholly in aesthetic terms. Conversely, ethics was seen as a dismal, dampening, depressing force which recognized sexual desire even as it tried to repress it or rechannel it.

Aesthetics, with its emphasis on process, represented both a fluid philosophy and a stylized mode of living. With its formal concerns with truth and beauty, aesthetics enhanced the life experience by contributing to the appreciation of its myriad manifestations, its rituals and their histories, and the attainment of the appropriate technical skills and attitudes. As Nietzsche put it:

> Art and nothing but art! It is the great means of making life possible, the great seduction to life, the great stimulant of life. Art as the only superior counterforce to all will to denial of life....Art as the redemption of the man of knowledge—of those who see the terrifying and questionable character of existence, who want to see it, the men of tragic knowledge. Art as the redemption of the man of action—of those who not only see the terrifying and questionable character of existence, but live it, want to live it, the tragic-warlike man, the hero. Art as the redemption of the sufferer—as the way to states in which suffering is willed, transfigured, deified, where suffering is a form of great delight.[64]

In *De Profundis*, Wilde cited Christ as the prime exemplar of the aesthetic life, because "living for others was not his aim. He did things for his own sake and because Love [was] more beautiful than Hate." In other words, Wilde envisioned Christ along Emersonian lines, as the "supreme individualist" who strove to express himself through his "artistic" life. For Wilde, as for Nietzsche, as for Christ, self-expression represented the ultimate truth of art.[65]

The "aesthetic" problem of "beauty" emerged obliquely during the trial and served to crack the neat aesthetic facade that Wilde had thus far been able to maintain. It arose late in the second day of the trial as Carson was questioning Wilde on the nature of his relationship with Walter Grainger, a sixteen-year-old servant who had waited table at Lord Alfred Douglas' house in the High Street, Oxford. When asked by Carson whether or not he had kissed Grainger, Wilde's response was "he was a peculiarly plain boy. He was unfortunately, very ugly. I pitied him for it." Wilde's answer was both callous and disingenuous, for it was indeed likely that Wilde had kissed Grainger. Kissing a boy was no crime from a legal standpoint, despite the serious aspersions it cast upon Wilde's character, but kissing an ugly boy was an unforgivable sin from an aesthetic point of view. Wilde lied about kissing Grainger, a reputedly ugly boy, in order to maintain the integrity of his artistic pose and the purity of his own aesthetic. The physical act of kissing Grainger was thus nullified aesthetically through Wilde's lie, in that the "beautiful" lie compensated for the hideous act.

From Wilde's remark, Carson inferred that Wilde preferred kissing only beautiful boys. Whereas for Carson it was Grainger's gender that was problematic, for Wilde it was his beauty, or lack thereof. Once having admitted

Grainger's ugliness, it was impossible to then admit that a kiss, indicating the possibility of love, followed. Clues to help us understand the complexity of Wilde's aesthetic quandary can be found in Plato's *Symposium*, a book that was very well known to Wilde during his days at Trinity and Oxford. In *The Symposium*, beauty is considered a property which is inseparable from the object that contains it, although the physical object is described merely as the temporary caretaker of the absolute ideal of Beauty.[66] According to Plato, the primary function of physical beauty was to induce love. Within the context of a suitable relationship, love was supposed to lead in turn to a transcendence of physical beauty and morality, and ultimately to an appreciation of the inner Beauty manifested in the beautiful soul.[67] The proper object of Platonic love in Wilde's case should have been a young man of the proper class—such as Alfred Douglas.[68] As an uneducated young man of the working classes, Grainger was an inappropriate object of Wilde's affection, and since he was not beautiful there could be no possibility of love or transcendence. An admitted attraction to Grainger thus would have grossly perverted the Platonic ideal which Wilde espoused, and even, at times, exemplified. Wilde's use of an "ugly boy" as a sexual object thus hinted of a mechanical functionalism, or instrumentality, which clashed with his own aesthetic precepts.

Indeed, Wilde's repeated concessions to utility in his manner of dealing with all the young men in question revealed some of the "cracks," or internal inconsistencies, in his aesthetic. The material, or class, basis of his aesthetic was particularly muddled. Certainly his own "elective affinities" lay with the power, privilege, prestige, manners, and "style" of the aristocratic classes. Yet despite his wealth, education, social skills, and talent, the sum of which constituted his "cultural capital," Wilde lacked the proper social pedigree and thus could never be accepted as an "equal" by any peer of the realm.[69] Within the larger picture, of course, he himself was a cultural "commodity" who was "consumed" by upper-class patrons and matrons of society, just as he, in turn, "consumed" the working-class bodies of the male prostitutes for his own pleasure.

The young men were valuable to Wilde primarily insofar as he could "use" them. In this situation, the very concept of "utility" had definite middle- and working-class connotations, which betrayed his aristocratic pretensions as well as the anti-utilitarian thrust of his highly stylized aesthetic.[70] Yet at the same time, Wilde's repeated efforts to "raise" the young men to his own discriminating levels of taste—especially in terms of the lavish dinners in fancy restaurants, the exotic wines and liqueurs, the "literary" dinner conversations, rooms in the best hotels, and extravagant and beautiful gifts such as the silver cigarette cases, and the silver-mounted walking stick and the blue serge suit presented to Alphonso Conway—can be seen as concessions to appearances, where the aesthetics of "appearance" have distinctly "aristocratic" connotations.[71] The locations of the trysts were also important, for the sites were chosen to put Wilde at ease, not the young men. The nice restaurants and hotels not only provided pleasant, luxurious, and "aesthetic" surroundings for the sexual acts themselves, but they also removed the young men from their own "element," in effect disorienting them socially and culturally and putting them in a position where their protests, if forthcoming, would either be disbelieved or dismissed. This is not to say that there was nothing in it for the young men. Besides the money and the relief from necessity it represented, Wilde's interest in them presented them with a unique opportunity to see, if only briefly, how the other half lived. But this was certainly no exercise in democratic good-will, as Wilde claimed.

The allegedly unreciprocated generosity of Wilde to all his youthful companions puzzled Carson as well. Carson could never escape the concepts of use-value and exchange-value. In the witness-box, Wilde portrayed himself as a paragon of "Christlike" kindliness, generosity, and selflessness.[72] In many respects, he was completely justified in doing so, for he certainly was kind, generous, and decent toward his youthful companions. But Wilde asked the Court to believe that he gave unstintingly of himself and his material resources to young men who were beneath him in age, station, and position, and who ostensibly shared with him only the possession of considerable leisure time. In return, he claimed he asked for nothing except the pleasure of their company and the philanthropic joy that came from being able to assist them materially.

The concept of "something for nothing" defied the logic implicit in the dominant ethos of British society—the Protestant work ethic—even as it fulfilled Christ's dictates. The Court's reluctance to believe in Wilde's "inner beauty," hinged in part on his lack of credibility as a witness on his own behalf. The Court might have been expected to respect Wilde's aesthetic even if it did not understand it, but his frequent self-contradictions, and the many apparent discrepancies between the aesthetic ideals he espoused and his actions, combined to create an image of him that was neither reliable nor sincere.[73] The Court's inability to believe in Wilde's "inner beauty," besides suggesting a heterosexist bias against the effeminacy of his appearance and the flamboyance of his manner, may have also been indicative of a more general cultural resistance to the physical embodiment of seemingly unattainable ideals. Whereas hypocrisy, representing the sacrifice of principles to utility, was understandable within the contemporary social context and thus generally accepted, Wilde's alleged "Christlike" behavior under the same conditions was theoretically incomprehensible and thus apparently intolerable.[74]

Immediately following the discussion of "The Phrases and Philosophies for the Use of the Young," and The Picture of Dorian Gray, Carson brought up the nagging problem of the public reception of Wilde's works:

CARSON: "People who have not the views you have might form another opinion of these passages?"

WILDE: "Undoubtedly; but don't cross-examine me about the ignorance of other people. [Laughter] I have a great passion to civilize the community."

And again:

CARSON: "May I take it that you are not concerned whether it ['The Phrases and Philosophies'] has a moral or an immoral effect?"

WILDE: "I do not believe that any book or work of art ever produced any effect upon conduct at all."

And again in a slightly qualified version:

CARSON: "You don't think that one person can exercise influence on another?"

WILDE: "I don't think, except in fiction, there is any influence, good or bad, of one person over another. It is a mere philosophic point."[75]

In an earlier letter to the *Scots Observer* in response to a review of *Dorian Gray*, Wilde had succinctly summarized the two dominant viewpoints on the matter of reception:

... the artist will always look at the work of art from the standpoint of beauty of style and beauty of treatment, and that those who have not got the sense of beauty—or whose sense of beauty is dominated by ethical considerations— will always turn their attention to the subject matter and make its moral import the test and touchstone of the poem or novel or picture that is presented to them, while the newspaper critic will sometimes take one side and sometimes the other, according as he is cultured or uncultured.[76]

In *Truth and Method*, Hans-Georg Gadamer draws a distinction between understanding and interpreting a text. Gadamer conceives understanding as the attempt to recover the original intentions of the author in the text, whereas interpretation tries to divine what the text actually said.[77] Within the context of the trial, Wilde sought to have his texts interpreted, whereas Carson preferred instead to try to understand them. Wilde's responses defended the experience of art as the experience of an entire world, separate and distinct from our own, which was complete and perfect in and of itself. Such a self-contained universe with its own logic, morality, and history lay outside the bounds of reality, and thus should have been from Wilde's perspective theoretically unassailable by objective criteria.[78] Carson, on the other hand, rejected Wilde's aesthetic stance and preferred instead to interpret the texts within the context of his own life experience and knowl-edge of the world.[79] Carson's position anticipated that of Theodor Adorno, for example, who described the purely aesthetic experience of reality as "negative," precisely because it was not grounded fully in *praxis*.[80]

Carson might also have concurred with Wolfgang Iser that narratives are not seamless, and that "gaps, blanks, and indeterminacies" within the text can be filled at the reader's discretion, regardless of what the author might have intended.[81] When Wilde claimed that "each man sees his own sins in Dorian Gray...[whoever] finds them has brought them," Carson addressed the indeterminacies in Wilde's texts in a way that was consistent with con-temporary reality, and in doing so, ironically recovered Wilde's original intentions.[82] Even Walter Pater, the critic to whom Wilde alluded as the only person in England whose opinion he respected, and who thus might be expected to have been Wilde's ideal reader, was careful to include in his review of *The Picture of Dorian Gray* a homiletic note which drew a positive moral from the "immoral" work. Pater noted that "[Wilde's] story is also a vivid, though carefully considered, exposure of the corruption of a soul, with a very plain moral, pushed home, to the effect that vice and crime make people coarse and ugly."[83]

As Carson saw it, the real problem with Wilde's "Phrases and Philosophies" was that they were indeed intended for "the Use of the Young." Fortunately, the axioms, and Wilde's other works as well, appeared relatively harmless when taken out of context, and Wilde was more or less able to take refuge among his own textual "gaps, blanks, and indeterminacies." Even as Carson exploited the same gaps for his own purposes, he was not able to create more than the shadow of a doubt, and the doubt concerning the literary evidence went to Wilde. Theoretically at least, the ideas within his texts remained just that—ideas, which were harmless unless acted upon.

From Carson's common-sensical viewpoint, however, ideas represented a form of power—the power to persuade and influence behavior. The problem with Wilde's literature was that it was attractively packaged and directed espe-cially at youth—representing the future of society—those developing individ-uals who were craving experience, whose minds had not yet been fully formed, and who were thus considered susceptible, and probably even attracted, to sub-versive influences. From society's standpoint, the ideas contained in Wilde's works were considered critical and anti-social, and were therefore branded as inflammatory and dangerous. Wilde certainly thought of them in that way, although from his perspective his ideas represented a positive tonic with invig-orating and rejuvenating medicinal properties. Whereas from society's per-spective, Wilde's ideas symbolized the dangers of "liberal" tolerance of dissent, for Wilde the same ideas represented a potent cure for the intolerance and repressiveness that ailed contemporary society.

The Politics of Pederasty

The most revealing exchange of Wilde's first criminal trial was his defense of a poem written by Lord Alfred Douglas and published in *The Chameleon*, an Oxford undergraduate publication with artistic pretensions and homosexual leanings. The poem was entitled "Two Loves," and as we have seen its last line read, "I am the Love that dare not speak its name." After reading the poem, Charles F. Gill, the Chief Counsel for the Prosecution, asked Wilde if "the love described relates to natural love and unnatural love?" Wilde's poetic reply seemed so beautifully composed and was delivered with such apparent conviction that it elicited a spontaneous outburst of applause from the spectators in the courtroom:

> "The love that dare not speak its name" in this century is such a great affection of an elder for a younger man as there was between David and Jonathan, such as Plato made the very basis of his philosophy, and such as you find in the sonnets of Michelangelo and Shakespeare. It is that deep, spiritual affection that is as pure as it is perfect. It dictates and pervades great works of art like those of Shakespeare and Michelangelo, and those two letters of mine, such as they are. It is in this century misunderstood, so much misunderstood that it may be described as the "Love that dare not speak its name," and on account of it I am placed where I am now. It is beautiful, it is fine, it is the noblest form of affection. There is nothing unnatural about it. It is intellectual, and it repeatedly exists between an elder and a younger man, when the elder has intellect, and the younger man has all the joy, hope, and glamour of life before him. That it should be so, the world does not understand. The world mocks at it and sometimes puts one in the pillory for it.[84]

Had Gill been as clever as Carson, he might have better exploited some of the weaknesses of Wilde's rhetoric. As it was, the speech had struck a chord within the audience. Their appreciative reaction only served to legitimate the sentiments that were expressed within it. But Gill had been as astonished by Wilde's reply as everyone else and could only think to ask the obvious question, "Did you feel this deep affection of an elder man to a younger towards all these boys?" When Wilde replied indignantly, "Certainly not! One feels that once in one's life, and only once, towards anyone," the Court was temporarily moved by Wilde's display of passion and principle. The next day, the correspondent for the *Daily Telegraph* reported that Wilde appeared a new man in the witness-box, and his subsequent responses seemed "quicker, sharper, and more confident." By his brilliant extemporization, Wilde and his counsels managed to regain the upper hand in the proceedings, if only for the moment.

Certainly the power of Wilde's rhetoric can be measured by its effect. Its content, however, is another matter. Wilde's "the love that dare not speak its name" speech contained a loose paraphrase of Socrates' espousal of the pederastic ideal of love in Plato's *Symposium*. In that dramatic dialogue, Socrates, after a series of speeches extolling the virtues of physical love, advocated what has come to be known as "Platonic love." Platonic love has been described as "a common search for truth and beauty by two persons of the same sex inspired by mutual affection."[85] Such a love transcends sensuality in favor of harmonic co-existence and mutual cultivation of the "higher"—intellectual, moral, and spiritual—aspects of the self. Within the context of the *Symposium*, Socrates promoted this lofty and noble ideal to an unsympathetic audience at a dinner party for the literati of Athens. The irony in Socrates' speech consisted in the fact that love for him contained a meaning which was spiritual, and therefore quite different from the meaning of love for the common man, which had sexual connotations.

In contrast, the irony in Wilde's speech consisted in his inversion of Socrates. The Platonic relationship described by Socrates was precisely the opposite of the kind of (sexual) love that Wilde had sought with Parker, Wood, and the rest of the young men. Wilde's disingenuous but skillful appeal to the authority of Plato and the Bible proved successful because it was interpreted literally by those in the courtroom. Wilde's ironic redeployment of the Platonic ideal was doubly devious—a fact that must have greatly amused him—since he was actually appealing less to the authority of the established literary, artistic, and religious canons than to the authority of one of his own works in which he had attempted to revaluate and subvert those same canons. In July of 1889, Wilde had published in *Blackwood's Edinburgh Magazine* the essay, "The Portrait of Mr. W. H." One purpose of that essay had been to hint strongly that many of Western civilization's greatest artists and thinkers, including Shakespeare, Marlowe, Bacon, and Michelangelo, preferred the company of boys to women, and not necessarily for spiritual reasons.[86]

It can be said that by lying in the witness-box, Wilde was simply following the dictates of his own philosophy. For his deceit to be successful, however, he depended upon what he perceived to be the "national stupidity" of the English.[87] Like his idol Baudelaire, Wilde's "diabolically passionate [dis]taste for stupidity" made him take peculiar pleasure in the fabrications of calumny.[88] Wilde was certainly not one to overvalue his audience, and his contempt for them was vindicated by their belief in his story. He also possessed a strong faith in his own talent for telling a convincing lie.[89]

It is not difficult to understand the reasoning behind Wilde's denial of his guilt—he wanted to keep the homosexual aspects of his life private and hidden, thereby maintaining the pretense of an admittedly bohemian but nevertheless respectable life. He certainly desired to keep intact his marriage, wealth, social position, and reputation, and to stay out of prison at all costs. But there was more to it than that. There was truth contained in the "love that dare not speak its name" speech, but not the whole truth. Wilde's rhetoric was at once duplicitous and honest, but the "code" necessary to distinguish fact from fiction was withheld. In any case, the speech reflected the degree to which hypocrisy over sexual matters pervaded society at this time. In many respects, Wilde's speech was an example of brilliant showmanship, the type of showmanship that the Court had expected to hear from someone of Wilde's reputation. It entertained them and impressed them, but more importantly, by talking about love, it glossed over the more uncomfortable issues of sexuality. The speech "addressed" sexuality by not addressing it, and by sublimating it instead. Physical desire was transmogrified and rendered instead as a spiritual ideal. Wilde's speech was phrased in a way which circumscribed the content of the speech within the generally acknowledged boundaries of social propriety, thereby maintaining a culturally comfortable compartmentalization of love and sex.[90]

It is apparent from the trial testimony that Wilde preferred having sex, not with men his own age, but with young men who were usually somewhere between the ages of seventeen to twenty-two.[91] Technically then, Wilde could, and perhaps should, be viewed as a pederast. Defined very broadly, pederasty signals the love of an older man for a younger man. It is important to note, however, that by late-Victorian standards, a young man of sixteen or seventeen years old, especially one of the working classes, would have been considered a fully emancipated adult.[92] I believe that Wilde's behavior with Charles Parker, Wood, and the other young men can be best understood if his sexuality is discussed within the aesthetic context of the ancient Athenian discourse on male homosocial desire and in terms of his personal "ontological aesthetic of dissent." As a prize-winning classicist at Trinity and Oxford, Wilde had been weaned academically on the culture of ancient Greece and Rome, and was thoroughly steeped in its virtues.[93] The values and ideals of the ancient Hellenes were a tremendous influence on the development of his own aesthetic, and their attitudes toward sexuality were incorporated—in modified form as I will show—within it.

Citing ancient Greek (primarily Athenian) sources, David Halperin argues that in ancient Athens, same-sex practices between free adult men were held in low esteem, and that pederasty was the only accepted form of sexuality between males.[94] The primary sexual distinction made by ancient Athenian men was between active and passive roles. Halperin represents sex in ancient Athenian culture as a deeply polarizing experience, one which had the effect of dividing and categorizing the participants ontologically.[95] Sex *per se* was penetrative, implying that only the active partner had "sex." Penetration connoted activity, which conferred agency, which in turn conferred "being." Conversely, receptivity was considered passive, which conferred an ontological status next to non-existence.

Halperin notes that sexual acts (both homo- and hetero-) were usually performed *without* the goal of mutual pleasure. Rather, they were typically performed for the pleasure of the dominant (male) partner only. Culturally, the proper sexual targets of adult male citizens of Athens were women, boys, foreigners, and slaves, i.e. those without any legal or political rights. The sexual acts of free adult males thus replicated and reinforced their social position, prestige, and political authority.[96] Adult male citizens of Athens had certain prerogatives: namely, the right to initiate the sex act, the right to obtain pleasure (since the passive partner was penetrated and his or her pleasure, even if forthcoming, was inconsequential), and the right to assume the insertive role. Sex between free adult male citizens was, therefore, theoretically inconceivable.[97] Halperin is careful to suggest that this represented the ideal, of course, and not always the reality. He also notes that "whatever the adult free male's sex object choice was: woman, slave, boy, or foreigner—that object choice was always different or 'hetero'—that is, the sexual object always had to belong to a different social category [or class]."[98] Wilde's sexual object choices might also be considered socially, economically, and culturally "hetero" from the same viewpoint.

Halperin argues that the ancient taxonomic strategies focused on the abnormality of gender deviance or ambivalence. For the ancient Athenians, men who willingly adopted the dress, gait, or manner of women were considered to suffer from mental and/or moral defects. For them, this suggested a perversion of desire, and indicated a condition of abnormality. What was most important for the free adult Athenian males was, as Halperin terms it, for their "phallocentric protocol" to be in order, which means that a free adult male was invariably identified with the insertive role. Therefore, as long as a male maintained a masculine phallocentric protocol, and assumed the insertive role, no matter what his sexual object choice—woman, boy, slave, or foreigner—he was, within the contemporary context, "politically correct" in terms of his sexuality.[99] Conversely, what was monstrous to the ancient Athenians were soft, effeminate, sexually submissive free adult males who willingly surrendered their autonomy, and who channelled their desire into passive, receptive modes.[100]

Wilde's gender and sexual identities were completely in concert with the ancient Athenian pederastic model and its correlative ethos of domination and penetration. Wilde's gender role was masculine and his phallocentric protocol was, as far as we know, insertive. Had Wilde lived in ancient Athens, his sexual object choices (young men) would have been appropriate and commensurate with his social position. As it was, however, it would have been ludicrous for Wilde to try to explain his behavior in 1895 by appealing to the authority of the ancient Greeks, for his tactical objective was not to tell the truth, but to stay out of prison. The ancient Athenian context resembled that of late-Victorian England in one crucial respect, however, which was that Wilde's sexual relations with young men were more than just sexual acts between willing partners. They were political acts as well, which reproduced patriarchal social norms and reinforced conventions of class privilege.

Theoretically, according to the ancient Athenian pederastic model, the youthful partner was supposed to benefit emotionally, intellectually, and spiritually from his relationship with the adult male. From their trial testimony it can be discerned that, despite being prostitutes, Wilde's youthful partners were much more conflicted than Wilde about what they were doing. Almost all of the young men, and especially Charles Parker and Alfred Wood, expressed shame, humiliation, and remorse concerning their roles as accomplices in the various enactments of Wilde's sexual fantasies. Although it cannot be assumed that they subscribed either morally or intellectually to the dominant values of society, it can be presumed that they were aware of existing prohibitions, and also aware that their actions violated established legal and moral codes.

Certainly the youths involved in the case were both Wilde's victims and his accomplices. They were victims in the sense that he clearly exploited their class position and economic circumstances, and also in the sense that their fulfillment of Wilde's desires appeared to have caused at least some of them great psychological distress. They can be seen as accomplices in the sense that they, as prostitutes, knowingly, and more or less willingly, participated in illegal activities. Conceptually, of course, the profession of prostitution lies at the intersection of the values of a modern industrialized society and a consumer culture: between the work ethic—especially the economic values of industry, discipline, and responsibility—and what sociologist Daniel Bell has described as the "adversarial" cultural values of narcissistic individualism, and the concomitant values of play and pleasure.[101]

The apparent unfairness with which Wilde's defense counsel attempted to characterize the prosecution's witnesses as accomplices in order to discredit their self-incriminating testimony against Wilde must be viewed within the context of the prevailing cultural attitudes toward prostitution. Had these witnesses been female prostitutes, it would almost surely have been they and not Wilde who were prosecuted. There existed a double standard in the way the law regarded "homosexual" prostitution. Whereas the male clients of female prostitutes for the most part went free, often both the clients of male prostitutes and the prostitutes themselves were prosecuted.[102] This indicates in part the extent to which same-sex practices were pathologized by the culture. In the case of heterosexual prostitution, the general perception was that it was the male client who was seduced, tempted, or victimized by the female prostitute. Conversely, in the case of "homosexual" prostitution, the prevailing perception was that it was the client who was guilty of seducing, and the prostitute who was perceived as having been the victim of the client's aberrant desires.

Necessity and Desire: The Metaphysics of Sodomy

The accusations alleged in Queensberry's initial plea of justification were corroborated by the evidence provided at Wilde's two criminal trials. Although he was not prosecuted on the more serious charge of sodomy, by the end of the second criminal trial there could have been little doubt in anyone's mind that Wilde was guilty of sodomitical practices. Parker and Wood both claimed Wilde sodomized them, and Parker's landlady and the Savoy Hotel employees described scenes which suggested that anal intercourse had taken place. Wilde never denied his guilt concerning these matters in *De Profundis*, but his admissions were cryptic, at best.

In *De Profundis*, Wilde referred to his "absurd and silly perjuries" in the witness-box, and admitted that he was accused of (and took credit for) one of Douglas' trysts at the Savoy. He also admitted other "acts" for which he was never indicted, and in a justly famous passage he compared his dalliances in the world of "rough trade" with "feasting with panthers":

> People thought it dreadful of me to have entertained at dinner the evil things of life, and to have found pleasure in their company. But they, from the point of view through which I, as an artist in life, approached them, were delightfully suggestive and stimulating. It was like feasting with panthers. The danger was half the excitement. I used to feel as the snake-charmer must feel when he lures the cobra ... they were to me the brightest of gilded snakes. Their poison was part of their perfection.[103]

What seems clear from both the trial testimony and Wilde's confessional writings[104] was the symbolic centrality of the act of sodomy to Wilde's sexual identity. I should like to develop this notion and, moreover, consider Wilde's practice of sodomy as a conscious expression of his "ontological aesthetic of dissent." In *De Profundis*, there are three passages in which Wilde compares his perceptions of his own historical notoriety to that of the Marquis de Sade.[105] This parallel is instructive, less for equating Wilde's actions with those of the most infamous of modern sexual libertines, than for comparing the ways in which their personal aesthetics justify acts of sodomy. Although the authority of Sade is invoked often in what follows, my own discussion draws equally from Sade and Pierre Klossowski's theorization of Sade and sodomy in his fascinating study, *Sade, My Neighbor*.

Like Michel Foucault and Jeffrey Weeks, Pierre Klossowski distinguishes between homosexuality and the sodomitical act.[106] The latter is considered a perversion whereas the former is not. Klossowski asserts that

> Sodomy is formulated as a specific gesture of countergenerality ... which strikes precisely at the law of propagation of the species in the individual. It evinces an attitude not only of refusal, but also of aggression; in being the simulacrum of the act of generation, it is a mockery of it.[107]

In a sense, Klossowski's formulation describes the results of the "social construction" of sodomy, in which an "empty," or theoretically meaningless, act is endowed with symbolic significance and inscribed with multiple layers of meaning. For Sade, the act of sodomy represented a "natural," if socially aberrant, performative gesture. In a normative state of Nature, the sodomitical act signified little more than a physical possibility.[108] Sade argued that possibility conferred permission: because of the way the human body is constructed, the act is possible, and because the act is possible, it is permissible. For Sade, there were no checks in Nature, and if Nature allowed it, then who was Man to refuse what Nature had offered?[109] In the predominantly heterosexual context that concerned him, Sade reasoned instrumentally that anal intercourse provided a convenient alternative to vaginal intercourse because it allowed for the same pleasure for the man, while eliminating the dangers of pregnancy for the woman. In regard to the Biblical proscriptions against onanism and the "wasting of seed," Sade claimed that sodomy could not be a crime, because "semen is not that precious a commodity to Nature that its loss is necessarily criminal."[110] Sade cited historical precedent—not just the ancient Greeks, but also the Turks, Persians, Gauls, Romans, North African Muslims, and Native Americans—to argue that sodomitical relations between men were acceptable, and perhaps even desirable, especially in a republic.[111] Pederasty was also described sympathetically as "the vice of the warrior races."[112]

Within the context of his own historical epoch, of course, Sade's intention was to exploit the material and moral conditions of the *ancien régime* for his own pleasure. The effect of his works, whether intentional or not, was to subvert the goals and rhetoric of the Enlightenment.[113] For Sade, these goals were unattainable, and hence "false," because they depended upon an unrealistically positive view of human nature. Paradoxically, however, Sade's work represents an "instrumental" use of Reason to attack and subvert the very idea that new societal "norms" and values could be derived through Reason and rationally constructed through social means. Ideas such as Rousseau's "social contract," for example, would have undoubtedly struck Sade as "artificial" constructs, which were contrary to Nature and to the pre-existing, and hence "naturally" established, hierarchies in which power was predominantly a function of (largely inherited) wealth and social position. Sade defended the personal free-doms of "natural man" against the "artificial" contraints represented by civil and religious proscriptions. As Maurice Blanchot suggests, Sade's philosophy was one of exclusive "self-interest" and "absolute egoism," in which all behav-ior was dictated by one law alone, "that of [one's] own pleasure."[114]

In Sade, one finds glimmerings of aesthetic or ideological positions devel-oped later in the nineteenth century by such thinkers as Freud, Darwin, Dostoyevsky, Nietzsche, and Wilde. Sade suggested that civilization repressed our true (physical) needs and constrained our desires, and asserted moreover that by nature, man was little more than a beast. He argued that since life was a struggle of all against all in which might was equated with right, everything was permissible, including murder.[115] Sade's radical justifications of "personal freedom" can be seen in Nietzschean terms as expressions of the "master-morality."[116] His relentless pursuit of personal pleasure at the expense of the personal freedoms (not to mention the civil rights) of others, can be seen as the "natural" right of the "strong" to act in accordance with the type and amount of power they possess. Pre-existing social hierarchies are thus "naturalized" and reinforced, and wealth and position once again function to eliminate con-straints which would limit the pursuits of "ordinary" individuals. Sade's aes-thetic of pleasure and "absolute egoism" also prefigures certain "camp" and hedonistic aspects of Wilde's "ontological aesthetic of dissent," and theorizes at least some of its more distinctive modes of expression, such as sodomy.

Klossowski theorizes that within Sade's naturalistic universe, the act of sodomy plays a role imbued with symbolic, if not spiritual, significance. Just as the rites ritualistically performed by priests constituted the forms of the estab-lished religions, so the Sadean "religion" of atheism was to have its own formal requirements, namely the dispassionate performance of acts of violation or transgression, with "sodomy as a simulacrum of the destruction of [social and cultural] norms. ..."[117] The sacralized performance of the sodomitical act was intended simultaneously to "negate" the constraints symbolized by God, reli-gion, and civilization, and to glorify man's "natural" impulses for brutality, lust, and physical satisfaction.

Like Sade's, Wilde's reasons for embracing the sodomitical act were intended to be subversive of the prevailing social status quo. Within the con-text of the material and moral conditions of late-Victorian England, his inten-tion was to subvert the "compulsory heterosexuality" of the middle classes; to subvert the class system by cultivating working-class sexual contacts; to subvert the law by engaging in illegal sexual acts; and to subvert contemporary moral-ity by aestheticizing his immoral actions. Like Sade, Wilde also desired to sub-vert the constraints of his own conscience, and to demonstrate his self-mastery, especially to himself. Through the private sodomitical act, Wilde transcended the effete and effeminate connotations of his dandified public image by emphasizing instead the exuberant bestiality of the act and the passion, power, and masculine virility its performance expressed. Unlike Sade, however, Wilde despised neither God nor civilization, and whereas Sade lauded the "naturalness" of the sodomitical act, Wilde prized it especially for its "artificiality."

According to Klossowski's criteria, Wilde's actions, too, although completely understandable, must be considered perverse. Klossowski defines the "pervert," as distinct from the ordinary licentious person, as one who is possessed by an "improper object," and who lives his life in the pursuit of a sole defining gesture.[118] Echoing Klossowski, Gilles Deleuze writes that the world of the pervert "is one where the category of the necessary has completely replaced the category of the possible."[119] The perversion is pathological because it represents an addiction, or a dependency upon a certain type of behavior. The perverse act has a sense of urgency and compulsion about it, and therefore is linked inextricably to the psychological survival of the person. The original reasons that created the psychological need for the signifying gesture may be unconscious or completely forgotten, but that does not dismiss the fact that such reasons once existed. Psychoanalytically, the repetition of the sodomitical gesture simultaneously serves two important psychic functions: it discharges tensions while serving to "maintain" the integrity of the ego—without the gesture, the self fragments.[120] The compulsive repetition of this single defining gesture represents the way in which the pervert reconstitutes himself psychically and gives meaning and wholeness to his life.

Certainly, Wilde's "perversion" was purposefully cultivated and constructed as a "gesture of countergenerality" which was aimed specifically against society. Wilde clearly endowed the sodomitical act with a greater symbolic importance than it generally possessed in late-Victorian society, and for that reason the act was for him, in all respects, an expressive and signifying gesture, and, indeed, an act of self-definition. Wilde also went to great lengths to justify the act aesthetically and historically. Although one can certainly argue that Wilde pursued other gestures of self-expression and self-definition besides sodomy, such as his critical, literary, and theatrical endeavors, and that he was, according to Klossowski's criteria, merely licentious as opposed to perverse, to do so is ultimately misleading. For whereas Wilde could and did take extended hiatuses from his artistic projects, he seemed unable to stop pursuing sexual contacts with young men—not only in England, but in France, Italy, and North Africa as well.[121] Even after his release from prison in 1897, Wilde freely admitted that old habits died hard. In a letter to Robert Ross from the Hôtel de Nice, Rue des Beaux-Arts, Paris, dated February 18? 1898, Wilde wrote:

My Dearest Robbie, ... It is very unfair of people being horrid to me about Bosie [Douglas] and Naples. A patriot put in prison for loving his country loves his country, and a poet put in prison for loving boys loves boys. To have altered my life would have been to have admitted that Uranian [same-sex] love is ignoble. I hold it to be noble—more noble than other forms. Ever yours—Oscar.[122]

Wilde described his thrall to his perversion in *De Profundis*, claiming that his perversity was a mask which hid his real (gentle, kindly, sympathetic) nature and that he wore the mask of perversity in order that his philosophy might appear consistent with his life, actions, and words.[123]

No doubt that was true, but then the opposite would have been equally true: his gentle, kindly, sympathetic nature was a disguise that masked the perverse and intolerable aspects of his self. In the end, Wilde was to give up on art before he gave up on young men.

When Wilde wrote in *De Profundis* of "feasting with panthers," he described "the danger as being half the excitement," and "their poison [implying their working-class status, and probably their criminal status as prostitutes as well] was part of their perfection."[124] His seduction of non-professionals, such as Shelley, Conway, and Grainger, may have provided him with an even greater and more exquisitely delicious pleasure, which Huysmans extolled in *A Rebours*, that is, the thrill of corrupting an innocent, and of creating another "criminal" in the process.[125]

It is interesting to note that matters of *hubris* connected with his actions only bothered Wilde while he was in Reading Gaol. Within the context of ancient Athenian pederasty, *hubris* connoted "any kind of behaviour in which one treats other people as one pleases, with an arrogant confidence that one will escape paying any penalty for violating their rights and disobeying any law or moral rule accepted by society."[126] In *De Profundis*, Wilde lamented,

Desire at the end was a malady, a madness, or both. I grew careless of the lives of others. I took pleasure where it pleased me and passed on. I forgot that every little action of the common day makes or unmakes character.[127]

Once he was released from prison, however, past memories were overridden by present concerns. His remorse was forgotten and *hubris* returned in the form of a renewed thrall to the pursuit of sexual experiences with young men.

From a Sadean perspective, of course, Wilde's greatest crime was in allowing himself to get caught, because from the confines of a prison cell he could no longer devote himself to "the philosophy of self-interest, of absolute egoism, bound by one law, that of one's pleasure."[128] Sade defined power as "the ability to get one's way."[129] According to this view, power was not a state of being, nor was it a necessary correlative of one's political, economic, or social position within society. Instead, Sade's definition of power anticipated

Nietzsche's, for in this sense, power was a choice that one willed and expended energy and effort to obtain.[130] In this sense, power represented the ability to control one's life and destiny. The power to do whatever one wants is predicated on not getting caught—for once one is caught, all one's power dissipates and one's glorious aesthetic disintegrates and disappears along with it.[131] The laws of pleasure are discovered to be contingent and ephemeral, and one is once again afraid of greater power and what it might do to one.

Reflecting upon the course of his past life and his present circumstances from his cell in Reading Gaol, Wilde wrote in *De Profundis*:

> I made art a philosophy, and philosophy an art. ... I altered the minds of men and the colours of things. ... I treated art as the supreme reality, and life as a mere mode of fiction. ... I awoke the imagination of my century so that it created myth and legend around me ... [then, at the height of his power]. ... I let myself be lured into long spells of senseless and sensual ease. I amused myself with being a flâneur, a dandy, a man of fashion. I surrounded myself with smaller natures and meaner minds. I became the spendthrift of my own genius, and to waste an eternal youth gave me a curious joy. Tired of being on the heights, I deliberately went to the depths in search of new sensations. ...[132]

After chronicling his descent, he illustrated Sade's concept of the loss of power.

> I ceased to be Lord over myself. I was no longer Captain of my soul. I allowed you [Douglas] to dominate me, and your father [Queensberry] to frighten me. I ended in horrible disgrace. There is only one thing for me now, absolute Humility.[133]

From society's point of view, Wilde's arrogance, or *hubris*, consisted in the fact that he was publicly characterized as an abscess on a healthy body, who paradoxically felt that he was authorized to speak on behalf of that body.[134] From society's perspective, Wilde was sick because he lacked the capacity to accept the current conditions of reality. From their viewpoint, Wilde's romanticized world may have been perfect, but it was also imaginary. Conversely, Wilde thought of himself as the healthy one, and society as sick. Unlike Sade, Wilde appreciated the artificiality of society—its unreality, as it were—with its constructedness, fragility, and contingency. Of course, society, such as it was, was necessary to his existence. Like Sade, the possibility of outraging society gave added meaning to his life. To deprive Wilde of his complacent bourgeois public would have been to deprive him of his *raison d'être*.

What Wilde lost as a result of "being found out" at the trials was the freedom to exploit the possibilities offered by society and the liberty to negate the ontological status of others that Klossowski calls "the power to dehumanize one's neighbor." Even more importantly, however, he lost the secrecy of his private life. From his prison cell, he lamented the loss of the society which he loved to hate. He especially missed the hypocrisy of English society—a hypocrisy that was negated by the iron bars of his cell—as well as his special and privileged place within it. In late-Victorian England, all things were indeed possible, and thus from Wilde's perspective, society was a virtual utopia of evil in which any vice imaginable could be had for a price.[135] He had labored long and hard to put himself into a position where he was able to exploit the opportunities that came his way. Wilde's position derived in part from his wealth, talent, and social position. Even more than that, it derived from his intelligence, imagination, and "will to power" over society. Before the trials, Wilde had his own way with society, and he could afford to ignore the public and to design and inhabit a private world of evil and fantasy instead. After the trials, of course, the tables were turned and it was society that had its way with Wilde. Even though he was eventually able to leave England behind, Wilde was never able to escape his notoriety or to reclaim the secrecy his private life had previously afforded him.

6

"SOCIAL PURITY" AND SOCIAL POLLUTION

Wilde and the National Health

Moral Revitalization and the "Social Body"

In the June 1895 issue of his own widely-respected journal, *The Review of Reviews*, W.T. Stead commented on the outcome of the Wilde trials.

> ...The trial of Oscar Wilde and Taylor at the Old Bailey, resulting in their conviction and the infliction of what will probably be a capital sentence—for two years' hard labour in solitary confinement always breaks up the constitution even of tough and stalwart men—has forced upon the attention of the public the existence of a vice of which the most of us happily know nothing. The heinousness of the crime of Oscar Wilde and his associates does not lie, as is usually supposed, in its being unnatural. It would be unnatural for seventy-nine out of eighty persons. *It is natural for the abnormal person who is in a minority of one* [italics added]. *If* the promptings of our animal nature are to be the only guide, the punishment of Oscar Wilde would savour of persecution, and he might fairly claim our sympathy as the champion of individualism against the tyranny of an intolerant majority. But we are not merely animal. We are human beings living together in society, whose aim is to render social intercourse as free and as happy as possible.[1]

Later in the same article, Stead seized upon the connection between the Wilde case and the cultural pervasiveness of the sexual double standard, and made the case (which was also made by HELVELLYN in the correspondence column of the *Star*) that if Wilde had ruined the lives of half a dozen young girls instead of indulging in indecent familiarities with young men, he would never have been prosecuted. In stating this, Stead was not calling for the repeal of the statute under which Wilde was convicted, but rather for the institution of equally strict statutes that would legally protect women from sexual exploitation by unscrupulous men.[2]

Stead expressed a hope that Wilde's conviction would also inspire a thorough house-cleaning of the Protestant public schools. He observed that "if all persons guilty of Oscar Wilde's offence were to be clapped in gaol, there would be a surprising exodus from Eton, Harrow, Rugby and Winchester, to Pentonville and Holloway."[3] Stead was not the only one to have remarked upon the connection between Wilde's offence and the alleged vices of public schoolboys. A letter to *Reynold's Newspaper* remarked, "Why does not the Crown prosecute every boy at a public or private school or half the men in the Universities? In the latter places 'poederism' [sic] is as common as fornication, and everybody knows it."[4] And an editorial in a special edition of the *Star* remarked that "the lesson of the trial ought not to be lost upon the headmasters, and all others who are responsible for the morals, of public schools. It rests with them, more probably than with anybody else, to exorcise this pestilence."[5]

Edward Bristow has argued that the Church of England Purity Society waged a "war on schoolboy masturbation" in the early eighteen-eighties. Drinking and "wild behavior" had been considered the main vices of the eighteen-seventies and had been supplanted, at least in the eyes of the CEPS, by self-abuse in the following decade.[6] Bristow says nothing about same-sex practices between schoolboys, but Jeffrey Weeks suggests that the "prevalent schoolboy homosexuality in public schools ... became a matter of major concern for a number of social-purity advocates from the 1880's onwards."[7] And in *Coming Out*, Weeks also notes that "in the United States and Britain there was a frequent linking of masturbation, 'the secret sin,' with homosexuality."[8] In the late-Victorian period, masturbation and same-sex practices were both seen essentially as the results of deficiencies of will. From a developmental perspective, however, masturbation was often seen as a prelude to same-sex practices.

Stead also expressed his desire that the natural ease of communication which he attributed to same-sex relationships could also become, in the future, a model for the "free and unfettered communion between individuals of the opposite sex." He noted that "at present, fortunately, people of the same sex can travel together, and live together in close intimacy, without anyone even dreaming of a scandal."[9] Stead's association of same-sex relationships and scandal was very suggestive. Stead implied that as a result of the publicity surrounding the Wilde trials, the previously assumed innocence of same-sex relationships was now threatened. If the Wilde trials demonstrated anything, it was that a Platonic relationship could serve as a "pose" which obscured a distinctly un-Platonic relationship underneath. While on the surface, perhaps, male–male

relationships would go on as before, from now on they would always be underlain by a new anxiety, fueled by unspoken doubts, "suspicions of impropriety,"
and "thoughts of indecency." Stead articulated this concern in a more explicit
manner in a private letter to Edward Carpenter, the "feminist,"[10] socialist, and
amateur sexologist: "A few more cases like Oscar Wilde's and we should find the
freedom of comradeship now possible to men seriously impaired to the permanent detriment of the race."[11]

In the article, Stead characterized Wilde's behavior as "unnatural for a normal person," but perfectly "natural" for an "abnormal person." By describing
sexual relations between people of the same sex as both "unnatural" and
"abnormal," Stead had, whether consciously or not, appropriated a pair of
ideologically-loaded terms from the professional discourses of the natural,
medical, and social sciences, and employed them as the criteria for assessing
Wilde's moral fitness. Implicitly, of course, Stead was defining normality in
psychosocial terms of "adaptedness," or instrumental subordination, to a particular environment or set of circumstances, that is, to a system of social determinants, or constraints, which were assumed to be good and desirable.[12] What
was perceived as Wilde's "maladaptation" was thus interpreted in terms of his
abnormality and sickness rather than in terms which might have questioned
the validity and desirability of the determinants themselves. In describing
Wilde's behavior as "natural for an abnormal person," Stead was essentially
characterizing Wilde's identity in pathological terms. In many respects,
Wilde's particular manifestation of "abnormality" resembled the medico-
psychiatric condition of "moral insanity." Clinically, this was a form of mental
derangement which had been described as early as 1830 as "consisting of morbid perversions of feelings, affections, and active powers, which often coexisted
with an unimpaired state of intellectual faculties, ... and which manifested itself
as the indulgence and gratification of every whim, caprice, and passion."[13] In
short, "moral insanity" did not signify a weak will, but rather a very willful
indulgence of one's every hedonistic impulse.

Stead's lay diagnosis was not meant to excuse Wilde's actions, but rather to
provide a rationale for his behavior, a rationale which might have reconciled
the apparent contradictions between Wilde's public life before the trials and his
private life as it was revealed during the trials. The concept of "moral insanity"
could have offered a "scientific" explanation for how a person such as Wilde
could have been cognizant of the existing cultural and social norms, and yet
perfectly capable of rationalizing his transgressions of those norms. At this
time, however, a legal defense of "moral insanity" was suspect in the eyes of the
courts, and was for the most part unacceptable to the public as well, because
the condition was popularly seen as representing a deficiency of will, which was
ultimately correctable through an act of personal resolve.[14] Stead's characterization of Wilde as "unnatural," "abnormal," and implicitly as "morally

insane," based as it was on a contested theory of ontological difference, can be seen as part of an ongoing process of labelling, marginalizing, and stigmatizing which was necessary to ensure Wilde's social death. Wilde's social death, I will argue, was in turn necessary to ensure the "health" of the "social body" itself.

Some readers today may find in Stead's comment that Wilde's behavior was perfectly "natural for an abnormal person" a rather tepid defense of Wilde's actions. Although Stead's intention was certainly not to justify Wilde's behavior, his comments at times give the impression of putting forth an honest effort to understand Wilde on his own terms. Contemporary readers of Stead, however, would have understood his comments in a different light altogether. To contemporaries, Stead's remarks would have been understood within the context of his long association with many of the causes of the "social purity" movement.

"Social purity" is an umbrella term which describes the loose association of a multitude of relatively small but very outspoken reform movements, or groups, in the eighteen-eighties and eighteen-nineties, which included the Social Purity Alliance, the Moral Reform Union, the National Vigilance Association, the Association for the Improvement of Public Morals, the Vigilance Association for the Defense of Personal Rights, the Church of England Purity Society, the National British Women's Temperance Association, in addition to hundreds of small local societies throughout Britain. Each of these groups united, more or less, in pursuit of the common goal of attaining public acceptance of an equal moral standard for men and women.[15]

It is easy to make too much of this common goal, however, and the heterogenous character of the social purity movement must not be overlooked. The impetus behind the movement derived predominantly from the twin influences of evangelical Christianity and feminism. Sheila Jeffries has pointed out that "feminist ideas and personnel played vitally important parts within the social purity movement, and shaped its direction and concerns."[16] Edward Bristow has also observed that much of the leadership of the social purity movement consisted predominantly of "Christians [like Stead] reborn in the revivalist missions of the 1860s and 1870s,"[17] and that much of its dynamism stemmed from the nature of a "militant holy alliance" between Christian feminists such as Josephine Butler[18] and Ellice Hopkins,[19] and "latter day puritans of church and chapel."[20] According to Bristow, the "holy alliance" united in opposing the sexual "double standard" as it was institutionalized at the time by the Contagious Diseases Acts of 1864, 1866, and 1869.[21] The efforts of the alliance were ultimately successful, and the Contagious Diseases Acts were finally suspended in 1883. In the early eighteen-eighties the same alliance opposed the issues of juvenile and enforced prostitution.

Yet, despite this record of success, Bristow's idea of a "holy alliance" is probably overstated. The alliances between the various groups within the "social purity" movement were almost always tenuous, temporary, and instrumental in purpose. The goals and direction of each group varied considerably, and the groups competed for membership and influence as often as they cooperated for the achievement of a common goal. The different organizations were able to find common ground and unite in support of some of the more important social legislation that lay before Parliament, such as the repeal of the Contagious Diseases Acts and the passage of the 1885 Criminal Law Amendment Act. However, they often opposed or supported different sections of the proposed bills, and opposed or supported them to greater or lesser extents.

Group unity was often illusory as well, as individuals competed for positions of leadership and power in an effort to sway their group's direction and purpose this way or that. The result of this internal dissent was that many individual members often found themselves at odds with the goals of their own organization. Many nineteenth-century feminists, for example, were able to find common ground with the evangelicals in their shared concern with eliminating vice and with raising moral standards for men. Radical Victorian feminists, however, were suspicious of those whose goals went no further than the improvement of men's morals, and of those whose positions were fundamentally repressive toward women. Previous legislation aimed ostensibly at moral reform, such as the Contagious Diseases Acts, had done little to alter the behavior of men, but much to curtail the civil rights of women. Feminist historians, such as Philippa Levine, Lucy Bland, and Judith Walkowitz, have rightly emphasized the diversity of feminist voices and concerns within the social purity movement. They point out that feminists within the groups were divided over issues regarding the nature of women's sexuality and the contemporary relevance of traditional gender roles.[22] Individual feminists were often torn between the pursuit of equal (that is, equally repressive or permissive) moral standards for both sexes, and advocacy for the civil liberties of women. Many of them found it difficult to balance their concerns with improving the position of women in society with their desires publicly to challenge traditional gender and sexual roles.

For instance, Lucy Bland points to the difference between social purity feminists and feminist "new moralists." According to Bland, social purity feminists emphasized "the right to control one's own body" and "the right to say 'No'" to all undesired male sexual advances, including advances from one's husband. They believed that sex should be reserved ideally for procreation, and that the use of contraception reduced women to the status of prostitutes. "New moralists," on the other hand, stood for "limited monogamy" and "free unions." They argued for the separation of sex from reproduction, and viewed contraception as a means which gave women control over their own bodies.[23]

Despite the plurality of ideological positions within the groups, and despite the fact that group agendas were passionately contested, social purity was a movement that was dominated publicly by a small number of powerful voices: Josephine Butler, Ellice Hopkins, William Coote, and W.T. Stead, among others. Stead's voice was particularly influential because he used his powerful position as editor of the *Pall Mall Gazette* as a means of keeping social purity issues continually before the public eye. Stead's position as a charismatic leader within the social purity movement was secured in 1885, when, as we have seen, he wrote a sensationalized journalistic *exposé* of child prostitution, entitled "The Maiden Tribute of Modern Babylon." The widespread sense of moral outrage that followed this series of articles served to re-focus public attention on the social purity agenda, and the increase in public pressure was instrumental in securing passage of the 1885 Criminal Law Amendment Act. This act was aimed specifically at the procurors of prostitution, and besides introducing new penalties for sex acts between men, it also attempted to suppress brothels and raised the age of consent for girls from thirteen to sixteen. In her recent treatment of Stead and the "Maiden Tribute" affair, Judith Walkowitz points out that Stead at once became a hero to feminists—who viewed him "as a 'champion' of women whose campaign broke down a great barrier of silence surrounding the sexual crimes of men"—and also to radical working men, trade unionists, and socialists, who saw in the "Maiden Tribute" series an attack on "upper-class profligates" and "Old Corruption."[24]

Following the passage of the 1885 Criminal Law Amendment Act, Stead played a key role in the founding of the National Vigilance Association, a voluntary organization whose expressed goals were to reform male sexuality and to press the government to mandate a more coercive policy of sexual regulation. Under the direction of William Coote, the NVA evolved into a network of highly aggressive, interventionist, self-authorized moral surveillance committees which first worked in consort with (and later came to dominate) local rescue societies and chastity leagues. The central office of the NVA involved itself in promoting important, exemplary prosecutions, such as Wilde's, and worked to suppress the works of progressive sexologists such as Havelock Ellis and others who were laboring mightily to educate the public about sex and sexuality.[25] Legislation to outlaw vice and promote public morality was the focus of social purity agitation for good reason. As William Coote explained,

> There is a very cant phrase that you cannot make men good by Acts of Parliament. It is false to say so ... you can, and do keep men sober simply by an Act of Parliament; you can, and do, chain the devil of impurity in a large number of men and women by the fear of the law.[26]

Coote's sentiment was hardly new, as we have seen. As early as the eighteen-sixties, many feminists had been pressing the government to legislate morality via their impassioned opposition to the Contagious Diseases Acts. However, the intent and tone of the morality advocated by the anti-CD feminists lacked the coercive intent and the totalitarian tone that characterized Coote's moral vision.[27] In many respects, the transition from the more compassionate and egalitarian impulses of the anti-CD feminists in the eighteen-sixties to the shriller, more strident and coercive impulses of the NVA in the eighteen-eighties and eighteen-nineties reflects the general tightening-up of the hetero-sexist structures of repression and the increasing sophistication of the heterosexist mechanisms of restraint.

Stead's remarks about Wilde and his ostensible threat to the nation must be understood within the context of the goals and ideology of the social purity movement, and, more importantly, within the context of the public's perception of the movement's goals and ideology. Recently, there has been considerable disagreement among historians over their assessments of the character and "identity" of the social purity movement. According to Sheila Jeffries, Edward Bristow's account has described the goals of the movement "negatively" in terms of the denial of the body and the repression of desire, and spiritually in terms of renewal.[28] Minimizing the differences between Victorian feminists, Jeffries argues instead that the movement's primary goal of eliminating the objectification and exploitation of women's bodies by men should be seen historically as a positive accomplishment in and of itself. Both Jeffrey Weeks' and Frank Mort's accounts of social purity are thoroughly imbued with Foucauldian concerns about the modalities of power. But whereas Weeks virtually dismisses the social purity movement "as a moment of moral panic over sex, [which condensed] wider social and political anxieties," Mort's view takes the movement much more seriously.[29] Approaching the social purity campaigns from what he terms a "medico-moral" perspective, Mort describes the significance of the purity movement in terms of its challenges to the traditional modes of regulating and discussing morality and sexuality, in terms of the movement's empowerment of women, and in terms of the public exposure of "the deeply misogynistic attitudes" which informed governmental policy making.[30]

Certainly all of the views expressed above are valid given the various contexts from which they emerge. Taken together, they represent the many nuances and contradictory aspects of a very complex social and cultural phenomenon. Social purity was simultaneously reactionary, repressive, and progressive. While the movement was peripheral to most people's lives, its impact was felt in some form by virtually everyone in late-Victorian society. I want to exploit the historical ambiguity and liminality of the social purity movement and cast it in yet another light. I want to portray it in even broader terms as a "proposed revolution in consciousness" and view it against the background of what I will suggest were more generalized *fin-de-siècle* anxieties about life and change.

Structurally, the social purity movements in Britain in the eighteen-eighties and eighteen-nineties resemble what anthropologist Anthony F.C. Wallace has termed "cultural revitalization movements."[31] Wallace defines these movements as "deliberate, organized, conscious efforts by members of a society to construct a more satisfying culture." They thus represent a "special kind of culture change phenomenon." According to Wallace's paradigm, the people involved in the revitalization process "must perceive their culture, or some major areas of it, as a[n organic] system," and feel that this system is somehow unsatisfactory or inadequate. They therefore desire "to innovate not merely discrete items, but a new cultural system, specifying new relationships as well as, in some cases, new traits."[32] Wallace ultimately sees revitalization movements constituting constructive responses to the cultural distortion which results from the build-up of long-term societal stresses, dislocations, and upheavals.[33]

Wallace's broad definition easily encompasses the ends and means of the British social purity movement. As I have noted previously, despite the splintering of factions within the larger movement, there was a public perception of general unity within the movement around the issue of the containment of male lust in its various forms—which included not only homosexuality and prostitution, but also masturbation, adultery, obscenity, white slavery, and the artistic depiction of nudes.[34] It was commonly perceived that the movement's goal was to stamp out vice and the prevalent hypocrisy which tolerated it, and to substitute instead a "higher," universal standard of behavior which was consistent with traditional Christian attitudes and beliefs.

Wilde was familiar with this aspect of social purity's moral agenda, and disagreed with it passionately. In *De Profundis*, for example, Wilde charged Queensberry with trying "to pose as a champion of [social] purity," and argued that "in the present condition of the British public ... the surest mode of becoming a heroic figure" was to stand up for morality and purity, a comment which revealed more about the influence of social-purity rhetoric on the social and intellectual climate of Britain than it did about Queensberry's highly personal motives in prosecuting Wilde.[35]

Considered as a movement of cultural revitalization, the social purity movement in Britain can be seen as a response to the popular fears which resulted from a wide variety of cultural dislocations and upheavals. In Chapter Four, I examined the public fears engendered by the ideas of "decadence" and "degeneration" and viewed those fears within the context of a threatening "modernity." Walter Houghton has observed that social purists, although by no means anti-scientific, were reacting in a fundamental way against what they saw as the cultural imposition of the secular values of "modernity," including the values of science and material consumption, and countered this by reaffirming traditional beliefs in faith and spiritual values.[36] The relationship between Christianity and modernity is complex, however. Matei Calinescu has suggested that "modernity" inherited from Christianity a fundamental hostility toward life, a hostility which Nietzsche characterized as "*ressentiment.*" While English Christians generally viewed Wilde as "decadent" from a perspective of moral asceticism, Wilde and Nietzsche could describe Christianity as "decadent" from an antinomian perspective. They viewed Christianity as "decadent" because it was essentially anti-life, or more precisely, it was against "this" world.[37] Without the concept of the redemptive afterlife, there is only the "here and now" of the material world—which is to say, there is only "modernity." Hence, the values that characterize modern Western culture resemble Christian values shorn of the concept of God. Within the *fin-de-siècle* context of the struggle between religious and secular world-views, Wilde's aesthetic "modernism" and his calculated practice of same-sex passion represented precisely the "new" values of experimentation, permissiveness, diversity, and tolerance which threatened the more stolid, traditional, and dogmatic of the religious faithful.

The threat to traditional Christian values represented by the increasing secularization of society was only one of many stresses that was contributing to a national psychological climate of anxiety, distress, and dysfunction. On a more prosaic level, Jeffrey Weeks argues that there was

> ... a perceived decline in moral standards in the 1850s and 60s ... associated with the economic prosperity of those years ... and 1885, the *annus mirabilus* of sexual politics, was also the year of the expansion of the electorate, fear of national decline following the defeat of General Gordon at Khartoum, anxieties about the future of Ireland, and all this in the context of socialist revival and feminist agitation.[38]

The list does not stop with anxieties over military defeat, the ever-present Irish problem, feminist and socialist agitation, and a nebulous fear of democracy. Retrospectively, of course, during the last quarter of the nineteenth century, there were many reasons for Britons to have agonized over the present condition and future potential of their nation. Declines in absolute and relative productivity and a decreased share in world markets gave credence to the widespread perception that Britain was in the throes of an economic depression.[39] Gareth Stedman Jones has argued that, especially in the eighteen-eighties and eighteen-nineties, the chronically unemployed, casually employed, and underemployed "residuum" of urban areas, who ostensibly represented both a moral and an aesthetic problem for the middle classes, were in fact symptomatic of the collapse of the industrial infrastructure and indicative of a wider social crisis as well.[40] Martin Weiner has suggested that mid-Victorian prosperity inspired a certain complacency in the younger generations. In the public schools, the privileged scions of the upwardly mobile middle and upper-middle classes received an education in the superiority of the leisured values of the aristocracy, an education which resulted in the wholesale rejection of the industrious values and acquisitive habits of their fathers. As a consequence, Weiner argues, along with the loss of its industrial might during the late-Victorian period England lost most of its "industrial spirit" as well.[41]

The forces of nationalism, which had only recently united the nations of Italy and Germany, were threatening to disintegrate both the United Kingdom and the British Empire.[42] Elie Halévy, the French historian, identified 1895 as a major watershed in British politics because that year witnessed the demise of traditional British Liberalism as it had been embodied in the person and political vision of Gladstone.[43] The traditional political allegiances of the middle classes had been gradually changing for some time. The middle classes were abandoning the Liberal Party and (symbolically) the working classes in droves, and generally realigning their traditional class interests upwards. As Michael Freeden has explained,

> The Liberal Party was losing—if it ever had enjoyed—the backing of actual and potential voters from the working class, while its traditional middle-class supporters were fragmented, among others, into a number of professional groups that maintained their progressive drive, and a growing number of property-holders whose creed became increasingly bound up with the preservation of acquired rights, non-intervention in economic affairs, legal encouragement for the profit motive, and the virtues of individually-based character and initiative.[44]

In addition, and unbeknownst to the public,[45] as I have tried to show earlier, Rosebery's Liberal Government had virtually ceased to function during the winter and spring of 1895, just as the Wilde trials were being held. I have already detailed Rosebery's personal problems, and an entry in Beatrice Webb's diary provides an insider's view of a dysfunctional Cabinet that conveys the impression of decay, degeneration, and lack of resolve at the very highest echelons of government:

> With the exception of Acland [Vice-President of the Council and education Minister], none of the ministers are doing any work: Rosebery sees no one but Eddy Hamilton, a flashy fast Treasury Clerk, his stud-groom, and various non-political fashionables; Sir W[illiam] Harcourt [Chancellor of Exchequer and Leader of Commons] amuses himself at his country palace and abroad, determined to do nothing to help Rosebery; even Asquith [Home Secretary], under the domination of his brilliant and silly wife, has given up attending to his

department and occupies his time by visiting rich country houses and learning to ride! "Rot has set in" says Haldane [M.P.]; "there is no hope now but to be beaten and then reconstruct a new party."[46]

From this broad view, one can imagine that the combined psychic weight of military defeat, Home Rule, economic depression, industrial malaise, social fragmentation, moral backsliding, generational angst, political transformations, governmental *ennui*, which—along with the perpetual problems of adaptation and environmental pollution resulting from continuing industrialization, urbanization, and technological innovation—must have seemed overwhelming to many individuals who were concerned about the fate of the nation and anxious to do something about it. Faced with such a multitude of seemingly insurmountable problems, the most viable practical solution to this situation of perpetual crisis was simply to choose one problem out of the many, and try to address it. In order to cope with the physical strains, psychological stresses and mental paralysis that represent the psychic correlate of the condition of modernity, it is logical to assume that people must have naturally sought to control whatever they could.

In the case of the social purists, this meant focusing on the issue they identified as the key problem, the one that was seen as a root cause of some of the other problems as well. This problem was morality, and by extension, sexuality.[47] Social purists like Stead felt that social change could be bearable as long as certain moral rules were inviolable. Because they were generally unable to comprehend and address the complexity and immensity of all the social and economic problems that plagued Britain, many social purists seized upon their personal beliefs about the centrality of morality to the public good. In many respects, such concerns reflected the importance of morality in their own private lives. Seen in this way, the larger public movement arose out of the combination of many small and private obsessions with morality, sexuality, and personal salvation.

While one cannot be absolutely sure about the motives of individual social purists, one can infer that although their public rhetoric announced that they were acting out of altruistic impulses for the benefit of society and the health of the nation, which was no doubt true to a large extent, it also seems likely that many individuals involved themselves in purity work in order to preserve their own mental stability in a period of incomprehensible social flux. The active promotion of social purity ideology was one way for these individuals to address their own deeply felt anxieties about change. On one hand, social purists projected their own psychological needs and insecurities about modernity and modernization upon society as a whole, in effect transforming personal anxieties into societal problems which could then be addressed through group action. On the other hand, individual social purists—ostensibly caring, concerned and sensitive individuals—may have experienced and internalized the external chaos and fragmentation to such a degree that the autonomy and integrity of their own "selves" was threatened. The effect was to transform social problems into personal problems which could then be worked through within the supportive confines of a group.[48]

There were others besides the social purists who were advocating a moral transformation of society, albeit for different reasons. Several influential political pundits were also trumpeting the Spencerian ideals of "self-development" and "ethical perfection" as social values, and indeed as values that the State ought to be promoting. The rhetoric of "New Liberalism" espoused by J.A. Hobson, the social theorist and reformer, L.T. Hobhouse, the political theorist and sociologist, and D.G. Ritchie, the Scottish metaphysician and Fabian, who addressed the nation through periodicals such as the *Speaker*, the *Nation*, and the *Manchester Guardian*, was thoroughly imbued with current biological and evolutionary views of society.[49] By accepting the basic premises of Spencer's evolutionism, "New Liberals" like Hobson could conceive of society as an integrated, interrelating social organism, "in which the welfare of the parts depended upon the health of the whole."[50]

This position pushed the notion of a "common good" in a more collectivist direction, and challenged the classical interpretations of liberalism, such as J.S. Mill's, which advocated the protection of individual rights against possible incursions by the State, and sought limitations of the State's power to interfere in the affairs of the individual. Leonard Hobhouse, for instance, replaced notions of individual liberty with concepts of "civic efficiency" and "social freedom," and represented the intellectual progression in political theory from the protection of individualism to the promotion of collectivism as evidence that society was indeed evolving in a more positive, altruistic direction.[51]

The widespread popular acceptance of the Spencerian synthesis of moralism and materialism provided the "New Liberal" thinkers with the leverage to challenge the traditional reluctance of the State to dictate public morality. T.H. Green, the Balliol idealist philosopher, defended the right of the state to promote public morality,[52] and D.G. Ritchie defined morality itself in terms of "the health of the social organism."[53] The "New Liberals" suggested that the State should play a greater role in the moral guardianship of the nation, and act as the primary agent of social improvement and the number one promoter of the common public good.[54] Within the context of the "New Liberal" vision of society, the government's prosecution of Wilde can be seen as representing an effort by the State to promote public morality and to protect its own health and viability.

In many ways, the exemplary prosecution of Wilde illustrates the internal logic of the social purists and the "New Liberal" idealists, who increasingly saw the moral authority of society as sacred, inviolable, and necessary for the maintenance of order within the society. From a Durkheimian sociological perspective (which in many ways parallels the views of "New Liberals" such as Green and Hobhouse[55]), "when flagrant individual breaches of morality are not followed by sanctions this is a clear sign that morality is in a state of flux," and hence a sign that society is unstable as well.[56] Similarly, when Wilde's crimes were revealed in the Queensberry trial, Wilde had to be prosecuted in order to demonstrate that society was indeed stable and secure. For Durkheim, it would not have been the intrinsic nature of Wilde's crime (the content of the act) that was problematic, but rather the fact that he violated one of society's pre-established sacred rules.[57] Symbolically then, Wilde's true crime was his refusal to subordinate himself to the rules of society, which implied both a failure to fulfill his social obligation to the nation and a failure to respect the authority of public opinion. As a side issue, Durkheim would have regarded Wilde's indirect appeals to the moral values of ancient Greece as specious and inappropriate, because "we cannot aspire to a morality other than that which is related to the state of our society."[58] Wilde's challenge to British society, like Socrates' challenge to Athens, can be seen in this context as constituting a willful flouting of reality.

Morality, for Durkheim as well as for Green, Ritchie, Hobhouse, and others, was necessarily a social concept which represented not a set of consensual social norms, but rather a set of social ideals and aspirations. As a set of ideals, morals served to shape the image of society, give it stability, and also supply it with an identity. Being unattainable, ideals also provided society with a rational goal and purpose as well.[59] Morality thus represented an integral part of the collective belief system, and as such was inseparable from society.[60] Taking their cue from Spencer, Durkheim and the "New Liberals" viewed society as a totalizing concept which encompassed both structure and content. Society therefore represented much more than just the sum of individuals. Rather, the association of individuals into a "social system" represented a separate and distinct ontological reality with its own salient characteristics.[61]

A Diseased State of Affairs

The imagery of health and disease within the context of "New Liberal" and social-evolutionary discourse was prevalent throughout the late-Victorian period.[62] Brougham Villiers, writing in 1904, argued that "the lives of men are so bound up with one another in the complex web of society, that it is impossible for social want or disease in any part of the body politic *not*, in the long run, to bring ruin to others."[63] Untended social diseases, therefore, whether physical or moral, would be passed on or otherwise transmitted, and eventually destroy the nation. The New Liberal solution to preserving the integrity of the social organism in many respects resembled that of the social purists. Echoing the sentiments expressed by William Coote, the director of the National Vigilance Association, cited above, D.G. Ritchie stated that "laws may produce those opinions and sentiments which go to the furtherance of morality."[64]

As Durkheim points out in his writings, shared ideals are necessary to assure social stability, and represent both the actual state of society and its aspirations. Social morality itself represents an ideal of health and an ideal of "normality" which are intended to reflect the assumed health and "normality" of society.[65] By defining morality in terms of normality, Durkheim was suggesting that the "normal" and "average" were socially desirable, not only because "normal" and "average" represented the abstract ideal of what "ought to be" and what everyone "ought to be like," but also because the "normal" was predictable and hence, from the State's point of view, easier to manipulate and control.

Certainly, if Durkheim can define morality in terms of normality, then normality can also be defined in terms of morality. Georges Canguilhem has pointed out that "normality," like morality, represents a behavioral goal or ideal which is significant for purposes of reference and regulation.[66] Within the parameters of medico-psychiatric discourse, "normality" represents the psychosocial ability to adapt to a particular environment at a particular point in time. This adaptation can be defined positively as the ability to "fit in," or defined negatively as the ability to "not stand out." Thus the "normal" is that which is able to conform to the rule, and also that which is temporarily viable.[67] Conversely, that which is "abnormal" is unable, for whatever reasons, to conform to the rule, and also that which is inappropriate for currently existing circumstances. Even more importantly, within a nineteenth-century context, "normal" was becoming a common term to designate the state of organic health.[68] The concept of the "normal" was thereafter linked and associated with the concept of "health" and the concept of the "good," all of which were defined primarily in social rather than individual terms. Thus ideologically loaded and imbued with the concept of "right," "normal" could be assimilated into popular discourse and deployed as a polemical concept.

With this in mind, we are now in a better position to grasp the full polemical import of W.T. Stead's indictment (cited at the head of this chapter) of Wilde as "abnormal" and "unnatural." Compared to some of the other descriptions of Wilde found in the press at this time, however, Stead's comments seem rather generous and benign. Other, more pointed and hurtful descriptions, which also appropriated metaphors from contemporary medico-psychiatric, biological, and evolutionary discourse, were commonplace in the daily newspaper commentaries on the Wilde case. After the first trial, for example, the *Daily Telegraph* attacked Wilde indirectly through the Aesthetic movement, which was described as a "French and Pagan plague which has [infested] the healthy fields of British life."[69] On the same day, the *Star* referred to the Aesthetes as "a parasite, an excrescence, an aberration."[70] In his summation during the second trial, chief prosecutor Gill referred to Wilde as "a sore which cannot fail in time to corrupt and taint [society]."[71] Justice Wills, in his summation after the third trial, referred to Wilde's "unclean sentiments and unclean appetites."[72] In a letter to the *Star*, Queensberry, no stranger to vitriolic diatribes, called Wilde "a sexual pervert of an utterly diseased mind."[73] The *Morning* regarded Wilde as a "canker" that needed to be "thoroughly cauterized."[74] Finally, after Wilde had been sentenced, the *Daily Telegraph* pronounced Wilde as "poisonous," "perverse," "unnatural," and "unhealthy."[75] The labels used to characterize Wilde's repulsiveness can be loosely categorized into two groups of metaphors: metaphors of dirt and disease, and metaphors of "otherness." Each of these types of phenomena—disease, dirt, and "otherness"—threaten, or appear to threaten, the social organism in different ways. Both groups of metaphors were used politically with the expressed purpose of labelling and stigmatizing their object, in this case Wilde, and thus should be seen as weapons wielded by the powerful to vilify, demonize, and ultimately to eliminate, their enemies. Once the processes of vilification, excoriation, and demonization have been successful—that is, once all the defenses and appeals have failed and the labels have been firmly and permanently affixed to the object—the victim fully appears to deserve whatever punishment is meted out to him, and the vengeance of the "majority" is rationalized and justified.[76] From the victim's perspective, the process of labelling and the stigmatization which results from it have a different consequence. The process of "accepting" the labels and stigmata, which occurs on both conscious and unconscious levels, privately constitutes an act of self-betrayal and publicly symbolizes an act of self-sacrifice on behalf of the greater good and the healthy "social organism." Symbolically, this self-sacrifice represents the "social death" of the individual. Robert Sherard, a friend of Wilde's and an observer at the trials, describes the finality of "social death" within the British context:

> In England, if a man fall, he falls never to rise again. There are in the British a certain bloodthirstiness and a certain instinctive cruelty, which not centuries of Protestant practice have been able to moderate. These qualities of the nation account for the facts that not only is our penal legislation the severest in the world, but that a conviction entails the immediate and irreparable social death of the offender.[77]

The metaphors of the ontologically different "other"—such as "aberration," "excrescence," and "abnormality"—are, because of their vagueness, somewhat unsatisfactory in terms of offering a rational explanation for the nature of the specific threat they represent to society. The very quality of "otherness" is both irrational and essentially devoid of meaningful content. Paradoxically, the power of metaphors of otherness appears to derive specifically from their vagueness and irrationality. Otherness only signifies difference without quantifying it and, in many cases, without explaining why difference, in and of itself, is necessarily bad. In signifying an ontological or qualitative difference, otherness simultaneously presents an insurmountable epistemological problem of knowing and evaluating that difference (according to what criteria?). In effect, stigmatizing someone as "other" implies that we know practically nothing about them. It also implies a willful blindness toward everything about them except their difference, where difference is categorically "bad" and thus to be dreaded. Psychoanalytically, the real threat of the "other" is the threat of our *own* ignorance, which is projected outward and then contained within the body of the "other." Thus objectified, the person of the "other" can then be hated irrationally, essentially for not being "us." In this regard, the polemical use of metaphors of "otherness" offers more information about the "in-group" and its ability to project power than it does about the "out-group" and its powerlessness.[78]

Compared to the abstract and irrational quality of metaphors of "otherness," metaphors of dirt and disease seem very concrete and rational. "Parasite," "canker," "plague," "poison," "sore," and so on, appear rational because they are essentially biological metaphors which are readily understandable through simple analogies. Although they are based on scientific knowledge and derive their authority from that source, they require no scientific knowledge on the part of the audience in order to comprehend or to use them.

From an anthropological perspective, Mary Douglas classifies the metaphors of dirt and disease as "pollution ideas" which signify social reactions to particular anomalies. Transgression of the ideas triggers a process which itself works somewhat mechanically, so that "recognition of the anomaly leads to anxiety and discomfort and from there to suppression and avoidance."[79] Pollution ideas typically originate in order to protect the sacred social body from contamination or profanation. From the standpoint of moral hygiene, "dirt" is a metaphor used to signify a state of (moral) disorder which threatens the very stability of a society. The elimination of the threat is not conceived as a negative act, but rather as a positive effort to reorganize the environment, and to make it conform to a generally shared idea of what is right, moral, and appropriate.[80] Pollution ideas function instrumentally to influence behavior and expressively to establish the tone of the society. From the standpoint of those in power, or in this case the State, the routine punishment of transgressors of pollution ideas is necessary to reinforce socially sanctioned behavior and beliefs.[81]

Ironically, as Georges Canguilhem indicates, the concept of disease reveals more about the state of "normalcy" (in society) than the state of normalcy discloses about the concept of disease. Canguilhem sees disease representing "the general concept of non-value which includes all possible negative values."[82] Disease, and its synonyms, sickness and illness, are here defined generally as the inverse of health. If "health" is conceptualized positively as life, long life, the possession of potential, capacity for reproduction and for physical work, strength, resistance to fatigue, absence of pain, and a joyous state of being, then "disease" represents a diminished life, an impaired, stunted, or shortened life, unfulfilled potential, a lack of capacity for or interest in work and reproduction, weakness, susceptibility to fatigue, the presence of pain, and a miserable state of being.

In *Illness as Metaphor*, Susan Sontag finds that illness or disease often provides a metaphor for the subjects of our deepest [social] dread, such as "corruption, decay, pollution, anomie, weakness." Sontag contends that "feelings about evil are projected onto a disease, and the disease [enriched with the new meanings] is then projected onto the world."[83] Without addressing them, Sontag's point raises the twin issues of communicability and impact, that is, how is the disease, theoretically isolated and contained within the person of someone like Wilde, transmitted to the larger society? And secondly, how does the disease affect society?

In response to the second question, it can be asserted that disease represents a very broad systemic threat. Canguilhem proposes that once disease enters into a (social) body, an internal struggle ensues which results in the disequilibrium of the body.[84] Disease is therefore described, metaphorically, as a destabilizing factor. According to "germ theory," disease is most often seen as an infectious foreign element, or pathological agent, which penetrates, invades, or otherwise enters the body. In another sense, as Sontag points out using the example of cancer, the disease could have been always present within the body, in a benign state of latency, and then suddenly triggered into an aggressive state of malignancy by the complex interaction of a constellation of factors, each factor of which alone would not have been enough to set off the disease.[85]

Within the context of the trials, Wilde himself was represented both by the Court and by the press as a pathological agent who had violated societal pollution laws and who thereby threatened to undermine the moral health of the social organism, in effect creating discord and destabilizing society in several ways. As I have discussed in Chapters Four and Five, the moral corruption of youth was one of the central issues of the State's case against Wilde. The idea of "corrupted youth" was disturbing to many contemporaries, for this implied that the very future of England was potentially imperiled by him. Although it was clear from the general rhetoric surrounding the trials that Wilde was perceived as threatening the social fabric of the nation, the *Daily Telegraph* went so far as to specify certain groups within society which they believed to be at greater risk.

> No sterner rebuke could well have been inflicted on some of the artistic tendencies of the time than the condemnation on Saturday of OSCAR WILDE at the Central Criminal Court ... the lesson of his life should not be passed over without some insistence of the terrible warning of his fate. Young men at Universities, clever sixth form boys at public schools, silly women who lend an ear to any chatter which is petulant and vivacious, novelists who have sought to imitate the style of paradox and unreality, poets who have lisped the language of nerveless and effeminate libertinage—these are the persons who should ponder with themselves the doctrines and the career of the man who has now to undergo the righteous sentence of the law. ...[86]

By addressing the lessons of the Wilde trial and holding them up as a warning to other potential deviants, who were identified as public school and university students, feminists, artists of different stripes, and effeminate men, the *Daily Telegraph* was, inadvertently or not, promoting the values of "social purity." Would that the potential deviants learned the lesson of Wilde's fate along with his fascinating artistic creed! The *Daily Telegraph*'s message can be distilled into two distinct, but related, warnings. The first was to avoid imitating Wilde because he represented almost every conceivable social evil. His philosophy, they were warned, was attractive on the surface, but dark and dangerous underneath. The second warning was not to deviate from the status quo. Of the two warnings, the second was undoubtedly the most important. In this jeremiad, the targeted readers were admonished to show some self-restraint and to rein in their youthful zeal for the unconventional and the daring, and somehow to find a way to accept the prevailing reality and their place in it. Echoing Nordau, those at risk were urged by the *Telegraph*'s editors to find a middle path and to avoid the extremes that Wilde represented:

> To be cultured is not necessarily to be in perpetual revolt ... a man can think deeply and yet live cleanly; a woman can be free and happy and yet recognize the obligations of law.[87]

In Chapter Four, I argued that Wilde's threat to society transcended his same-sex practices and embraced the notion of gender deviancy which is contained within the concept of male effeminacy. In Chapter Five, I suggested that Wilde's promotion of his personal "ontological aesthetic of dissent" was viewed by contemporaries as having vast (and overwhelmingly negative) social and political implications. At this point, I want to introduce two additional components to this very potent constellation of threats that Wilde represented to the social body. These are the public's perceptions of Wilde's "elitism" and what might be described benignly as his "internationalism" and more maliciously as his "foreignness"—both of which are inextricably connected with his aristocratic pose. In what follows I will develop some linkages between these four aspects (same-sex practices and effeminacy, the "ontological aesthetic," elitism, and foreignness) in order to show how their combination represented much more than the sum of their parts.

We have already examined the class angle in relation to Wilde's sexual exploitation of working-class youths. A separate but related class issue concerns the discrepancy between the treatment accorded middle-class persons who were accused of crimes and the treatment accorded aristocratic persons who were accused of the same crimes. In a letter to the *Star* following the Queensberry libel trial, Robert Buchanan argued that Wilde was treated like a criminal before his conviction solely because he was not an aristocrat.[88] Had Wilde been a peer of the realm, Buchanan suggested, he would have been treated with all due respect, his innocence or guilt notwithstanding, and he certainly would not have been deprived of his much-needed cigarettes. COMMON-SENSE responded to the underlying class aspect in Buchanan's letter, and foregrounded it in his comment which made a reference to Dickens' character Bill Sykes and his "clay" (pipe). COMMON-SENSE compared Wilde unfavorably to Bill Sykes, suggesting that a manly, if criminal, representative of the lowest rung of the (productive) working classes was preferable to an "unmanly" artist with "effeminate" and "aristocratic" airs who represented the parasitism and uselessness of the upper classes. Whereas Buchanan felt that Wilde's commoner status had been a disadvantage during the trials and had led to unfair treatment, COMMON-SENSE argued that Wilde had very little resemblance to the common man at all.

COMMON-SENSE was not the only one to have made such a charge against him. Certainly, to people of limited means and relatively simple outlooks, Wilde's flamboyant and luxurious lifestyle, exotic tastes, extravagant spending habits, cultivated manner, and arrogant attitude must have been easy to confuse with the lifestyles, manners, and attitudes of many aristocrats. The careless dissipation of time and energy associated with his debauched and hedonistic lifestyle precluded its undertaking by anyone deficient in capital, vigor, or leisure time.[89] Wilde's friend, Robert Sherard, believed that class hatred was the basis of the popular dislike of Wilde, and claimed that Wilde had been identified with the aristocratic "element." While observing the crowd's reaction to Wilde's conviction, Sherard noted that "to the crowd [outside the courtroom], Wilde represented the aristocrat, and they [the crowd] were exulting in [what they thought was] the fall of an aristocrat."[90]

Wilde's "foreignness," on the other hand, stemmed less from his Anglo-Irish heritage than from the fact that he was perceived to be the ambassador of an insidiously subversive French school of art. In castigating Wilde for maliciously importing the French taste for exotic vice and degenerate modern art (the Impressionists!), the *Daily Telegraph* juxtaposed the "healthy fields of British life" and the "sanctity and sweetness of [the British] home" against the "profligate tastes" and "salacious impulses" of Wilde's Francophile dandyism.[91] Paris especially was seen as the center of artistic and moral corruption, and Wilde was portrayed as its representative:

> We speak sometimes of a school of Decadents and Aesthetes in England, although it may well be doubted whether at any time its prominent members could not have been counted on the fingers of one hand; but quite apart from any fixed organization or body such as may or may not exist in Paris, there has lately shown itself in London a contemporary bias of thought, an affected manner of expression and style, and a few loudly vaunted ideas which have had a limited but evil influence on all the better tendencies of art and literature. Of these the prisoner of Saturday constituted himself a representative. He set an example, so far as in him lay, to the weaker and the younger brethren; and, just because he possessed considerable intellectual powers and unbounded assurance, his fugitive success served to dazzle and bewilder those who had neither experience nor knowledge of the principles which he travestied, or of that true temple of art of which he was so unworthy an acolyte. Let us hope that his removal will serve to clear the poisoned air, and make it cleaner for all healthy and unvitiated lungs.[92]

The *Daily Telegraph*'s advocacy of Wilde's "removal" from the "temple of art," and implicitly from the national "body," was described in terms analogous to that of a medical operation which was necessary to save the patient's life. The newspaper's fantasized existence of an artistic cabal in Paris, a sort of Comintern, and covertly perhaps, a "Homintern," for Art, appeared to advance the possibility of an insidious foreign "political" conspiracy aimed at corrupting the weak-brained and sensitive youth of England, and through them putting the future security of the English race in dire jeopardy.[93]

While we have already explored some of the conceptual links between the aristocracy, same-sex practices, and male effeminacy, the time is ripe to add a xenophobic twist to all of this. There were, and still are, long-standing associations in Britain between "foreignness," the aristocracy, and same-sex practices. In his study of the Oxford Movement of the eighteen-forties, David Hilliard has shown the connection between Anglo-Catholicism—a "foreign" religion associated with France and Ireland, traditional enemies of England—and the male "homosexual" subculture in England. Hilliard suggested that "for many homosexual men in the late nineteenth and early twentieth centuries, Anglo-Catholicism provided a set of institutions and religious practices through which they could express their sense of difference in an oblique and symbolical way."[94] Wilde had flirted with Roman Catholicism since his early days at Oxford, and ultimately underwent a deathbed conversion in 1900.

In his own work on the history of "homosexuality" in England, H.M. Hyde has traced the spread of sodomitical habits in France and England to the Normans in the eleventh century, and described how the "gilded youth of Norman England" cultivated a deliberately effeminate appearance and manner.[95] When Thomas Paine discussed the omnipresent "Norman yoke" in England in *The Rights of Man*, we can be reasonably sure that he was not speaking of homosexual bondage, although in retrospect it can perhaps be read that way. But he was alluding to both a class and a cultural difference between the working and middle classes, descended predominantly from indigenous Anglo-Saxons, and the English aristocracy, many of whom were of Norman descent. Historically, the possession of power, wealth, leisure, and privacy meant that aristocrats could do as they pleased within the confines of their estates, so in terms of sexuality, aristocrats have stereotypically perhaps, but often deservedly, been regarded as having more interest in, more time and opportunity for, and hence a greater tolerance of, libertinism and other "deviant" sorts of sexual activities.

Even more pertinent than the content of the public imagination, however, was the popular association, as evinced in the trial testimony and in various letters commenting on the trials, such as those of Stead and Millard at the beginning of this chapter, between same-sex practices and the English public schools and universities.[96] Of course, education may have played a more important role than class in establishing this linkage,[97] but the class factor must not be overlooked. Long the province of the sons of the aristocracy, the public schools and universities had only in the mid-nineteenth century begun to open their doors to the sons of the middle classes. If we accept Martin Weiner's thesis that the public schools provided the means whereby the privileged middle-class youth of the day were socialized into the world-view and values of the ruling classes,[98] then we must also believe that the sons of businessmen, professionals, and bureaucrats were also being socialized into a world where same-sex practices had long been established and thus comprised a virtual norm. At the same time as the students were learning the values of the aristocrats, they were learning their vices as well.[99]

In short then, Wilde's image was invested with much more than just a deviant sexuality. Rather, he represented a frightening constellation of threats which conflated all these disparate elements and associations: he represented foreign vice, foreign art, and indirectly, the legacy of foreign rulers; he represented the useless, lawless, effeminate, and sexually debauched upper classes; he represented an elite and effete form of art, and an atheistic and anarchistic aesthetic; finally, and tragically, he represented the abuse of privilege and the misuse of talent. Thus when the newspapers attacked Wilde and condemned his immoral vice, they were also expressing their xenophobic fear of foreigners and foreign influences, their hatred of a useless and parasitic aristocracy, and their intolerance for useless artists and for anyone else who would actively try to subvert the status quo. In sum, they were expressing fear, hatred, and intolerance for everything that was not bourgeois, useful, rational, procreative, "right-thinking," and patriotic. In effect, then, Wilde represented a constellation of fears and ideas which was antithetical to the representative middle-class values of the nation, particularly as they were construed in terms of class, gender, and sexuality, and as they were construed in moral and political terms as well.

Epilogue

In retrospect, Wilde is often seen as *the* representative English writer of the eighteen-nineties, and said to exemplify the frivolous concerns and superficial preoccupations of the *fin-de-siècle*.[100] Although Wilde's reputation and importance as a writer has grown continually in the years since his death in 1900, it is important to remember that while contemporaries generally regarded him as a writer of great style who was often brilliant, witty, and humorous, he was hardly ever accused of being a writer of great substance. Literarily, therefore, Wilde was held in lesser esteem by contemporaries than several of his more serious rivals, such as Shaw and Ibsen, who, while they could not match Wilde's technical virtuosity and verbal flair, more than compensated for that lack by addressing through their work some of the great social, political, and philosophical questions of the day.

To understand Wilde's fall as it is represented in the trials, it is useful to understand exactly from whence he fell. Despite an impressive string of literary and theatrical successes since 1890, Wilde was hardly considered a national treasure. His superior intellect and huge talent brought him, along with success, considerable notoriety. His flamboyant and extravagant lifestyle, disdain for common values, and disrespect for tradition alienated him from the middle classes who comprised the bulk of his audiences, even as his comedic works, which lampooned the leisured classes, amused them. So even though there was great respect for his work in general, that respect did not necessarily translate to his person. His private life was in a shambles as well. His marriage had fallen apart long before the trials, and was dissolved while he was in prison. Financially, Wilde was in equally bad shape. By the time of the libel trial, he had already squandered most of his considerable wealth on high living, and was ultimately forced into bankruptcy by Queensberry after losing the libel case.

This investigation was initially motivated by the question, why were the Wilde trials historically important? What made Wilde's conviction of this particular crime any more significant than the conviction of any other person who had committed the same crime—Alfred Taylor, for example? Certainly Wilde's celebrity status, talent, success, and flamboyant lifestyle made him a public curiosity. In essence, Wilde belonged to the public domain. People had been following his well-publicized escapades in London, America, and the Continent for a decade and a half. People wanted to know about him, and they fully expected to be startled, amused, and even scandalized by him, within limits. What separated Taylor from Wilde in the public mind was that whereas nobody had ever heard of Taylor, Wilde was rightly perceived as a person with the power, charisma, and talent potentially to affect large numbers of people. Because Wilde had access to the public—through his works and through exposure in the print media—he possessed the capability of altering public judgment.

Celebrity status is in great part based on either public ignorance or the willful denial of the many facts of a person's life, facts that, once they emerge in the context of a criminal trial, invariably contradict the image that has been publicly constructed, the image in which the public wants to believe, and which the public idealizes. As long as no crime has been committed, the denial or ignorance of the celebrity's private life can be perpetuated, and icon status can be maintained. However, once innuendo is confused with fact and the public knows more about the public figure's private life than about his or her positive public achievements, the image of the celebrity is invariably tarnished and irrevocably damaged, and redemption is virtually impossible. Once the possibility of idealization is diminished or revoked, the celebrity (as icon) is no longer able to represent the values, ideals, and aspirations he or she used to represent, and can no longer command the public's awe and respect.

All Wilde's positive achievements were erased as negative public knowledge of his scandalous private life displaced the positive public knowledge of his literary accomplishments. As long as knowledge of Wilde's sexual activities remained out of the public domain, his illicit activities could be, and were, tolerated by an increasingly suspicious public. But once knowledge of his sexuality entered the public domain via the Queensberry libel trial and those suspicions were confirmed, his actions could no longer be tolerated. He ultimately had to be prosecuted for two main reasons, one based on widespread public knowledge and the second based on highly confidential information. First of all, within the context of the cultural and intellectual climate in England, the successful prosecution of Wilde was necessary in order to appease a capricious public whose threshold of tolerance had been breached and to protect the moral integrity and cohesion of the social body. Secondly, if my hypothesis concerning Rosebery's inclinations toward same-sex practices is correct, then we may suppose that the successful prosecution of Wilde was necessary to prevent another, potentially larger and infinitely more damaging scandal, involving the Prime Minister himself. Such a scandal would have possessed the power—like Watergate—to rip the social body apart.

Although the backstairs governmental maneuvering and legal stacking of the deck against Wilde can only be hypothesized, and not convincingly proved, based on our knowledge of the behavior of contemporary governments, one wants to believe in such a high-level cover-up and the conspiracy theory which supports it, if only for Wilde's sake. It seems clear from *De Profundis* and his letters, and also from his conduct during the trial and in and after prison that Wilde had a very strong sense of self, and high self-esteem. When he was in Reading Gaol, Wilde resisted the efforts of the State to rehabilitate him because he basically believed that he was fine just the way he was.[101] Wilde's oft-quoted petition to the Home Office requesting an early release from Reading Gaol—in which he cited the work of Lombroso and Nordau and argued that his perversion was a result of "sexual madness," and thus a form of insanity that deserved a doctor's treatment, and not a crime that deserved imprisonment—must ultimately be seen as little more than a deliberate ruse to fool his captors and not as an honest self-assessment.[102] For Wilde, it was always the State that needed improvement, and never himself. He regretted the social stigmatization and ostracism that resulted from his conviction and imprisonment, but he rejected the labels that were attached to him. He recognized the power of the labels, and acknowledged the opinions of others regarding himself, but he could not accept those opinions because he did not respect the people who were labelling him. Ultimately he felt that the public was incapable of understanding or appreciating the complexities and nuances of his multi-faceted personality.

As the verdict was read at the conclusion of the trials, Wilde bowed, for the first time in his life, to the public will. He consented to his social death and went willingly to his martyrdom on behalf of art. He thought he had been sentenced to jail for his supreme arrogance and *hubris* in thinking he would be able to put a peer (Queensberry) into prison.[103] Thus he was in a sense aware that his real crime had been less his specific same-sex practices, and more his general efforts to subvert and undermine the official status quo. In a peripheral and oblique way that did not really interest him, Wilde knew that his punishment was meant to restore and reinforce the ideals of the collective. But to die socially for a public ideal does not necessarily signify a belief in that ideal. He fully understood that everyone else believed in it, but he himself did not care. That his social death was perceived as constituting public atonement for his crime was of no personal consequence. Rather, Wilde saw his social death as fated, and thus as necessary to attain a private redemption and to mark a new phase in his life.

Ironically, it was in prison that Wilde's quest for self-knowledge and self-acceptance was finally completed. In *De Profundis*, Wilde wrote that prison had been good for him. He had finally discovered the humility which was the perfect complement for his *hubris*, and this allowed him to round out his antinomian persona.[104] Ultimately, Wilde might have wished that society could have known the good that was in his heart, for if they had, society might have been transformed in a positive way. Sadly, however, Wilde knew that this particular threat represented no particular danger to society, for "in sublimity of soul there is no contagion."[105]

NOTES

Introduction

1. Holbrook Jackson, *The Eighteen Nineties*, New York: Capricorn Books, 1913, p. 72.
2. The highlights of Wilde's literary production for the first half of the decade are the following. In 1890, *The Picture of Dorian Gray* was published in *Lippincott's Monthly Magazine*, causing great furor and debate in the press on the subject of art and morality. In 1891, Wilde published "'The True Function and Value of Criticism" in two parts, later retitled "The Critic as Artist" when collected with three previously published essays ("The Decay of Lying," "The Truth of Masks," and "Pen, Pencil, and Poison") in *Intentions*. Also in 1891, Wilde published *The Soul of Man Under Socialism*, the revised version of *The Picture of Dorian Gray* as a novel, *Lord Arthur Savile's Crime and Other Stories*, and the play *A House of Pomegranates*. The play *A Duchess of Padua*, was anonymously produced in New York under the title of *Guido Ferranti*. In 1892, Wilde wrote *Salomé*, in French. It was refused a license for production in England, but was later débuted in Paris in 1896. In 1892, *Lady Windermere's Fan* was Wilde's first theatrical success in London, followed by *A Woman of No Importance* in 1893. *An Ideal Husband* and *The Importance of Being Earnest* both opened in early 1895.

3. In E.M. Forster's novel *Maurice* (finished in 1914, published in 1971), for example, the character Maurice makes a reference to "unspeakables of the Oscar Wilde sort." Quoted in Alan Sinfield, *The Wilde Century: Effeminacy, Oscar Wilde, and the Queer Moment*, New York: Columbia University Press, 1994, p. 140. Similarly, in Robert Roberts' memoir of growing up in working-class Salford during the Edwardian period, he writes that the working classes had been fascinated with the Wilde trials in 1895, and that "as late as the first world war the ribald cry heard in factories, 'Watch out for

oscarwile!' mystified raw young apprentices." Quoted in *ibid.*, p. 146.

4. The Marquess of Queensberry was also, of course, famous for supervising the formulation of the basic rules of modern boxing, which provide for the use of gloves, the division of the match into rounds, the separation of the contestants by weight class, etc.

5. Richard Ellmann, *Oscar Wilde*, New York: Alfred A. Knopf, 1988.

6. Norbert Kohl, *Oscar Wilde: The Works of a Conformist Rebel*, Cambridge: Cambridge University Press, 1989. See also Gary Schmidgall, *The Stranger Wilde: Interpreting Oscar*, New York: Dutton, 1994.

7. Melissa Knox, *Oscar Wilde: A Long and Lovely Suicide*, New Haven: Yale University Press, 1994.

8. Regenia Gagnier, *Idylls of the Marketplace: Oscar Wilde and the Victorian Public*, Stanford: Stanford University Press, 1986.

9. Those that stand out are Jonathan Dollimore, *Sexual Dissidence: Augustine to Wilde, Freud to Foucault*, Oxford: Clarendon Press, 1991; Ed Cohen, *Talk on the Wilde Side: Towards a Genealogy of a Discourse on Male Sexualities*, London: Routledge, 1993; Neil Bartlett, *Who Was That Man? A Present for Mr. Oscar Wilde*, London: Serpent's Tail, 1988; Alan Sinfield, *The Wilde Century: Effeminacy, Oscar Wilde, and the Queer Moment*, New York: Columbia University Press, 1994. Several other books also deserve inclusion even though Wilde is not the only subject considered: Eve Kosofsky Sedgwick, *Between Men: English Literature and Male Homosocial Desire*, New York: Columbia University Press, 1985

and *Epistemology of the Closet*, Berkeley and Los Angeles: University of California Press, 1990; James Eli Adams, *Dandies and Desert Saints: Styles of Victorian Manhood*, Ithaca and London: Cornell University Press, 1995.

10. Another relatively recent book also focused on Wilde's trials, albeit in a very uncritical manner: Jonathan Goodman, ed., *The Oscar Wilde File*, London: Allison & Busby, 1989.

11. The accusation was contained in an article published in *Revue Blanche*, June 1, 1896, entitled "Une introduction à mes poemes avec quelque considérations sur l'affaire Wilde," parts of which are reprinted in H. Montgomery Hyde, *The Trials of Oscar Wilde*, New York: Dover, pp. 346–7.

CHAPTER 1
The Queensberry Libel Trial

1. H. Montgomery Hyde reports that despite the crowd, "no ladies were present." H.M. Hyde, *The Trials of Oscar Wilde*, New York: Dover, 1962, p. 98.

2. *Daily Telegraph*, April 4, 1895.

3. Richard Ellman notes that Carson had reservations about accepting the brief from Charles Russell, Queensberry's new solicitor. Carson did not like the fact that he would be going up against a fellow Irishman from the same university, and he initially thought the case against Wilde "too weak." This was before Detective Littlejohn, furnished with information from Charles Brookfield and Charles Hawtrey, turned up incontrovertible evidence against Wilde. Richard Ellmann, *Oscar Wilde*, New York: Alfred A. Knopf, 1988, p. 441.

4. H.M. Hyde reports that in early March, Lord Alfred Douglas wished Wilde to consult with Sir George Lewis, a prominent lawyer who specialized in settling awkward society cases out of court. Hyde maintains that Lewis knew a great deal more about Wilde's private life than Clarke or Humphreys did, and therefore would have probably dissuaded Wilde from attempting to prosecute Queensberry. At the time, however, Lewis was receiving instructions from Queensberry himself. A week later, for some unknown reason, Lewis declined to act further in the defense of Queensberry, and returned his instructions. Lewis was then replaced by Mr. Charles Russell. Hyde, *op. cit.*, pp. 79, 81. Richard Ellmann states that Lewis withdrew out of friendship for Wilde. Ellmann, *op. cit.*, p. 441.

5. Lord Douglas of Hawick, the eldest surviving son of Lord Queensberry and brother of Lord Alfred Douglas, had been acquainted with one of the youths mentioned in Queensberry's plea of justification—Ernest Scarfe—whom he had met on his way to Australia in 1893. Hence Lord Douglas thought it best that he be legally represented at the trial. Hyde, *op. cit.*, p. 97n.

6. The card was just the latest in a series of insults that dated back to early 1894. Hyde speculates that if Wilde had prosecuted Queensberry for criminal libel at this time, Queensberry would have been convicted and silenced. *Ibid.*, p. 72.

7. The libel itself was not printed in the *Daily Telegraph*.

8. H.M. Hyde reports that pleas of justification to charges of criminal libel were inadmissible in Court before 1843. The Libel Act of 1843 permitted such a tactic, provided the

defendant could also prove that the libel had been published for the public benefit. Hyde states that "although the prosecution had been furnished a copy of this plea, counsel in opening the case did not put it in detail to the jury, because the onus lay with the defendant to prove the truth of the libel." Hyde, *op. cit.*, p. 100.

9. *Ibid.*, p. 98.

10. Richard Ellmann claims that "public sentiment against Wilde was overwhelming: Queensberry's charges were generally regarded as true." Ellmann, *op. cit.*, p. 442. In this appraisal of the situation, Ellmann generally follows the account of Frank Harris, Wilde's flamboyant, unscrupulous friend. Harris says he spent time "trying to find out what was known about Oscar Wilde and what would be brought up against him. I wanted to know how he was regarded in an ordinary middle-class English home. My investigations had appalling results. Everyone assumed that Oscar Wilde was guilty of the worst that had ever been alleged against him ... to my horror, in the Public Prosecutor's office, his guilt was said to be known and classified. All 'people of importance' agreed that he would lose his case against Queensberry." During a subsequent lunch with Wilde and George Bernard Shaw, Harris tried to confront Wilde with this information in order to convince him to drop his prosecution of Queensberry. Harris' plans were squashed when Lord Alfred Douglas interrupted the gathering, created a scene, and pressured Wilde to leave with him. Frank Harris, *Oscar Wilde*, New York: Carroll & Graf, Inc., 1992, p. 115. Although Harris' biography of

Wilde is notorious for its exaggerations and embellishments, the palpability (indicating prevalence) of negative public sentiment against Wilde is also corroborated by virtually all the newspaper accounts of the (overwhelmingly negative) crowd reaction whenever Wilde entered or left the Court.

11. A variation of the "Phrases and Philosophies for the Use of the Young" had been published as the Preface to the revised, bound version of *The Picture of Dorian Gray,* which appeared in April, 1891. The celebrated preface was written in response to criticism of the original version of the novel which appeared in *Lippincott's Monthly Magazine* in July 1890 (46 [1890] 271: 3–100), and first appeared in the March 1891 edition of Frank Harris' *Fortnightly Review* (49 [1891] 291: 480–81) as "A Preface to Dorian Gray." Donald L. Lawler, ed., *Oscar Wilde: The Picture of Dorian Gray,* New York: W.W. Norton, 1988, p. x. In comparing the Preface to the "Phrases and Philosophies for the Use of the Young," Lawler notes that the "paradoxes are not so plentiful in the former as in the latter, and the manner is less insolent [in the Preface], but the intent is to be provocative." *Ibid.,* p. 3n.

12. Quoted from Queensberry's Plea of Justification. The plea was signed by Charles F. Gill, dated and filed March 30, 1895 by Charles Russell, Queensberry's solicitor. Hyde, *op. cit.,* pp. 326, 327.

13. Rupert Hart-Davis notes that the exact date of the letter is conjectural, but that it was written sometime during the month of January, 1893, from Babbacombe Cliff, a house near Torquay owned by Lady Mount-Temple but rented by Wilde from mid-November 1892 until February 1893. Rupert Hart-Davis, ed., *Selected Letters of Oscar Wilde,* Oxford: Oxford University Press, 1979, pp. 107, 107n. A sonnet in French by Pierre Louys based on this letter was published in the May 4, 1893 issue of *The Spirit Lamp,* an Oxford undergraduate magazine edited by Lord Alfred Douglas.

14. Lady Queensberry had won a divorce from her husband on January 22, 1887, on grounds of his adultery with Mabel Gilroy, of 217 Hampstead Road, Camden Town. Ellmann, *op. cit.,* p. 388.

15. Hyde states that the letters came into Wood's possession when Douglas gave him an old suit of his clothes after befriending him. The letters were in the jacket pockets and had been carelessly overlooked by Douglas. Wood, an unemployed clerk, in conjunction with two professional blackmailers, Allen and Clibborn, then used the letters to extort money from Wilde. Hyde, *op. cit.,* pp. 66–7.

16. One example is Queensberry's letter to his son, Lord Alfred Douglas, dated April 1, 1894: "Your intimacy with this man Wilde must either cease or I will disown you and stop all money supplies. I am not going to try and analyse this intimacy, and I make no charge; but to my mind to pose as a thing is as bad as to be it. With my own eyes I saw you both in the most loathsome and disgusting relationship, as expressed by your manner and expression. Never in my experience have I seen such a sight as that in your horrible features. No wonder people are talking as they are. Also I now hear on good authority, but this may be false, that his wife is petitioning to divorce him for sodomy and other crimes. Is this true, or do you not know of it? If I thought the actual thing was

true, and it became public property, I should be quite justified in shooting him at sight." Douglas' celebrated reply to this amazing effusion was sent in a telegram, which said: "What a funny little man you are." Hyde, *op. cit.*, p. 71.

17. Wilde remembered asking Queensberry if he seriously accused his son and himself of criminal behavior, and Queensberry's reply was "I don't say you are 'it' but you look 'it.'" *Daily Telegraph*, April 4, 1895.

18. Ellmann, *op. cit.*, p. 430.

19. In actuality, the story had been written by John Francis Bloxam of Exeter College, Oxford. Bloxam was the editor of *The Chameleon*, which lasted for only one issue (December 1894). Bloxam later went on to become an Anglo-Catholic priest in 1897. David Hilliard, "UnEnglish and Unmanly: Anglo-Catholicism and Homosexuality," *Victorian Studies*, 25, no. 2 (Winter 1982), p. 197.

20. Hyde, *op. cit.*, p. 105.

21. Travers Humphreys reported Wilde as having said, upon learning Queensberry's case was being handled by Edward Carson, "No doubt he will perform his task with the added bitterness of an old friend." Richard Ellmann also notes that Wilde had been advised by his friend Reggie Turner, a barrister himself, to get Carson and Clarke to represent him as leaders, and Gill and Mathews as juniors. However, since Carson and Gill had already been retained by Queensberry, Wilde got Clarke, Mathews, and Travers Humphreys instead. Ellmann, *op. cit.*, pp. 441, 441n.

22. Carson went so far as to try to intercede on Wilde's behalf just before the first criminal trial began, suggesting that Wilde had suffered enough. Ellmann, *op. cit.*, p. 462.

23. The text of "In Praise of Shame" is as follows:
Last night unto my bed bethought there came/Our lady of strange dreams, and from an urn/She poured live fire, so that mine eyes did burn/At sight of it. Anon the floating flame/Took many shapes, and one cried: "I am Shame/That walks with Love, I am most wise to turn/Cold lips and limbs to fire; therefore discern/And see my loveliness, and praise my name." //
And afterwards, in radiant garments dressed/With sound of flutes and laughing of glad lips,/A pomp of all the passions passed along/All the night through; till the white phantom ships/Of dawn sailed in. Whereat I said this song,/"Of all sweet passions Shame is loveliest."
The poem *Two Loves* contained these lines:
"Sweet youth,/Tell me why, sad and sighing, dost thou rove/These pleasant realms? I pray thee tell me sooth,/What is thy name?" He said: "My name is Love",/Then straight the first did turn himself to me,/And cried: "He lieth, for his name is Shame./But I am Love, and I was wont to be/Alone in this fair garden, till he came/Unasked by night; I am true Love, I fill/The hearts of boy and girl with mutual flame."/Then sighing said the other: "Have thy will;/I am the Love that dare not speak its name."
Quoted in Hyde, *op. cit.*, pp. 199, 200.

24. David Hilliard notes that "The Priest and the Acolyte" was the first piece of English fiction to mimic the already established French literary genre of the "naughty priest" story. Hilliard, *op. cit.*, p. 198.

25. *Daily Telegraph*, April 4, 1895.

26. Mikhail Bakhtin, *Epic and Novel*, in

Michael Holquist, ed., *The Dialogic Imagination: Four Essays,* trans. Caryl Emerson and Michael Holquist, Austin: University of Texas Press, 1990, p. 23. Bakhtin argues that defamiliarization is freedom from preconceptions and freedom to explore new possibilities.

27. Walter Houghton states that "of all the criticisms brought against them by the Lytton Stracheys of the twentieth century, the Victorians would have pleaded guilty to only one. They would have defended or excused their optimism, their dogmatism, their appeal to force, their straight-laced morality, but they would have confessed to an unfortunate strain of hypocrisy." Walter E. Houghton, *The Victorian Frame of Mind, 1830–1870,* New Haven: Yale University Press, 1985, p. 394.

28. Wilde said that of "the two hundred and sixteen criticisms of 'Dorian Gray' that have passed from my library table into the waste-paper basket I have taken public notice of only three. One was that which appeared in the *Scots Observer.* I noticed it because it made a suggestion, about the intention of the author in writing the book, which needed correction. The second was an article in the *St. James Gazette.* It was offensively and vulgarly written, and seemed to me to require immediate and caustic censure.... The third was a meek attack in a paper called the *Daily Chronicle.* I think [this response] was an act of pure willfulness. ... I believe they said that 'Dorian Gray' was poisonous, and I thought that, on alliterative grounds, it would be kind to remind them that, however that may be, it is at any rate, perfect." Oscar Wilde, *Art and Morality: A Defence of "The Picture of Dorian Gray",* ed. Stuart Mason, London: J.

Jacobs, 1908, pp. 75–6.

29. Pater's review of the revised edition of *The Picture of Dorian Gray* appeared in the *Bookman,* November 1891. Walter Pater, *Essays on Literature and Art,* ed. Jennifer Uglow, Everyman's Library, London: J.M. Dent & Sons, 1990, pp. 161–4. Donald L. Lawler gives the date of the *Bookman* as October 1891. Lawler, *op. cit.,* p. 352.

30. *Daily Telegraph,* April 4, 1895.

31. The reference is to Wilde's essay, "The Portrait of Mr. W.H.," which originally appeared in *Blackwood's Magazine,* July 1889. Wilde attempted in the essay to demonstrate that Shakespeare's sonnets had been inspired by his love for a boy named Willie Hughes. Carson's point was based on this fact. Wilde's rebuttal was based on his view that same-sex passion was neither an "unnatural vice" nor a "perversion."

32. Hyde, *op. cit.,* p. 112–13.

33. Here Wilde was generally reiterating what he had said more specifically in a letter, dated July 9, 1890, to the Editor of the *Scots Observer* in response to an unflattering review of *The Picture of Dorian Gray.* The relevant part says: "Each man sees his own sins in Dorian Gray. What Dorian Gray's sins are no one knows. He who finds them has brought them." Lawler, *op. cit.,* p. 347.

34. This is one instance where Wilde should be taken at his word. Wilde's reply that he could not answer apart from art is in my opinion the key to interpreting the whole of his testimony. This thesis will be developed in Chapter Five.

35. "Bosie" was Lord Alfred Douglas' childhood nickname. Wilde employed it throughout their relationship as a term of endearment.

36. Rupert Hart-Davis reports that the words in square brackets were apparently considered too shocking or too obscure to be read out. Hart-Davis supplies the missing passage, "I would sooner be [blackmailed by every renter in London]..." from a later reference to this letter in *De Profundis*. A "renter" was a slang term for a man who "participates in male homosexual affairs for a reward (originally perhaps for the rent)." Hart-Davis, *op. cit.*, pp. 111, 111n.

37. *Daily Telegraph*, April 4, 1895.

38. Hyde describes one point in Carson's cross-examination where Wilde was recounting a dinner with Shelley at which another gentleman was present. Hyde says Carson caused some surprise by asking Wilde not to mention the gentleman's name, but instead to write it down upon a piece of paper. The gentleman in question was Maurice Schwabe, who was the nephew of Lady Lockwood, wife of Sir Frank Lockwood, the Solicitor-General, who would prosecute Wilde in the third trial.

39. Hyde, *op. cit.*, p. 120.

40. *Ibid.*, p. 122.

41. Their actual ages were several years younger, usually between sixteen and eighteen.

42. *Ibid.*, p. 127.

43. Richard Ellmann states that "one of the Parker brothers had been promised immunity by ex-Inspector Littlefield if he would turn state's evidence against Wilde, but that he nobly refused." Yet, later on the same page, Ellmann claims that Charles Parker and his brother William had been under the protection of a Crown detective (apparently having decided to testify without immunity?). Ellmann also says that it was "apparently true" that "all the witnesses had been receiving £5 a week [from Queens-

berry] from the beginning of Wilde's prosecution of Queensberry until his conviction." Ellmann, *op. cit.*, pp. 474–5.

44. Coincidentally, Wilde related, sometime before this, Scarfe had come into contact with Lord Douglas of Hawick, Lord Alfred Douglas' elder brother, on an Australian-bound ship. By including this detail, Wilde was trying to legitimize Scarfe by connecting him with the respectable Hawick.

45. Hyde reports that Scarfe had been a valet. Hyde, *op. cit.*, p. 132.

46. *Daily Telegraph* (April 5, 1895) says "door-posts" instead of "door-mats."

47. Hyde, *op. cit.*, p. 134.

48. The reasons why Lord Alfred Douglas was not called are examined on p. 24.

49. Hyde, *op. cit.*, p. 138.

50. Interestingly, Carson portrayed the young men as victims, noting "they are men who have been more sinned against than sinning." *Daily Telegraph*, April 6, 1895.

51. Hyde, *op. cit.*, p. 149.

52. *Daily Telegraph*, April 6, 1895.

53. Hyde, *op. cit.*, p. 152.

54. *Ibid.*, pp. 219–20.

55. H. Montgomery Hyde, *Carson: The Life of Sir Edward Carson, Lord Carson of Duncairn*, London: William Heinemann, 1953, p. 143.

56. Ellmann quotes Douglas, "Oscar Wilde is now suffering for being a uranian, a Greek, a sexual man. ... I have already said that such men are the salt of the earth." Ellmann, *op. cit.*, p. 502.

57. Alfred Douglas, letter to *La Revue Blanche*, June 1, 1895, trans. Regenia Gagnier, in Regenia Gagnier, *Idylls of the Marketplace: Oscar Wilde and the Victorian Public*, Stanford: Stanford University Press, 1986, pp. 205–6.

58. H. Montgomery Hyde, *Oscar Wilde*,

New York: Da Capo, 1975, p. 171; Ellmann, *op. cit.*, p. 426.

59. Hyde reports his own conversation with Francis Douglas, the 11th Marquess of Queensberry, who "was positive his uncle Drumlanrig had taken his own life in the shadow of a suppressed scandal. ..." Hyde, *op. cit.*, p. 171.

60. Ellmann, *op. cit.*, p. 404.

61. *Ibid.*, p. 426.

62. H.M. Hyde, *Lord Alfred Douglas: A Biography*, London: Methuen, 1984, p. 8. See also Rupert Croft-Cooke, *Bosie: The Story of Lord Alfred Douglas, His Friends and Enemies*, London: W.H. Allen, 1963, pp. 22–30.

63. Hyde, *Oscar Wilde*, *op. cit.*, p. 171; Ellmann, *op. cit.*, p. 427.

64. Ellmann, *op. cit.*, p. 441.

65. *Ibid.*, p. 475.

66. Hyde, *Oscar Wilde*, *op. cit.*, p. 270; Ellmann, *op. cit.*, p. 467.

67. Ellmann, *op. cit.*, p. 538.

68. *Ibid.*, p. 450.

69. Letter from Queensberry to Alfred Montgomery, dated July 6, 1894, in Ellmann, *op. cit.*, p. 450.

70. *Daily Telegraph*, April 5, 1895.

71. Ellmann, *op. cit.*, p. 463.

72. David Brooks, *The Destruction of Lord Rosebery*, London: The Historian's Press, 1986, p. 220.

73. Peter Stansky, *Ambitions and Strategies: The Struggle for the Leadership of the Liberal Party in the 1890s*, Oxford: Clarendon, 1964, p. 148.

74. Brooks, *op. cit.*, p. 60.

75. The comparative chronology between the events surrounding the three trials and Rosebery's "breakdown" is close enough to be very suggestive. Rosebery's illness lasted from late February to late May. Although Queensberry had left the infamous card for Wilde at the Albemarle Club on February 18,

Wilde did not receive it until the 28th. Two days later, on March 2, Queensberry was arrested and indicted at Wilde's behest. The Queensberry libel trial went from April 3–5, and Wilde's first criminal trial from April 26 to May 1. Wilde's second trial began on May 22, and he was finally convicted on May 25.

76. Stansky, *op. cit.*, p. 153; Brooks, *op. cit.*, p. 59.

77. Beatrice Webb claimed that Rosebery saw no one but "Eddy Hamilton, a flashy fast Treasury Secretary, his stud-groom, and various non-political fashionables." Beatrice Webb, *Our Partnership*, London, 1948, p. 121, quoted in Stansky, *op. cit.*, p. 121.

78. Brooks, *op. cit.*, p. 224.

79. *Ibid.*, p. 225.

80. *Ibid.*, p. 228.

81. Entry: April 4, 1895, diary of Sir Edward Hamilton, in *ibid.*, p. 236.

82. Entry: April 5, 1895, *ibid.*, p. 236.

83. See Chapter Three, p. 58 for the contents of the letter, dated April 7, 1895. In Hyde, *The Trials of Oscar Wilde*, *op. cit.*, p. 161.

84. Brooks, *op. cit.*, p. 239.

85. *Ibid.*, p. 243.

86. *Ibid.*, p. 247.

87. *Ibid.*, p. 250.

88. *Ibid.*

89. In Ellmann, *op. cit.*, pp. 557–8.

90. *Ibid.*, pp. 429–31, 557–8.

91. *Ibid.*, p. 551. In December 1897, Wilde had experienced a devastating break-up with Douglas (for the last time), and he recorded his anger, bitterness, and "paralysis" in a letter to Robert Ross. March 2, 1898, in Hart-Davis, *op. cit.*, p. 330. This probably accounts for Wilde's seclusion in Neville-Rolfe's report to Rosebery.

92. George Cecil Ives founded a secret homosexual society, "The Order of Chaeronea," which was supposedly

organized according to Masonic principles. One of the major concerns of the society was the reform of laws pertaining to homosexuality. Jeffrey Weeks, *Sex, Politics and Society*, London: Longman, 1989, pp. 112–14.

93. Ellmann, *op. cit.*, p. 462.

94. Stansky, *op. cit.*, p. 177. "Beer" referred to Harcourt's crusade on behalf of Local Option. Harcourt's 1894 budget also raised taxes on brewers and distillers, and was thus widely perceived as "taxing the poor man's beer." Brooks, *op. cit.*, pp. 16–18.

95. Although poor in seats, the Liberals were rich in votes. The Liberals received 2,380,000 votes out of 4,800,000, indicating that only 221,000 accounted for the Unionist majority of 152 seats in Parliament. Stansky, *op. cit.*, p. 178.

CHAPTER 2
Wilde's Criminal Trials

1. *Star*, April 26, 1895. Rupert Hart-Davis writes that *Reynold's Evening News* and the *Daily Chronicle* were the only two newspapers that reported Wilde's trials impartially. Rupert Hart-Davis, ed., *Selected Letters of Oscar Wilde*, Oxford: Oxford University Press, p. 313n. Hart-Davis' comment implies that every other newspaper in Britain came out against Wilde to a greater or lesser extent. I have chosen the *Star*'s version of events to drive this chapter precisely because its bias was more or less overt, and also because its coverage of the trials was the most thorough of the major London newspapers.

2. *Star*, April 26, 1895.

3. H.M. Hyde, *The Trials of Oscar*

Wilde, New York: Dover, 1962, p. 171.

4. *Ibid.*, p. 172.

5. *Ibid.*, p. 176.

6. *Ibid.*, p. 178.

7. *Ibid.*, p. 177.

8. *Ibid.*, p. 181.

9. *Star*, April 27, 1895.

10. *Ibid.*; and Hyde, *op. cit.*, p. 185. See also note 38, Chapter One.

11. Hyde, *op. cit.*, p. 188.

12. *Ibid.*, p. 189.

13. *Ibid.*, p. 188.

14. *Ibid.*, p. 190.

15. *Star*, April 27, 1895.

16. *Star*, April 29, 1895.

17. *Star*, April 30, 1895.

18. Note how Clarke always phrased the alleged offense innocuously as "misconduct," whereas Gill always phrased it pejoratively, as "abominable" acts, "immoral" acts, or "indecent" acts.

19. *Star*, April 30, 1895.

20. *Daily Telegraph*, May 1, 1895.

21. *Ibid.*

22. *Ibid.*

23. *Ibid.*

24. *Ibid.*

25. *Ibid.*

26. *Ibid.*

27. *Star*, May 1, 1895.

28. *Ibid.*

29. *Ibid.*

30. Hyde, *op. cit.*, p. 216.

31. *Star*, May 1, 1895.

32. Hyde, *op. cit.*, p. 217.

33. *Ibid.*, p. 217.

34. *Ibid.*, p. 227. Wilde lived at 16 Tite Street in Chelsea and Wills lived at 46 Tite Street. Vyvyan Holland, *Son of Oscar Wilde*, New York, 1954.

35. H.M. Hyde gives the name as John Peter Grain. Hyde, *op. cit.*, p. 166. Richard Ellmann gives the name as J.T. Grein. Richard Ellmann, *Oscar Wilde*, New York: Alfred A. Knopf, 1988, p. 462.

36. *Star*, May 20, 1895.

37. Hyde, *op. cit.*, p. 228.

38. *Star*, May 21, 1895.
39. *Ibid.*
40. *Ibid.*
41. *Ibid.*
42. The *Star*'s headline for Tuesday, May 21, read: "The Wilde Scandal: Taylor Found Guilty on Two Counts." *Star*, May 21, 1895.
43. The *Star* noted that "there are three courts sitting, and the juries frequently changed. Jurors are sometimes in waiting for a week before being called in the order of their names on the list, and never know until they are called what case they will have to hear." *Star*, May 22, 1895.
44. *Ibid.*
45. The contents of two of these letters from Queensberry to the wife of Lord Percy Douglas are reproduced in Francis Archibald Kelhead Douglas Queensberry (with Percy Colson), *Oscar Wilde and the Black Douglas*, London: Hutchinson, 1949, pp. 59, 64–5. Francis Douglas was the son of Percy Douglas.
46. The *Star*'s headline for Thursday, May 23, was, "Wilde, Weak, Ill, and Utterly Dejected in the Dock." *Star*, May 23, 1895.
47. *Ibid.*
48. *Star*, May 24, 1895.
49. *Ibid.*
50. Hyde, *op. cit.*, p. 252.
51. *Star*, May 24, 1895.
52. *Star*, May 25, 1895. Although curiously, Charles Gill had had the final word in the previous trial.
53. Jeffrey Weeks states that because of the prohibitions against all sexual activities between men, whether committed in public or in private, the 1885 Criminal Law Amendment Act was referred to as the "Blackmailer's Charter." Jeffrey Weeks, *Coming Out: Homosexual Politics in Britain, from the Nineteenth Century to the Present*, London: Quartet

Books, 1977, p. 22.
54. *Star*, May 25, 1895.
55. The *Star*'s description of Justice Wills' summing-up as "colorless" and "discursive" demonstrated the extent of its bias against Wilde. *Star*, May 25, 1895.
56. Ellmann, *op. cit.*, p. 476.
57. *Star*, May 25, 1895.
58. *Ibid.* In a question to the judge, the foreman of the jury intimated that any guilt associated with the letters must be ascribed to Douglas as much as to Wilde, but Wills replied that Douglas' involvement in the case was not the present business of the jury to decide, and that they should focus on the matter at hand. Wilde visibly demonstrated his relief at the outcome of Wills' brief colloquy with the jury foreman.
59. Wills stated that "The medical evidence would have thrown light on what has been alluded to as marks of grease or vaseline smears. Then, with reference to the condition of the bed, there was the diarrhea line of defence. That story, I must say, I am not able to appreciate. I have tried many similar cases, but I have never heard that before." Hyde, *op. cit.*, pp. 267–8. Wills did say in all fairness that the lapse of time was indeed a factor in the jury's consideration of the Savoy Hotel servants' testimony. In summation of the Savoy affair, he remarked "it is a condition of things one shudders to contemplate in a first-class hotel." *Ibid.*, p. 268.
60. *Ibid.*, p. 269.
61. *Star*, May 27, 1895.
62. The jury deliberated for just over two hours before reaching the verdict. Hyde, *op. cit.*, p. 269.
63. This sentence found in the *Daily Chronicle*, May 27, 1895.
64. *Star*, May 27, 1895.
65. *Ibid.*

CHAPTER 3
The Reception of the Trials in the Press

1. *Star*, 25 May 1895, reported that "a great buzz of excited conjecture filled the courtroom, and that "the general opinion in court was that the jury would again disagree." On May 27, the *Star* said "the end of the trial ... was a tragic surprise." The *Westminster Gazette*, May 27, 1895, reported that "the general impression was that a verdict of guilty would only be found on one of the counts." These were the exceptions among newspaper accounts. The *News of the World*, May 26, 1895, reported that "the cries of 'Shame' with which the sentence pronounced by Mr. Justice Wills was received, indicate that a certain section of the public in court regarded the verdict with disfavor, and that feeling will very possibly be shared by a section of the public outside."

2. Alan Lee stresses the fact that the London Press was not a "national press" in the modern sense. Although a newspaper's importance and influence is not a direct correlative of circulation figures, they are useful for gauging the relative popularity of the various newspapers. Presenting circulation figures of the eighteen-eighties, Lee notes that of the London morning "penny dailies," the *Daily Telegraph* had a circulation of over 300,000, the conservative *Standard* was 250,000, the *Daily Chronicle* and the *Daily News* were just under 100,000, and *The Times* was 60,000. No figures are given for the major evening dailies: the paper of the club set, the *Pall Mall Gazette*, the *Evening News*, and the more plebeian and radical papers, the *Echo*, and the *Star*. Of the weekly press, the Sunday papers—although this was a strictly honorific title since it was illegal to sell newspapers on the Sabbath—had the widest circulation. In 1896, *Lloyd's Weekly News* circulation topped 1,000,000, quickly followed by *News of the World* and *Reynold's News*. Alan Lee, "The Structure, Ownership, and Control of the Press, 1855–1914," in George Boyce, James Curran, and Pauline Wingate, eds., *Newspaper History: From the Seventeenth Century to the Present Day*, London: Constable, 1978, pp. 120–23.

3. John Stokes, *In the Nineties*, Chicago: University of Chicago Press, p. 9.

4. *Ibid.*, p. 21. Raymond Williams attributes the appellation, "New Journalism" to Matthew Arnold. Raymond Williams, *The Long Revolution*, New York: Columbia University Press, 1961, p. 195.

5. Although Lee states that "the ideal [the penny paper as the organ of educated democracy] had always been a provincial rather than a metropolitan one, and one born directly from the repeal of the stamp." Lee, *op. cit.*, pp. 118, 122.

6. Alan J. Lee, *The Origins of the Popular Press in England, 1855–1914*, London: Croom Helm, p. 38.

7. Michael Palmer, "The British Press and international news, 1851–99: of agencies and newspapers," in Boyce, Curran, and Wingate, *op. cit.*, p. 211. *The Times* was unique in that regard, however, because foreign news and analysis was expensive to come by, and *The Times* was the only paper to employ its own legion of foreign correspondents.

8. Attributed to Kingsley Martin. Steve Chibnall, "Chronicles of the

Gallows: The Social History of Crime Reporting," in *The Sociology of Journalism and the Press*, Sociological Review Monograph 29 (October 1980), p. 206. Raymond Williams quotes Burnham's history of the *Daily Telegraph*, "Reviewing the files, the honest biographer cannot dispute that the *Daily Telegraph* thrived on crime." Williams, *op. cit.*, p. 196.

9. Judith R. Walkowitz, *City of Dreadful Delight: Narratives of Sexual Danger in Late-Victorian London*, Chicago: University of Chicago Press, 1992. See also Edward J. Bristow, *Vice and Vigilance: Purity Movements in Britain since 1700*, Totowa, NJ: Rowman & Littlefield, 1977, pp. 106–10.

10. Jeffrey Weeks, *Sex, Politics, and Society: The Regulation of Sexuality since 1800*, London: Longman, 1989, p. 86.

11. Steve Chibnall describes how Alfred Harmsworth (later Lord Northcliffe, who was one of the driving forces behind the creation of a tabloid press with the founding of the national morning halfpenny paper, the *Daily Mail*, in 1896) had interviewed the murderer of a pregnant girl, and how his reports of the interview helped double the circulation of the recently taken over *Evening News* (1984) to almost 400,000. Chibnall, *op. cit.*, p. 206.

12. Raymond Williams states that in the period from 1855 to 1896, "an attention to crime, sexual violence, and human oddities made its way from the Sunday into the daily papers. ..." Williams, *op. cit.*, p. 195. Regarding middle-class reading habits, Alan Lee notes that "the morning papers were also read at the breakfast table, particularly by the middle classes, where the head of the family would not have usually had to leave home before the morning delivery. When the evening papers came into their own towards the close of the century they were read at the tea-table, and as early as the 1870's suburban trains were left strewn with the litter of thousands of newspapers every morning ... in 1866, commuter reading was credited with saving people half an hour at the office every morning, and with enabling them to avoid having to stare at advertisements or other people during the journey." Lee, *Origins of the Popular Press in England, op. cit.*, p. 39.

13. Chibnall, *op. cit.*, p. 209.

14. *Ibid.*, p. 209.

15. Wilde, "The Critic as Artist," in Richard Ellmann, *The Artist as Critic: The Critical Writings of Oscar Wilde*, Chicago: University of Chicago Press, 1982, p. 393. Wilde also commented that "Somebody— was it Burke?—called journalism the fourth estate ... at the present moment it is the only estate. It has eaten up the other three. The Lords Temporal say nothing, the Lords Spiritual have nothing to say, and the House of Commons has nothing to say and says it!" Wilde, *The Soul of Man Under Socialism*, in *The Soul of Man and Prison Writings*, ed. Isobel Murray, Oxford: Oxford University Press, 1991, p. 23.

16. *Ibid.*, pp. 23, 25.

17. Wilde, *The Critic as Artist, op. cit.*, p. 403.

18. Søren Kierkegaard, *The Present Age*, trans. Alexander Dru, New York: Harper & Row, 1962, pp. 60–66.

19. Wilde, *The Soul of Man, op. cit.*, p. 24.

20. *Ibid.*, p. 25.

21. *Ibid.*, p. 25.

22. *Ibid.*, p. 24.

23. *Illustrated Police News*, 6 April 1895.

24. *Echo*, April 6, 1895.

25. Stokes, *op. cit.*, p. 17. The other so-called "Clubland" papers were the *St. James Gazette* and the *Westminster Gazette*.

26. *Pall Mall Gazette*, April 6, 1895.

27. The *Daily Telegraph*, April 6, 1895.

28. *Ibid.*, in Jonathan Goodman, ed., *The Oscar Wilde File*, London: Allison & Busby, 1989, p. 76.

29. *Daily Telegraph*, April 6, 1895. p. 76.

30. *Ibid.*, pp. 76, 77.

31. *National Observer*, April 6, 1895, quoted in H.M. Hyde, *The Trials of Oscar Wilde*, New York: Dover, 1962, p. 156. Hyde notes that the article was probably written by Charles Whibley, whom Donald L. Lawler refers to as the "henchman" of editor W.E. Henley. Whibley and Wilde had been at each other's throats previously in their extended literary debate in July 1890 over the artistic merits of *The Picture of Dorian Gray* which was conducted in the pages of the *Scots Observer*, a newspaper also edited by Henley. Donald L. Lawler, ed., *The Picture of Dorian Gray*, New York: W.W. Norton & Co., 1988, p. 346n.

32. *Star*, April 6, 1895.

33. *Ibid.*

34. *Ibid.*

35. *Ibid.*

36. Wilde remained in custody from the date of his arrest through the end of his first criminal trial nearly a month later. After the jury failed to reach a verdict, Wilde was finally granted bail. Hyde, *op. cit.*, p. 162.

37. *Ibid.*, p. 157.

38. *Star*, April 8, 1895.

39. Hyde, *op. cit.*, p. 156.

40. *Star*, April 8, 1895.

41. *Star*, April 11, 1895.

42. A caption under an illustration entitled "Scene at the Old Bailey" refers to the first criminal trial of Wilde as "the most sensational trial of the century." *Illustrated Police Budget*, May 4, 1895.

43. The *Illustrated Police News*, April 20, 1895, reported that a "fortnight's confinement in Holloway Gaol has told severely on Wilde. He has lost a great deal of flesh. His face looked almost bloodless, and his eyes heavy and weary. He entered the dock [for his committal] with faltering steps, and, having obtained Sir John Bridge's permission to be seated, sank with a sigh of relief upon the narrow oak plank which does duty for a seat in the dock."

44. *Star*, April 8, 1895.

45. *Illustrated Police News*, April 27, 1895.

46. *Daily Telegraph*, April 8, 1895.

47. *Le Figaro* (Paris), April 11, 1895, trans. Jonathan Goodman, in Goodman, *op. cit.*, p. 95.

48. *Star*, April 18, 1895.

49. An excerpt from a letter from Charles Gill, the attorney who led the Crown's prosecution of Wilde and Taylor, to Hamilton Cuffe, the Director of Public Prosecutions, dated 19 April 1895: "My dear Cuffe ... having regard to the fact that Douglas was an Undergraduate at Oxford when Wilde made his acquaintance—the difference in their ages—and the strong influence that Wilde has obviously exercised over Douglas since that time, I think that Douglas, if guilty, may fairly be regarded as one of Wilde's victims. ... I am afraid there is little room for doubt that immoral relations existed between them, yet if an attempt were made to prove anything definite, it would be found, I think, that the evidence available only disclosed a case of grave suspicion. ... Comments will no doubt be made as to Douglas not being prosecuted, but these comments are made by people who do not under-

50. Letter dated April 7, 1895, less than two days after Wilde's arrest. In Hyde, *op. cit.*, pp. 161–2.

51. On April 24, Mr. Charles Mathews, one of Wilde's solicitors, applied for a postponement of the criminal trial against him until the next criminal sessions, on the grounds that the present state of public feelings against Wilde would prohibit an impartial trial. Mathews suggested that "the lapse of a month or so will give time for that feeling to subside and increase the chances of a fair and impartial trial." *Star*, April 24, 1895.

52. Hyde, *op. cit.*, p. 164n.

53. The notable exceptions (i.e. those friends who stuck by Wilde) included Douglas, Robert Ross, More Adey, Robert Sherard, and Ada and Ernest Leverson. Richard Ellmann, *Oscar Wilde*, New York: Alfred A. Knopf, 1988, p. 457.

54. A pseudonymous correspondent of Buchanan's, who signed himself "DIKE," remarked that "Mr. Buchanan's pen has often adorned the columns of the Daily Telegraph." *Star*, April 25, 1895.

55. *Star*, April 16, 1895.

56. *Ibid.*

57. *Star*, April 19, 1895.

58. *Star*, April 20, 1895.

59. *Star*, April 19, 1895.

60. In *De Profundis*, Wilde also postulates Douglas' secret guilt over his complicity in Wilde's downfall. Wilde, *De Profundis*, in *The Soul of Man*, p. 140.

61. *Star*, April 22, 1895. An editor's note reads: "We have received a host of other letters bearing on the Wilde case, which, for various reasons, we have decided not to publish."

62. Stokes, *op. cit.*, pp. 10–11.

63. *Star*, April 22, 1895.

64. *Ibid.*

65. *Star*, April 23, 1895.

66. *Ibid.*

67. *Ibid.*

68. *Star*, April 24, 1895. The sale of Wilde's effects was described as a "sorrowful sight," in part because "the buyers were for the most part brokers of a very ordinary character with loud voices and much chaff, and they smoked shag to the general discomfort. Shag in Oscar Wilde's sanctum!"

69. The *Star*, April 24, 1895.

70. Walter Pater, "A Novel By Mr. Oscar Wilde," in Jennifer Uglow, ed., *Walter Pater: Essays on Literature and Art*, London: Everyman's Library, 1990, pp. 163–4.

71. The *Star*, April 25, 1895.

72. Wilde, *De Profundis*, *op. cit.*, p. 140.

73. *Ibid.*, p. 147.

74. *Morning*, May 2, 1895.

CHAPTER 4

The Cultural Climate of the Trials: Heterosexism and Homophobia as Historical Constructs

1. I have arrived at the term "heterosexism" third-hand. "Adrienne Rich attributes to the black political scientist Gloria I. Joseph the thought 'that homophobia is an inaccurate term, implying a form of uncontrollable mental panic, and that heterosexism better describes what is really a deeply ingrained prejudice. ...'" Alan Sinfield, *The Wilde Century: Effeminacy, Oscar Wilde and the Queer Moment*, New York: Columbia University Press, 1994, p. 187.

2. David Halperin states that the *Oxford English Dictionary* credits Charles Gilbert Chaddock, an early

translator of Krafft-Ebing's *Psycho-pathia Sexualis*, with having intro-duced "homosexuality" into the English language in 1892, "in order to render a German cognate twenty years its senior." David M. Halperin, *One Hundred Years of Homosexuality: and Other Essays on Greek Love*, New York and London: Routledge, 1990, p. 15. As Halperin describes in his extensive notes, "homosexuality" was not originally juxtaposed with "heterosexuality," a concept which had connotations approximating our usage of the term "bisexual," but with the German term "*normalsexual.*" So even in its inception, it is interesting to note that the concept "homosex-uality" signified not just difference, but also illness or abnormality (p. 159, n. 17).

3. The best discussion of the substan-tive and stylistic problematics of the term "homosexual" is found in John Boswell, *Christianity, Social Tolerance, and Homosexuality: Gay People in Western Europe from the Beginning of the Christian Era to the Fourteenth Century*, Chicago and London: University of Chicago Press, 1980, pp. 41–60.

4. For example, in the United Kingdom Margaret Thatcher's sec-tion 28 legislation of 1988 forbade municipalities to spend public money in ways that might promote homosexuality. Similarly, in the United States, especially within the past decade, there have been numerous state and local ordi-nances passed which have effec-tively mandated heterosexism under the moralistic guise of "family values."

5. Jeffrey Weeks' awe-inspiring oeuvre is perhaps the only notable exception. See, for example, Jeffrey Weeks, *Coming Out: Homosexual Politics in Britain from the Nineteenth Century to the Present*, London: Quartet Books, 1977; *Sex, Politics and Society*, London: Longman, 1989; *Against Nature: Essays on History, Sexuality, and Identity*, London: Rivers Oram Press, 1991; *Sexuality and Its Dis-contents: Meanings, Myths and Modern Sexualities*, London: Rout-ledge and Kegan Paul, 1985; and Weeks and Kevin Porter, eds., *Between the Acts: Lives of Homosexual Men, 1885–1967*, Lon-don: Routledge, 1990. Historians, unfortunately, always seem to lag behind their counterparts in other academic disciplines such as English literature, gay/gender stud-ies, and even philosophy. The work of Michel Foucault, at once bril-liant, original, and exhilarating, has now become a bit dated. The best of the gender theorists today, despite being intellectually indebted to Foucault, have moved beyond him and are charting new territory. The books that have been most helpful to me in thinking about issues of gender and sexuality have been Eve Kosofsky Sedgwick, *Between Men: English Literature and Male Homosocial Desire*, New York: Columbia University Press, 1985; Sinfield, *op.cit.*; Judith Butler, *Gender Trouble: Feminism and the Subversion of Identity*, London and New York: Routledge, 1990; James Eli Adams, *Dandies and Desert Saints: Styles of Victorian Manhood*, Ithaca and London: Cornell University Press, 1995; Halperin, *op. cit.*; Michel Foucault, *The History of Sexuality, Vol. 1: An Introduction*, New York: Vintage, 1980; Keith Plummer, *The Making of the Modern Homosexual*, London: Hutchinson, 1981; Ed Cohen, *Talk on the Wilde Side: Towards a*

Genealogy of a Discourse on Male Sexualities, London: Routledge, 1993; Neil Bartlett, *Who Was That Man? A Present for Mr. Oscar Wilde,* London: Serpent's Tail, 1988; Joseph Bristow, ed., *Sexual Sameness: Textual Differences in Lesbian and Gay Writing,* London and New York: Routledge, 1992; Jonathan Dollimore, *Sexual Dissidence: Augustine to Wilde, Freud to Foucault,* Oxford: Oxford University Press, 1991.

6. Daniel Pick, *Faces of Degeneration: A European Disorder, c. 1848–1918,* Cambridge: Cambridge University Press, 1993, pp. 44–59, 203. The theory of *dégénérescence* originated with French medical psychiatrist, Bénédict Morel in the eighteen-forties and eighteen-fifties. Morel was initially concerned with the social implications of cretinism and their relation to questions of social hygiene, but his concerns with social health, patterns of heredity, and deviations from the "normal" type were seized upon by others and easily transferred to any and all social anomalies, including sexual inverts. Morel's work, along with that of the Italian criminal anthropologist, Cesare Lombroso, was influential in British medical circles; for example, Henry Maudsley, the important Victorian medical psychiatrist, was greatly influenced by Morel and Lombroso.

7. The related concepts of "sexual inversion," and the "sexual invert" (which historically preceded and were later displaced by the modern concepts of "homosexuality" and the "homosexual") had been formulated and articulated by the time of the trials, but the meaning of these terms was still contested and hence ambiguous (an ambiguity that still persists today), and besides

that, the terms could not have been circulated widely in the public domain. On the other hand David Halperin remarks that the term "sexual inversion" was a "common designation throughout the 1880s." "Inversion" implied gender deviance rather than deviance in sexual object choice, and thus represented "an age-old outlook on sexual nonconformity...[rather than the] sharp break with traditional ways of thinking" implied by the term "homosexuality." Halperin, *op. cit.,* p. 156.

8. Although, as Jeffrey Weeks points out, decriminalization did not mean legalization. Weeks states that "the threat of conspiracy charges continued to hang over homosexuals; and the prosecution for offences in public vastly increased over the next decade." Weeks, *Sex, Politics and Society, op. cit.,* p. 267. Interestingly, Weeks also notes that in 1965, statistics revealed that while 65 percent of a given sample were in favor of homosexual law reform, 93 percent of those saw homosexuality as a form of illness requiring medical treatment. *Ibid.,* p. 265.

9. Peter J. Bowler, *Darwinism,* New York: Twayne, 1993, p. 79. Bowler describes Spencerian-Darwinism as a "seamless web" in the public mind since it seemed to explain adequately existing conditions of society. Daniel Pick notes that "Spencer's evolutionary sociology was assimilated in England by such influential psychiatrists as Henry Maudsley...who was the Victorian psychiatrist most widely read and quoted in Italy, France, and Germany at the time." Pick, *op. cit.,* p. 205.

10. See Mary Poovey, *Making a Social Body: British Cultural Formation 1830–1864,* Chicago and London:

University of Chicago Press, 1995, pp. 7–8, 40–42. The "body politic" is a medieval legacy and "the great body of the people" derives from Adam Smith's *The Wealth of Nations* (1776).

11. "Darwin insisted that even under civilized conditions there is a constant tendency for antisocial individuals to be eliminated." Bowler, *op. cit.*, p. 99.

12. Herbert Spencer, *Herbert Spencer: Selected Writings*, ed. J.D.Y. Peel, Chicago: University of Chicago Press, 1972, *passim*.

13. Mary Douglas, *Purity and Danger: An Analysis of the Concepts of Pollution and Taboo*, London: ARK, 1966, p. 14. Green sought to deemphasize the revealed aspects of Christian doctrine and elevate morality as the essence of religious practice and belief. Green was essentially Erastian and did not think the State should have a role in promoting morality. His idea was "to revive religion in the educated, make it intellectually respectable, create a new moral fervor and so produce a reformed society."

14. Spencer, *op. cit.*, *passim*.

15. Bowler, *op. cit.*, pp. 38–44.

16. Spencer's and Weber's views of society overlap on this point. Max Weber, *The Protestant Ethic and the Spirit of Capitalism*, trans. Talcott Parsons, New York: Charles Scribner's Sons, 1958.

17. In contrast to Spencer and Weber, psychoanalyst Karen Horney advances a theory of "cultural neurosis" based, among other things, on the irreconcilability of Christian values with competitive capitalist values. Karen Horney, *The Neurotic Personality of Our Time*, New York: W.W. Norton, 1937, pp. 246–7.

18. Jose Harris, *Private Lives, Public Spirit: Britain 1870–1914*, London: Penguin, 1994, 225.

19. *Ibid.*, p. 224.

20. J. Edward Chamberlin, "Images of Degeneration: Turnings and Transformation," in J.E. Chamberlin and Sander L. Gilman, eds., *Degeneration: The Dark Side of Progress*, New York: Columbia University Press, 1985, p. 270.

21. Robert Nye, "Sociology and Degeneration: The Irony of Progress," in Chamberlin and Gilman, eds., *Degeneration: The Dark Side of Progress*, New York: Columbia University Press, 1985, pp. 64, 67.

22. William Ewart Gladstone, "Locksley Hall and the Jubilee," in *The Nineteenth Century*, no. CXIX, Jan. 1887, pp. 1–18. Gladstone's article was a response to Alfred Lord Tennyson's poem, "Locksley Hall Sixty Years Later," which criticized contemporary conditions in Britain. Gladstone's response was in part an *ad hominem* attack on Tennyson, and in part a recitation of the litany of material advances in British society since the Reform Bill of 1832.

23. Alfred Lord Tennyson, "Locksley Hall Sixty Years Later" (1886), in C. Ricks, ed., *The Poems of Tennyson*, London: Longman, 1969. Georges Sorel, *The Illusions of Progress*, trans. John and Charlotte Stanley, Berkeley and Los Angeles: University of California Press, 1972, pp. xlii–xlv.

24. Pick, *op. cit.*, pp. 44–59, 109–38, 203–16.

25. *Ibid.*, pp. 100, 120, 126.

26. *Ibid.*, pp. 54, 218.

27. Bernard Shaw, "The Sanity of Art," in *Major Critical Essays*, New York: Wm. H. Wise and Co., 1931, p. 297. Nordau's book was published in 1893 under the title *Entartung*. It was translated and published in

England in early 1895 with the title, *Degeneration*.

28. Max Nordau, *Degeneration*, 6th edn, New York: D. Appleton and Co., 1895, pp. 296–337.

29. *Ibid., passim.*

30. *Ibid.*, p. 16.

31. *Ibid.*, pp. 20–22. Other characteristics Nordau identifies are: mental weakness, despondency, misanthropy, pessimism, self-hatred, an aversion to action or work, mysticism, short attention-span, rejoicing in the imaginary.

32. *Ibid.*, pp. 319, 320. Compare Nordau's comments with those of Henry Labouchere in Chapter Three (p. 56).

33. *Ibid.*, p. 318.

34. *Ibid.*, pp. 318–38.

35. See Chapter Three on the public reception of the trials. Virtually all the newspapers characterized Wilde as an "aesthete" or a "Decadent," often using the terms interchangeably.

36. Richard Ellmann, *Oscar Wilde*, New York: Alfred A. Knopf, 1988, pp. 26–34. Ellmann points out that even when Wilde was attending Trinity College in Dublin, he could be seen accumulating "the elements of his Oxford behaviour—his Pre-Raphaelite sympathies, his dandiacal dress, his Hellenic bias, his ambiguous sexuality, his contempt for conventional morality"—which would eventually form the cornerstone of his mature aesthetic. *Ibid.*, p. 34.

37. *Ibid.*, pp. 47–52.

38. *Ibid.*, pp. 225–31, 335–61. Briefly, Rollinat, a poet and tragedian, was described by contemporaries as a "second Baudelaire." Lorrain was one of the first to "take up the theme of homosexuality." Goncourt was a publisher and champion of decadent literature.

Bourget was a novelist and major theorist of decadence. Richard Ellmann notes that Wilde's aestheticism, as it had been developed within the context of his American speaking tour on the subject of the contemporary English Renaissance of arts and letters, had been "celebrated in America for its lofty idealism." Whereas in America Wilde had argued that aestheticism was commensurate with surrounding oneself with beautiful objects, in Paris he was exposed and immediately attracted to the "decadent" aspects of the total aestheticization of one's life. *Ibid.*, p. 229.

39. Huysmans' book, *A Rebours* (1884) was an inspiration for Wilde's *The Picture of Dorian Gray*. Ellmann, *op. cit.*, pp. 252–3.

40. Nordau, *op. cit.*, pp. 296–301. Also, Jean Pierrot, *The Decadent Imagination: 1880–1900*, trans. Derek Coltman, Chicago: University of Chicago Press, 1981, *passim*.

41. This is from Gautier's justly famous preface to the 2nd edition of Baudelaire's *Les Fleurs du Mal* (Paris, 1869, pp. 17–18). Quoted in Nordau, *op. cit.*, p. 299. See also Richard Gilman, *Decadence: The Strange Life of an Epithet*, New York: Farrar, Straus, and Giroux, 1980, p. 89.

42. Gilman, *op. cit.*, pp. 5–6.

43. *Ibid.*, p. 79.

44. Nordau, *op. cit.*, p. 301.

45. *Ibid.*, p. 302.

46. Pierrot, *op. cit.*, p. 9.

47. *Ibid.*, p. 49.

48. Pierrot states that reference to Schopenhauer's theories from the eighteen-eighties was "one of the commonplaces of the age," and that Schopenhauer was ranked with Darwin as one of the major influences of the last decades of the nineteenth century. Schopenhauer's

influence in France prior to 1886—the date of the translation of *The World As Will and Idea* into French—was limited to a small group of specialists. The book was first published in 1819, but there was little interest in it even in the German states before the eighteen-fifties. *Ibid.*, p. 56.

49. According to Schopenhauer, with the historical demise of the Christian goal of eternal salvation, life becomes a meaningless process without a *telos* or endpoint. Schopenhauer's solution to the conditions of modern life was to advocate, following the Hindu mystics, a quietistic withdrawal from this life of constant and futile struggle, and to adopt instead a purely intellectual and disinterested attitude toward the world. Schopenhauer believed that a life of indifferent contemplation would lead, paradoxically, to freedom from the cares of the world. Such a tactic circumvents the necessity of the *telos* of Christian salvation, and life on earth becomes a *telos* unto itself. Georg Simmel, *Schopenhauer and Nietzsche*, trans. Helmut Loiskandl, Deena Weinstein, and Michael Weinstein, Urbana and Chicago: University of Illinois Press, 1991, *passim*.

50. "Schopenhauer's philosophy is the absolute philosophical expression for this inner condition of modern man. The center of his doctrine is that the essential metaphysical essence of the world and of ourselves has its total and only decisive expression in our will. The will is the substance of our subjective life because and insofar as the absolute of Being as such is precisely an urge that never rests, a constant movement beyond. Thus, as the exhaustive reason of all things, it condemns to eternal dissatisfaction. Inasmuch as the will can no longer find anything outside itself for its satisfaction, and because it can only grasp itself in a thousand disguises, it is pushed forward from every point of rest on an endless path. Thus, the tendency of existence toward a final goal and the simultaneous denial of this goal are projected into a total interpretation of reality (*Gesamtweltanschauung*). It is precisely the absoluteness of will, which is identical with life, that does not permit an external resting place: there is nothing outside of the will. Contemporary culture is also aptly described through its desire for a final goal in life, a goal which is felt to have disappeared and is gone forever." *Ibid.*, p. 5.

51. Bernard Porter, *Britain, Europe and the World, 1850–1986: Delusions of Grandeur*, London: Unwin Hyman, 1987, pp. 56–81.

52. In London, in the eighteen-eighties, "the Artisans' Dwellings Acts demolished rookeries and slums and dispersed their inhabitants." Gareth Stedman Jones, *Languages of Class: Studies in English Working Class History, 1832–1982*, Cambridge: Cambridge University Press, 1987, p. 191. A decade earlier, the "Haussmannization" of Paris had the same effect: "Haussmann's slum 'clearance' simply broke up working-class neighborhoods and moved the eyesores and health hazards of poverty out of central Paris and into the suburbs." Susan Buck-Morss, *The Dialectics of Seeing: Walter Benjamin and the Arcades Project*, Cambridge: MIT Press, 1991, p. 89.

53. The literature on "modernity" and "postmodernity" is enormous and varied in quality. The texts which have been most influential in form-

ing my own opinions on the subject are: Andreas Huyssen, *After the Great Divide: Modernism, Mass Culture, Postmodernism,* Bloomington and Indianapolis: University of Indiana Press, 1986; Daniel Bell, *The Cultural Contradictions of Capitalism,* New York: Basic Books, 1976; Matei Calinescu, *The Five Faces of Modernity,* Bloomington and Indianapolis: University of Indiana Press, 1977; Marshall Berman, *All That Is Solid Melts Into Air: The Experience of Modernity,* New York: Simon & Schuster, 1982; Hal Foster, *The Anti-Aesthetic,* Port Townsend: Bay Press, 1984; Jean-François Lyotard, *The Postmodern Condition,* Minneapolis: University of Minnesota Press, 1984; David Harvey, *The Condition of Post-modernity,* Oxford: Blackwell, 1989; Gianni Vattimo, *The End of Modernity: Nihilism and Herme-neutics in Postmodern Culture,* trans. Jon R. Snyder, Baltimore: Johns Hopkins University Press, 1991; Buck-Morss, *op. cit.*; Jürgen Habermas, *The Philosophical Discourse of Modernity,* trans. Frederic Lawrence, Cambridge: MIT Press, 1987; Stephen Toulmin, *Cosmopolis: The Hidden Agenda of Modernity,* New York: The Free Press, 1990.

54. Pierrot, *op. cit.*, p. 53.

55. *Ibid.*, p. 52.

56. *Ibid.*, pp. 11–16. Sigmund Freud, *Civilization and Its Discontents,* trans. James Strachey, New York: W.W. Norton & Co., 1962, *passim.*

57. Oscar Wilde, *The Soul of Man Under Socialism,* in Isobel Murray, ed., *Oscar Wilde: The Soul of Man and Prison Writings,* Oxford: Oxford University Press, 1991, p. 33.

58. The schizophrenic metaphor of society has been used most promi-nently by Gilles Deleuze and F. Guattari in *Anti-Oedipus: Capit-alism and Schizophrenia,* trans. Robert Hurley, Mark Seem, and Helen R. Lane, New York: Viking Press, 1977, and by Fredric Jameson in his essay, "Postmodernism and Consumer Society" (1982), in Hal Foster, *The Anti-Aesthetic,* Seattle: Bay Press, 1983, p. 119. For Jameson, pastiche and schizophrenia are the metaphors which best describe the postmodern world. See also Daniel Bell, *The Cultural Contradictions of Capitalism,* New York: Basic Books, 1976.

59. I am essentially describing Wilde's aesthetic in Kohutian Self-Psycho-logical terms as a "self-object" which performs both mirroring and idealizing functions, and which thus contributed significantly to the sustenance of his "self" and his self-image. Heinz Kohut, *The Restoration of the Self,* New York: International Universities Press, 1977, especially pp. 171–219.

60. Pierrot, *op. cit.*, p. 20.

61. Donald L. Lawler, ed., *Oscar Wilde: The Picture of Dorian Gray,* New York: W.W. Norton, 1988, pp. 329, 285. Wilde also borrowed heavily from Walter Pater's *The Renais-sance: Studies in Art and Poetry* (1873).

62. Lawler, *op. cit.*, p. 330. *The Picture of Dorian Gray* was published only sixty days after the "Cleveland Street affair"—the press coverage of which had persisted for about five months—had come to an end.

63. Adams, *op. cit.*, p. 4.

64. H. Montgomery Hyde, "The Prevalence of Male Homosexuality in England," Appendix E in *The Trials of Oscar Wilde,* New York: Dover, 1962, p. 350.

65. Weeks, *Against Nature, op. cit.*, p. 17.

66. Alan Bray, *Homosexuality in*

Renaissance England, London: Gay Men's Press, 1982, pp. 34, 88, 130–31. See also the histories of homosexuality presented in Weeks, *Sex, Politics and Society, op. cit.,* and Cohen, *op. cit.*

67. Randolph Trumbach, "Gender and the Homosexual Role in Modern Western Culture: The 18th and 19th Centuries Compared," in Dennis Altman, Carole Vance, Martha Vicinus, Jeffrey Weeks, and others, *Homosexuality, Which Homosexuality?,* London: Gay Men's Press, 1989, pp. 152, 156, quoted in Sinfield, *op. cit.,* pp. 36, 49.

68. Sinfield, *op. cit.,* p. 45.

69. *Ibid.,* pp. 39–45. "Molly houses" were a prominent feature of this underground homosocial subculture, in which men could dress in women's clothes, mimic women's behavior, manners, and language, and generally act like women. Most "mollies" seem to have been lower- to middle-class men, and Sinfield is clear on the fact that not all mollies were effeminate.

70. Alan Sinfield argues that working-class men were regarded by many in the middle and upper classes as something less than men (in the social and cultural sense) since they lacked any form of self-determination in the workplace, and therefore that there is a distinct class basis for the concept of "manliness." Sinfield, *op. cit.,* p. 64.

71. Leonore Davidoff and Catherine Hall, *Family Fortunes: Men and Women of the English Middle Class 1780–1850,* Chicago: University of Chicago Press, 1987, p. 402.

72. Adams, *op. cit.,* pp. 14, 150.

73. Weeks, *Sex, Politics and Society, op. cit.,* p. 104.

74. John Addington Symonds, *Studies in Sexual Inversion,* privately printed, 1928, pp. 132–42. Symonds was a friend of Wilde's, and although this work was written as a polemic against such views as Krafft-Ebing's, Ulrichs', and Lombroso's, it still provides us with a discrete perspective on the harsh and unsympathetic climate of contemporary professional opinions about "sexual inversion."

75. *Ibid.,* pp. 164–5.

76. Weeks, *Sex, Politics and Society, op. cit.,* pp. 104–5. These early congenital theories were later given credence by the research of the German biologist August Weisman, whose "germ plasm" theory (1893), along with the "rediscovery" in 1900 of Gregor Mendel's theory of particulate inheritance, identified the (genetic) "mechanism" which could be used to explain how the "disease" was transmitted. Bowler, *Darwinism, op. cit.,* pp. xii, 15, 33.

77. This theme reappears frequently in the eugenic literature of the *fin-de-siècle.* Symonds, *op. cit.,* pp. 143–7.

78. Weeks, *Sex, Politics and Society, op. cit.,* p. 104.

79. For the reconceptualization of the criminal and lunatic, see especially Michel Foucault, *Discipline and Punish: The Birth of the Prison,* trans. Alan M. Sheridan, New York: Vintage, 1979 and *Madness and Civilization: A History of Insanity in the Age of Reason,* trans. Richard Howard, New York: Vintage, 1973.

80. Foucault, *History of Sexuality, op. cit.,* p. 43.

81. Michel Foucault, *The Birth of the Clinic: An Archaeology of Medical Perception,* trans. A.M. Sheridan Smith, New York: Vintage, *passim.* Foucault's general thesis was that medical science, through the medical establishment, which according to its own Hippocratic oath was supposed to serve society and thus improve humanity, has come

instead to manipulate, control, and ultimately to oppress us.

82. Some may find it strange that Freud was one of the few in his profession who did not find in "inversion" a synonym for degeneracy. Sigmund Freud, *Three Contributions to the Theory of Sex, in The Basic Writings of Sigmund Freud*, trans. and ed. Dr. A.A. Brill, New York: Modern Library, 1938, pp. 554–5. Freud argued that "inverts were not degenerates, because, 1. inversion is found in people who otherwise show no marked deviation from the normal, 2. it is found in people whose mental capacities are not disturbed, who on the contrary are distinguished by especially high intellectual development and ethical culture, and 3. inversion must be contextualized historically and cross-culturally, so that one finds that inversion was practiced by [highly advanced] ancient civilizations at the height of their culture, and that it is currently prevalent among savages and primitive races [without social stigma]."

83. Certainly by the mid-nineteenth century, physicians and surgeons, along with barristers and the clergy, were generally regarded as constituting the pinnacle of the middle class. As a result of the 1858 Medical Act, English doctors had acquired professional status and in subsequent decades their expert advice was increasingly sought on matters of public policy and social reform. Frank Mort, *Dangerous Sexualities: Medico-Moral Politics in England since 1830*, London: Routledge & Kegan Paul, 1987, pp. 65–8. Harold Perkin states that the professionalization of science also took place in the late-Victorian age. Perkin generally describes the period 1880–1914 in terms of what he calls the ascendancy of the "professional ideal." Harold Perkin, *The Rise of Professional Society: England since 1880*, London: Routledge, 1989, p. 86.

84. Weeks, *Sex, Politics and Society, op. cit.*, pp. 99, 102.

85. *Ibid.*, pp. 99, 102.

86. *Ibid.*, p. 101.

87. One of the more prominent examples was the prosecution of Charles Bradlaugh and Annie Besant in 1877 for privately republishing and circulating the pro-contraception tract, *The Fruits of Philosophy, or The Private Companion of Young Married People*. Norman and Jeanne MacKenzie, *The Fabians*, New York: Touchstone, 1977, p. 47.

88. Weeks, *Sex, Politics and Society, op. cit.*, pp. 141–5.

89. Symonds' work contained two separate studies, *A Study in Greek Ethics* (first printed privately in 1883) and *A Study in Modern Ethics* (first printed privately in 1891). *Studies in Sexual Inversion, op. cit.*

90. John Marshall, "Pansies, Perverts and Macho Men: Changing Conceptions of Male Homosexuality, in Kenneth Plummer, ed., *The Making of the Modern Homosexual*, Totowa, NJ: Barnes & Noble, 1981, pp. 133–54.

91. Marshall's evidence is corroborated in Sinfield, *op. cit.*, pp. 121–56, *passim*.

92. Marshall, *op. cit.*, p. 151.

93. *Ibid.*, p. 149.

94. *Ibid.*, p. 139.

95. H. Montgomery Hyde, *The Other Love: An Historical and Contemporary Survey of Homosexuality in Britain*, London: Heinemann, 1970, p. 135.

96. Marshall, *op. cit.*, pp. 140–41. One exception that comes to mind is

Queensberry's rant (recorded in Chapter Three) which describes Wilde as a "sexual pervert" with a "diseased mind." However, even in this instance, Queensberry's insult is clearly intended as a moral rather than a "medical," "legal," or psychiatric indictment of Wilde.

97. Adams, *op. cit.*, pp. 98, 99.

98. Sinfield, *op. cit.*, p. 67.

99. Ross Poole, *Morality and Modernity*, London and New York: Routledge, 1991, pp. 46–50.

100. "Mapping the 'feminine' onto the aristocracy" is a phrase of Sedgwick's. Sedgwick, *op. cit.*, pp. 93–4.

101. *Ibid.*, p. 93; Sinfield, *op. cit.*, p. 40; Adams, *op. cit.*, pp. 98–9.

102. Sinfield, *op. cit.*, pp. 91, 92.

103. *Ibid.*, *op. cit.*, p. 121.

104. *Ibid.*, *op. cit.*, pp. 69–71.

105. *Ibid.* p. 122.

106. Weeks, *Sex, Politics and Society, op. cit.*, p. 103.

107. *Ibid.*, p. 141.

108. The Cleveland Street Scandal of 1889–90 was the obvious precursor to the Wilde scandal in this regard. For different perspectives on the feminist viewpoint, see especially Philippa Levine, *Feminist Lives in Victorian England: Private Roles and Public Commitment*, Oxford: Basil Blackwell, 1990, p. 92; Sheila Jeffries, *The Spinster and Her Enemies: Feminism and Sexuality 1880–1930*, London, Boston, and Henley: Pandora, 1985, p. 8; Lucy Bland, "Purity, Motherhood, Pleasure or Threat? Definitions of Female Sexuality, 1900–1970's," in *Sex and Love: New Thoughts on Old Contradictions*, ed. Sue Cartledge and Joanna Ryan, London: The Women's Press, 1983, pp. 12–15.

109. Sedgwick, *op. cit.*, p. 216.

110. *Ibid.*, p. 12.

111. Weeks, *Sex, Politics and Society, op. cit.* p. 103.

112. Weeks, "Discourse, Desire, and Sexual Deviance," in *Against Nature, op. cit.*, p. 40.

113. Weeks, *Sex Politics and Society, op. cit.*, p. 103.

114. Weeks, "The Fabians and Utopia," in *Against Nature, op. cit.*, pp. 174–5. Weeks cites G.B. Shaw and Robert Blatchford in this context.

115. As defined by Judith Butler, in Butler, *op. cit.*, p. 154. See Jacques Lacan, *Écrits: a selection*, trans. Alan Sheridan, New York and London: W.W. Norton & Co., 1977, p. 327.

116. Butler, *op. cit.*, p. 64. Butler's argument expands upon the ideas expressed in Gayle Rubin, "The Traffic in Women: The 'Political Economy' of Sex," in *Toward an Anthropology of Women*, ed. Rayna R. Reiter, New York: Monthly Review Press, 1975.

117. Butler, *op. cit.*, p. 65.

118. *Ibid.*, pp. 25, 112, 119.

119. *Ibid.*, pp. 8, 18.

120. *Ibid.*, p. 33.

121. *Ibid.*, p. 140.

122. Sedgwick, *op. cit.*, p. 88. Sedgwick attributes this to "homophobia" and not "heterosexism." While the sensationalization of the Wilde trials by the press is a good example of the conscious and often malicious manipulation of a "heterosexist" cultural climate for ideological ends, such arguments of "social control" ascribe an initial intentionality that is untraceable. I would assert that while one can certainly examine the effects of such widely pervasive social phenomena as "heterosexism," "homophobia" or "racism," and can trace changes in the collective expressions of such attitudes at particular times and in particular cultures, the origins of such phenomena are rarely, if ever, recoverable.

123. J. Laplanche and J.-B. Pontalis, *The*

Language of Psychoanalysis, trans. Donald Nicholson-Smith, London and New York: W.W. Norton, 1973, pp. 103–11. I have mixed my Durkheimian and Freudian paradigms to create a metaphor with mass-psychological implications.

124. Ibid., pp. 103–7. The "mechanism" itself—that is, the potential for repression—is always present in a covert fashion, and "on call," which is to say that the mechanism is capable of being evoked or summoned whenever potential threats appear.

125. Frank Mort, Dangerous Sexualities: Medico-Moral Politics in England since 1830, New York: Routledge & Kegan Paul, 1987, p. 148. Social purists felt that radical feminists posed a similar threat to the family and to the traditional separation of spheres.

126. Wilde, De Profundis, op. cit., pp. 64–5, 71. Wilde says, "You knew what my Art was to me, the great primal note by which I had revealed, first myself to myself, and then myself to the world; the real passion of my life; the love to which all other loves were as marsh-water to red wine, or the glow-worm of the marsh to the magic mirror of the moon."

127. Ibid., pp. 42, 129.

CHAPTER 5
The Pathology of Pleasure and the Eschatology of Immanence: Theorizing Wilde's Identity and Desire

1. Daily Telegraph, April 4, 1895.
2. Wilde defined "Philistines" as those who "uphold and aid the heavy, cumbrous, blind, mechanical forces of Society, and who [do] not recognize a dynamic force when [they meet] it." De Profundis, in Isobel Murray, ed., Soul of Man and Prison Writings, Oxford: Oxford University Press, 1991, p. 133.

3. But whereas "Society often forgives the criminal, it never forgives the dreamer." Wilde, "The Critic as Artist," in Richard Ellmann, ed., The Artist as Critic: Critical Writings of Oscar Wilde, Chicago: University of Chicago Press, 1982, p. 380. Wilde also examined the peculiar confluence of art, liminality, and criminality in the character of the notorious art-critic/forger/murderer/comedian, Thomas Griffiths Wainewright, in the appreciative essay, "Pen, Pencil, and Poison. Pen, Pencil, and Poison: A Study in Green," (originally published 1889), in Ellmann, op. cit., pp. 320–40.

4. Hans-Georg Gadamer, Truth and Method, New York: Crossroad, 1988, p. 63.

5. Ibid., p. 87. Gadamer traces the origin of the concept "world-view" or Weltanschauung, to Kant and Fichte, where it referred generally to a "moral world order." Gadamer finds that Hegel was the one who first aestheticized the term, thus allowing for a multiplicity of "world-views," each with its own frame of reference, and thus its own "truth."

6. Allan Megill, Prophets of Extremity: Nietzsche, Heidegger, Foucault, Derrida, Berkeley and Los Angeles: The University of California Press, 1987, pp. 31–3.

7. Wilde, De Profundis, op. cit., p. 98.

8. See J. Laplanche and J.-B. Pontalis, The Language of Psychoanalysis, trans. Donald Nicholson-Smith, New York: W.W. Norton, 1973, pp. 255–7. Sigmund Freud, On Narcissism (1914), in General

Psychological Theory, New York: Collier, 1963, pp. 56–82, especially p. 76.

9. Heinz Kohut, *The Restoration of the Self*, New York: International Universities Press, 1977.

10. Wilde, *The Soul of Man Under Socialism*, in Murray, *op. cit.*, p. 17.

11. *Ibid.*, pp. 1–37.

12. Friedrich Nietzsche, *The Will to Power*, ed. Walter Kaufmann, trans. Walter Kaufmann and R.J. Hollingdale, New York: Vintage, 1967, p. 377 (708).

13. *Ibid.*, p. 22

14. *Ibid.*, p. 32.

15. *Ibid.*, p. 19.

16. Susan Sontag, "Notes on Camp," in *Against Interpretation*, New York: Anchor, 1990, pp. 275–92. Sontag's essay was written specifically with Wilde in mind.

17. *Ibid.*, p. 287.

18. Jack Babuscio, "Camp and the Gay Sensibility," in Richard Dyer, ed., *Gays and Film*, New York: Zoetrope, 1984, pp. 40–57. Babuscio defines the "gay sensibility" as: "a creative energy reflecting a consciousness that is different from the mainstream; a heightened awareness of certain human complications of feeling that spring from the fact of social oppression; in short, a perception of the world which is coloured, shaped, directed and defined by the fact of one's gayness" (p. 40).

19. *Ibid.*, p. 41.

20. *Ibid.*, pp. 45, 46.

21. *Ibid.*, pp. 46–8.

22. Matei Calinescu, *Five Faces of Modernity*, Durham: Duke University Press, 1987, pp. 225–62.

23. *Ibid.*, p. 230.

24. *Ibid.*, p. 244.

25. Herbert Marcuse, "On Hedonism," in *Negations: Essays in Critical Theory*, trans. Jeremy J. Shapiro, London: Free Association Books, 1988, p. 162. Herbert Marcuse has distinguished between two varieties of hedonism, which he identified as the Cyrenaic and the Epicurean. The Cyrenaic school suggested that happiness is found in experiencing pleasure as often as possible, whereas the Epicurean school saw happiness in the avoidance of pain. The goal of both was ultimately self-knowledge, self-mastery, and self-realization, which was equated with perfection. Walter Pater agreed with Marcuse in substance, but refers to the Epicurean mode of hedonism as merely the Roman counterpart of the Greek original. Walter Pater, *Essays on Literature and Art*, ed. Jennifer Uglow, London: Everyman, 1990, p. 166.

26. *Daily Telegraph*, April 4, 1895.

27. *Oscar Wilde: Art and Morality: A Defence of "The Picture of Dorian Gray,"* ed. Stuart Mason (pseud., Christopher Sclater Millard), London: J. Jacobs, 1908.

28. *Daily Telegraph*, April 4, 1895.

29. Wilde, *The Soul of Man Under Socialism*, *op. cit.*, p. 9.

30. *Ibid.*, p. 7.

31. Nietzsche, *op. cit.*, p. 375. The Wilde/Nietzsche connection is very strong, but yet to be developed in any systematic scholarly way.

32. In *The Soul of Man Under Socialism*, Wilde described social conformity as the enemy of freedom, and sinning as a possible mode of perfection." *Op. cit.*, p. 11.

33. *Ibid.*, p. 19.

34. Nietzsche, *op. cit.*, pp. 419–20.

35. In *The Birth of Tragedy*, Nietzsche discusses these disparate pulls in terms of "Dionysian" and "Apollonian" impulses. *The Birth of Tragedy*, in *The Birth of Tragedy and The Case of Wagner*, trans. Walter Kaufmann, New York: Vintage,

1967, *passim.*

36. The term "anomie" is primarily associated with the work of Durkheim, and denotes a state of society in which normative standards of conduct and belief are weak or lacking, or a similar condition in an individual characterized by disorientation, anxiety, and isolation. Durkheim uses "anomie" to denote "the spiritual costs [to society] of unrestricted [individual] desires." Rosalind Williams, *Dream Worlds: Mass Consumption in Late Nineteenth-Century France*, Berkeley and Los Angeles: University of California Press, 1991, p. 338. As Talcott Parsons develops the concept in relation to the individual, "anomie" represents a generalized psychological condition which results when expectations are first confronted and then crushed by reality—a mixture of despair, anguish, and frustration. Talcott Parsons, "The Life and Work of Emile Durkheim," in Emile Durkheim *Sociology and Philosophy*, trans. D. F. Pocock, New York: The Free Press, 1974, p. lvii.

37. Wilde, *The Critic as Artist, op. cit.,* p. 396.

38. This view likens the modern artist's need of creative expression to that of "God as the supreme artist, amoral, recklessly creating and destroying, realizing himself indifferently in whatever he does or undoes, ridding himself by his acts of the embarrassment of his riches and the strain of his internal contradictions." Friedrich Nietzsche, from *The Birth of Tragedy*, quoted in Daniel Bell, "Beyond Modernism, *Beyond Self*," in *The Winding Passage: Essays and Sociological Journeys, 1960–1980*, New York: Basic Books, 1980, p. 286.

39. Ralph Waldo Emerson, "Self-Reliance," in Brooks Atkinson, ed. *The Complete Essays and Other Writings of Ralph Waldo Emerson*, New York: The Modern Library, 1950, pp. 145–70. Upon the occasion of Emerson's death in 1883, Wilde memorialized him as "New England's Plato," and considered him as one of America's two most influential thinkers (Whitman was the other). While incarcerated in Reading Gaol, a book of Emerson's essays was on the first of three (existing) lists of books requested by Wilde. Ellmann, *op. cit.,* pp. 167, 181, 508.

40. Fredric Jameson, "Postmodernism and Consumer Society," in Hal Foster, ed., *The Anti-Aesthetic*, Seattle: Bay Press, 1983, pp. 111–25. Philosopher Charles Taylor describes the condition of modernity similarly as "atomistic." The ancient reference is, of course, to Democritus, but as regards the modern world, Taylor's "atomism" refers to the results of the breakdown of the (perhaps mythic) sense of community associated with the *ancien régime*, and the subsequent growth of unrestricted forms of radical individualism. Charles Taylor, *The Ethics of Authenticity*, Cambridge: Harvard University Press, 1992, *passim.*

41. Simmel describes an "adventure" as "a part of our existence, directly contiguous with other parts which precede and follow it; at the same time, in its deeper meaning, it occurs outside the usual continuity of this life ... it is a foreign body in our existence which is yet somehow connected with the center; the outside, if only by a long and unfamiliar detour, is formally an aspect of the inside." Georg Simmel, "The Adventurer," in Donald N. Levine, ed., *Individuality*

and Social Forms: Selected Writings, Chicago: University of Chicago Press, 1971, p. 188.

42. Georg Simmel, "The Stranger," in *The Sociology of Georg Simmel,* trans. and ed. Kurt H. Wolff, New York: The Free Press, 1950, pp. 402–8.

43. *Ibid.,* p. 189.

44. Simmel describes the adventurer experiencing the segmental, episodic character of life and experiencing the wholeness of life within each segment: "A fragmentary incident, it is yet, like a work of art, enclosed by a beginning and an end. Like a dream, it gathers all passions into itself, and yet, like a dream, is destined to be forgotten; like gaming, it contrasts with seriousness, yet, like the *va banque* of the gambler, it involves the alternative between the highest gain and destruction. Thus the adventure is a particular form in which fundamental categories of life are synthesized." *Ibid.,* p. 192.

45. A state of idleness also suggests a state of uselessness. While both these virtues were praised and elevated into a creed of contemplative inaction by the Taoist sage, Chuang Tzu, they represented anti-social virtues in late Victorian England.

46. *Daily Telegraph,* April 4, 1895.

47. Wilde, "The Critic as Artist," *op. cit.,* p. 389.

48. Wilde, "The Truth of Masks," in Ellmann, *op. cit.,* p. 432.

49. Nietzsche, *The Will to Power, op. cit.,* p. 435.

50. Wilde, "The Critic as Artist," *op. cit.,* p. 305.

51. "The Decay of Lying," in Ellmann, *op. cit.,* p. 316.

52. *Ibid.,* p. 320.

53. Susan Sontag compares Jean Genet's statement, "the only criterion of an act is its elegance," with Wilde's, "in matters of great importance, the vital element is not sincerity, but style." Sontag, *op. cit.,* p. 288.

54. Wilde's emphasis on the value of uselessness was in part inspired by his fascination with the Taoist sage, Chuang Tzu. Chuang Tzu, like Wilde, pointed out the ultimate uselessness of useful things in the grand scheme, and preached the creed of Inaction—"to resolve action into thought, and thought into abstraction, was his wicked transcendental aim." Wilde, "A Chinese Sage: Chuang Tzu," in Ellmann, *The Artist as Critic, op. cit.,* pp. 221–8. In Wilde's book review, Chuang Tzu echoes the sentiments of Baudelaire, Schopenhauer, and Rimbaud: he was a "mystic who held that the aim of life was to get rid of self-consciousness, and to become the unconscious vehicle of a higher illumination." He was characterized as a combination of "Heraclitus, Böhme, Eckhart, Hegel, and Rousseau." *Ibid.,* p. 223.

55. George Simmel, "Fashion," in *On Individuality and Social Forms, op. cit.,* p. 295.

56. Simmel describes how this becomes an increasingly important historical issue in the late nineteenth century, when the forces of democracy and mass production have a pronounced effect upon fashion. Because more and more people have access to similar styles of dress, fashion is no longer the strict indicator of class it had been previously. In this way, fashion became a great social leveller. In Simmel's thesis, people were attracted to fashion as an expression of the present moment, because "the great, permanent, unquestionable convictions (God, Church, State, and Progress) were increasingly being

doubted." Thus, fashion, and "posing," represent modes of coping with what we have described as the schizophrenic, or atomistic, condition of modern society. Simmel, "Fashion," *op. cit.*, pp. 295–311.

57. In a letter (dated June 25, 1890) to the editor of the *St. James Gazette* in response to a review of *Dorian Gray*, Wilde said, "The sphere of art and the sphere of ethics are absolutely distinct and separate; and it is to the confusion between the two that we owe the appearance of Mrs. Grundy, that amusing old lady who represents the only original form of humour that the middle classes in this country have been able to produce." In Donald L. Lawler, ed., Oscar Wilde, *The Picture of Dorian Gray*, New York: W.W. Norton, 1988, p. 336. The review Wilde responded to was entitled "A Study in Puppydom" (*St. James Gazette*, June 24, 1890). "Puppyism" was a colloquialism which meant "affectation or excessive art in costume or posture." *Ibid.*, p. 331n.

58. The *Scots Observer* review was dated July 5, 1890, and Wilde's response was dated July 9, 1890. The outlawed nobleman and perverted telegraph boys refer to the Cleveland Street Scandal, 1889–90. Lawler, *op. cit.*, p. 346n.

59. Mason, *op. cit.*, pp. 68–9. Wilde's allusion to the "colours of the palette" refers to Gautier's statement on decadent style: "... taking colors from all palettes, notes from all keyboards. ..." Max Nordau, *Degeneration*, New York: D. Appleton and Co., 1895, p. 299.

60. Wilde, letter to the Editor of the *St. James Gazette*, June 26, 1890, in Lawler, *op. cit.*, pp. 337–9.

61. Walter Pater expressed a similar sentiment: "What is important then, is not that the critic should possess a correct abstract definition of beauty for the intellect, but a certain kind of temperament, the power of being deeply moved by the presence of beautiful objects." Walter Pater, *From the Preface to The Renaissance*, in Jennifer Uglow, ed., *Essays on Literature and Art*, London: J.M. Dent & Sons, 1990, p. 91.

62. Wilde, "The Critic as Artist," *op. cit.*, p. 352.

63. *Ibid.*, p. 406.

64. Nietzsche, *The Will to Power*, *op. cit.*, p. 452.

65. Wilde, *De Profundis*, *op. cit.*, pp. 110–17.

66. Georg Simmel, "Eros, Platonic and Modern," in Levine, *op. cit.*, p. 238. In *The Symposium*, Absolute Beauty is described as "unique, eternal" and incorporeal. Diotima tells Socrates that the "highest life" is that spent in the contemplation of absolute beauty." Plato, *The Symposium*, trans. Walter Hamilton, New York: Penguin, 1951, pp. 92–4.

67. As Ideal Forms, beauty, truth, love, and "the good" are virtually indistinguishable. Plato, *op. cit.*, p. 94.

68. Simmel, "Eros, Platonic and Modern," *op. cit.*, p. 240. Within the pederastic context of love between an adult male citizen and a boy of the same class, the sensual element is ideally absorbed, transformed, and elevated by the intellectual element. David Halperin notes that the ancient Greek concept of beauty, *to kalon*, implies not only physical comeliness, but "a constellation of physical and moral attributes or endowments." David M. Halperin, "Two Views of Greek Love: Harald Patzer and Michel Foucault," in *One Hundred Years of Homosexuality: and Other Essays on*

Greek Love, New York: Routledge, 1990, p. 57. John Addington Symonds lists the attributes associated with beauty: "male beauty was associated with strength at rest (physical potential), spirit in repose (spiritual potential), suavity, casual nonchalance, dignity in carriage and deportment" and these qualities were seen in turn to embody the following moral qualities: "excellence, virility, self-discipline, intelligence, health, energy, ability to enjoy life, temperance, and an indomitable spirit." Symonds, "A Study in Greek Ethics," in *Studies in Sexual Inversion*, privately printed, 1928, p. 91.

69. Pierre Bourdieu, *Distinction: A Social Critique of the Judgement of Taste*, trans. Richard Nice, Cambridge: Harvard University Press, pp. 11–96.

70. *Ibid.*, especially pp. 41–59.

71. *Ibid.*

72. I use the word "Christlike" to avoid the word "Christian," which I feel has been tainted with inflections of hypocrisy.

73. Wilde's instrumental attitude toward his aesthetic is discussed in an excerpt from the opening of Carson's case for the defense: "In relation to his books, Mr. Wilde took up the position of an artist: that he wrote only in the language for artists. Contrast that with the position which he took up as regarded his acquaintances. They included Parker, a gentleman's servant; Conway, a boy who sold papers on the pier at Worthing; and Scarfe, who was also a gentleman's servant. Then Mr. Wilde's case was no longer that he was dwelling in the regions of art, but that he was such a noble, such a democratic soul that he drew no social distinctions, and that it gave him exactly the same pleasure to have a sweeping boy from the street to lunch or drive with him as to sit down with the best educated artist or the greatest literateur in the whole kingdom." *Daily Telegraph*, April 5, 1895.

74. Wilde's comparison of himself with Christ was developed at length in *De Profundis*. Wilde noted that there were Christians before Christ, but hardly any since, with the exception of St. Francis. In Wilde's interpretation, Christ was the first person to offer an aesthetic critique of mechanical bourgeois society. Christ treated everyone as individuals, not as equals. For him there were no universal laws, only exceptions, and self-realized, self-expressive artists were seen as those most worthy of exceptional status. Wilde, *De Profundis, op. cit.*, pp.119–25.

75. *Daily Telegraph*, April 4, 1895.

76. Letter, dated August 13, 1890, in Stuart Mason, *op. cit.*, p. 77. In a previous letter, dated August 2, 1895, he expressed the identical sentiments: "For if a work of art is rich and vital and complete, those who have artistic instincts will see its beauty, and those to whom ethics appeal more strongly than aesthetics will see its moral lesson." *Ibid.*, p. 70.

77. Gadamer, *op. cit.*, pp. 263–6. Of the two, understanding is the most difficult, for it requires the suspension of one's own biases, prejudices, and ideologies.

78. *Ibid.*, pp. 63–87.

79. Carson's viewpoint is reflected in Georg Simmel's notion of the alloplastic origins of "subjective culture:" "Culture exists only if man draws into his development something that is external to him ... forms of comportment, the refine-

ment of taste expressed in judgements, the education of moral tact ... are all cultural formations in which the perfection of the individual is routed through real and ideal spheres outside of the self. The perfection does not remain a purely immanent process, but is consummated in a unique adjustment and teleological interweaving of subject and object." Simmel, "Subjective Culture," in Levine, *op. cit.*, p. 230.

80. Theodor W. Adorno, *Kierkegaard: Construction of the Aesthetic*, trans. and ed. Robert Hullot-Kentor, Minneapolis: University of Minnesota Press, 1989, pp. 1–23. Speaking generally, Adorno argues the superiority of the ethical over the aesthetic principle: "The aesthetical in a man is that by which he is immediately what he is, the ethical is that whereby he becomes what he becomes. ... Aesthetic deportment appears as an absence of decisiveness from the perspective of the ethical ... in the face of the "leap" of faith, the aesthetic is deprecatorily transformed from a level in the dialectical process, that of the failure of decisiveness, into simple creaturely immediacy." *Ibid.*, p. 15.

81. Wolfgang Iser, *The Act of Reading: A Theory of Aesthetic Response*, Baltimore: Johns Hopkins University Press, 1978, p. 9.

82. Wilde, letter to *Scots Observer*, dated July 9, 1890, in Mason, *op. cit.*, p. 69.

83. Walter Pater, "A Novel by Mr. Oscar Wilde," in Uglow, *op. cit.*, pp. 161–4.

84. *Daily Telegraph*, Wednesday, May 1, 1895.

85. Plato, *op. cit.*, p. 26.

86. "The Portrait of Mr. W.H.," in Ellmann, *op. cit.*, especially pp. 184–7.

87. Wilde, "Decay of Lying," in *op. cit.*, p. 291.

88. Charles Baudelaire, "Third Draft of a Preface to the Flowers of Evil," in Marthiel and Jackson Mathews, eds., *The Flowers of Evil*, New York: New Directions, 1989, p. xxix.

89. The issue, of course, was not whether Wilde lied, for all the evidence points to the fact that he did, repeatedly. We know Wilde was lying concerning the commission of the acts for which he was accused because, on one hand, we have the testimony of Parker, Wood, and the others describing Wilde's actions, and on the other hand, we have Wilde's own admissions of both the acts and the lying in *De Profundis*. Wilde, *De Profundis*, *op. cit.*, pp. 47, 133.

90. Showing great tact, Wilde purposely refrained from subverting what Steven Marcus referred to as "the characteristic Victorian arrangement in which the existence of a whole universe of sexuality and sexual activity was tacitly acknowledged and actively participated in, while at the same time [every]one's consciousness of all this was, as far as possible, kept apart from one's larger, more general, and public consciousness of both self and society." Steven Marcus, *The Other Victorians: A Study of Sexuality and Pornography in Mid-Nineteenth Century England*, New York: W.W. Norton & Company, 1985, pp. 162–3.

91. *Star* (May 1, 1895) reports Frederick Atkins was 20 years old when he testified, which makes him 17 or 18 years old when the alleged events took place in November of 1892. Charles Parker was 21 when he testified, placing him in the 18–19-year range (*Star*, April 26, 1895). Edward Shelley testified that he was "a lad of 18 or 19" when he met Wilde (*Star*,

May 22, 1895). Alfred Wood was referred to as "the lad" (*Star*, April 27, 1895), as indeed were Atkins, Parker, Shelley, and all the rest of the young men who gave evidence against Wilde. Alfred Taylor's landlady testified that those who frequented Taylor's apartment were "young men of 16 and upward" (*Star*, April 26, 1895).

92. Jose Harris, *Private Lives, Public Spirit: Britain 1870–1914*, New York: Penguin, 1994, pp. 84–9. Harris says that in the early and mid-Victorian periods, "for the vast majority of children 'childhood,' if it existed at all, was effectively over by the age of 10" (p. 84). By the end of the century, "childhood" had been extended a couple of years, to the ages of 12 or 13 (pp. 88, 89).

93. Ellmann, *Oscar Wilde, op. cit.*, pp. 26–100.

94. I agree with David M. Halperin when he writes that "The real issue for cultural historians, or critics of contemporary culture, is to recover the terms in which the experiences of individuals belonging to past societies were actually constituted and to measure and assess the differences between those terms and the ones we currently employ." Halperin, "One Hundred Years of Homosexuality," in *One Hundred Years of Homosexuality, op. cit.*, p. 29.

95. *Ibid.*, p. 30.

96. Symonds also notes the fact that "Paederasty was a masculine passion closely associated with love of political independence, with contempt for Asiatic luxury, with sport, with self-mastery, and with intellectual pursuits which distinguished the Hellenes from the Barbarians." He also notes that the social customs encouraged the seclusion of free women in the homes, leaving the public sphere exclusively to the males. Moreover, Symonds contends, women were not generally educated and therefore were never considered the intellectual equals of men. Therefore, a true commonality of interests between men and women was impossible. For this reason, all the higher intellectual pursuits and passions associated with them became the exclusive privileges of men, and the exaltation of emotions was reserved solely for the male sex. John Addington Symonds, "A Problem in Greek Ethics," in *Sexual Inversion, op. cit.*, p. 71.

97. Halperin, *One Hundred Years of Homosexuality, op. cit.*, pp. 30–31.

98. *Ibid.*, p. 34n.

99. Halperin argues that "sexual object preferences are not the single defining principle of the personal identity: to categorize people by gender roles and sexual object choices is just as arbitrary, contingent, and conventional as any other form of classification." *Ibid.*, p. 28n.

100. *Ibid.*, p. 24.

101. "In *The Cultural Contradictions of Capitalism*, Daniel Bell argues that the crises of the developed societies of the West are to be traced back to a split between culture and society. ... Because of the forces of modernism, the principle of unlimited self-realization, the demand for authentic self-experience and the subjectivism of a hyperstimulated sensitivity have come to be dominant. This temperament unleashes hedonistic motives irreconcilable with the discipline of professional life in society. ... Moreover, modernist culture is altogether incompatible with the moral basis of a purposive, rational conduct of life. In this manner, Bell places the burden of responsibility for the dissolution of the Protestant ethic on the

'adversary culture.' Culture in its modern forms stirs up hatred against the conventions and virtues of everyday life, which has become rationalized under the pressures of economic and administrative imperatives." Jürgen Habermas, "Modernity—An Incomplete Project," in Hal Foster, *The Anti-Aesthetic: Essays on Postmodern Culture*, Seattle: Bay Press, 1983, p. 6.

102. "If Oscar Wilde, instead of indulging in dirty tricks of indecent familiarity with boys and men, had ruined the lives of half a dozen innocent simpletons of girls, or had broken up the home of his friend by corrupting his friend's wife, no one could have laid a finger upon him. The male is sacrosanct: the female is fair game." W.T. Stead, *The Review of Reviews*, June 1895. In H. Montgomery Hyde, *The Trials of Oscar Wilde*, New York: Dover, 1962, p. 341.

103. In Murray, *op. cit.*, pp. 47, 75, 101, 133.

104. At one point in *De Profundis* Wilde cites confession as a "noble endeavour" and a "purifying experience." Recalling Lockwood's scathing denunciation of him in his final statement to the jury, Wilde wrote: "How splendid it would be, if I was saying all this about myself! I saw then at once that what is said of a man is nothing. The point is who says it." Wilde, *De Profundis, op. cit.*, p. 145.

105. *Ibid.*, pp. 47, 81, 82.

106. See Jeffrey Weeks, *Sex, Politics and Society*, London: Longman, 1989, pp. 99–100; and Michel Foucault, *The History of Sexuality, Volume I: An Introduction*, New York: Vintage, 1980, p. 43.

107. Pierre Klossowski, *Sade, My Neighbor*, trans. Alphonso Lingis,

Evanston: Northwestern University Press, 1991, p. 24.

108. Marquis de Sade, "Philosophy in the Bedroom," in *Justine, Philosophy in the Bedroom, and Other Writings*, trans. Richard Seaver and Austryn Wainhouse, New York: Grove Weidenfeld, 1990, p. 326.

109. *Ibid.*, pp. 326, 327.

110. *Ibid.*, p. 326.

111. *Ibid.*, p. 327.

112. *Ibid.*, p. 328. Sade notes that "the wars fought to sustain the republic brought about the separation of the two sexes, and hence the propagation of the vice, and when its consequences, so useful to the State, were recognized, religion speedily blessed it."

113. In addition to Sade's rejection of bourgeois morality and "Kantian" optimism, Horkheimer and Adorno, for example, find in Sade's work a critique of Enlightenment ideals such as "solidarity with society, duty, and family." Max Horkheimer and Theodor W. Adorno, *Dialectic of Enlightenment*, trans. John Cumming, New York: Continuum, 1989, pp. 81–119.

114. Maurice Blanchot, "Sade," in Marquis de Sade, *op. cit.*, p. 40.

115. *Ibid.*, pp. 329–37. His rationale was that since Nature killed indiscriminately, and the State murdered arbitrarily, why should not individuals be accorded the same right of committing immoral acts? Compared to murder, sodomy seemed a trifling offence.

116. See Nietzsche's discussion in *Beyond Good and Evil* (section 260, pp. 394–8), and in the first essay of *On the Genealogy of Morals*, pp. 460–93 in *Basic Writings of Nietzsche*, trans. and ed. Walter Kaufmann, New York: The Modern Library, 1968, pp. 460–93.

117. Klossowski, *op. cit.*, p. 6. Alphonso

Lingis, in his introduction to Klossowski's text, elaborates on the meaning of sodomy within this context: "Sodomy is not simply anal eroticism, a natural and animal pleasure; it is anal eroticism biblically and theologically interpreted as an act that functions neither for the reproduction of the species nor for species bonding, [but] as an act done to gore the partner and release the germ of the species into his excrement. Thus sodomy, theologically interpreted, is an assault on the human species as such, an act of monstrous singularity, and an act directed against God, the ultimate formula for all norms." *Ibid.*, p. xiii.

118. *Ibid.*, p. 22.
119. Gilles Deleuze, "A Theory of the Other," in Constantin V. Boundas, ed., *The Deleuze Reader*, New York: Columbia University Press, 1993, pp. 59–68.
120. Laplanche and Pontalis, *op. cit.*, p. 80.
121. Ellmann, *Oscar Wilde, op. cit., passim.*
122. Oscar Wilde, *Selected Letters of Oscar Wilde*, ed. Rupert Hart-Davis, Oxford: Oxford University Press, 1979, p. 327.
123. Wilde, *De Profundis, op. cit.*, p. 80.
124. *Ibid.*, p. 132.
125. Joris Karl Huysmans, *Against the Grain*, New York: Dover, 1969, pp. 65–70.
126. K.J. Dover, *Greek Homosexuality*, Cambridge, MA: Harvard University Press, 1989, p. 34.
127. Wilde, *De Profundis, op. cit.*, p. 96.
128. Blanchot, *op. cit.*, p. 40.
129. *Ibid.*, p. 41.
130. *Ibid.*
131. *Ibid.*, p. 44.
132. Wilde, *De Profundis, op. cit.*, p. 95.
133. *Ibid.*, p. 96.
134. Klossowski, *op. cit.*, p. 64.
135. Marcus, *op. cit., passim.*

CHAPTER 6
"Social Purity" and Social Pollution: Wilde and the National Health

1. W.T. Stead, *The Review of Reviews*, June 1895, quoted in H. Montgomery Hyde, *The Trials of Oscar Wilde*, New York: Dover, 1962, p. 340.
2. *Ibid.*, p. 341. Henry Labouchere stated that the amendment he introduced, which ultimately became section 11 of the Criminal Law Amendment Act of 1885, was inspired by a report on male prostitution sent to him by W.T. Stead. Jeffrey Weeks, *Sex, Politics, and Society: The Regulation of Sexuality since 1800*, 2nd edn, New York: Longman, 1989, p. 102.
3. Hyde, *op. cit.*, p. 341.
4. Letter by C.S.M. (Christopher Sclater Millard) in *Reynold's Newspaper* May 29, 1895, quoted in Hyde, *op. cit.*, p. 357. Millard later became Wilde's bibliographer.
5. *Star*, special edition, May 27, 1895.
6. Edward J. Bristow, *Vice and Vigilance: Purity Movements in Britain since 1700*, Totowa, NJ: Rowman and Littlefield, 1977, p. 133.
7. Weeks, *op. cit.*, p. 109.
8. Jeffrey Weeks, *Coming Out: Homosexual Politics in Britain, from the Nineteenth Century to the Present*, London: Quartet, 1977, p. 25.
9. Stead, in Hyde, *op. cit.*, pp. 340–41.
10. Elaine Showalter, *Sexual Anarchy: Gender and Culture at the Fin-de-Siècle*, New York: Penguin, 1990, pp. 172, 173, 178. Carpenter's "feminism" was apparently limited to notions of intellectual equality. Carpenter advocated economic liberation for women, but maintained a traditional attitude toward women's roles and responsibilities

in the household and toward child-rearing. Both these views were consistent with contemporary socialist beliefs (which were hardly progressive regarding women's roles in the home). His "progressive" view of women was also tainted by a misogyny which stemmed from his "aesthetic" preference for the male body.

11. Stead to Edward Carpenter (Ms 386–54 [1–2], June 1895, Edward Carpenter collection, Sheffield City Library), in Weeks, *Sex, Politics, and Society*, pp. 109, 120.

12. Georges Canguilhem, *The Normal and the Pathological*, trans. Carolyn R. Fawcett and Robert S. Cohen, New York: Zone Books, 1991, p. 282.

13. James Cowles Pritchard, "A Treatise on Insanity" (1830), in Michael Stone, ed., *Essential Papers on Borderline Disorders: One Hundred Years at the Border*, New York: NYU Press, 1986, pp. 14–15.

14. C.H. Hughes, *Moral (Affective) Insanity–Psychosensory Insanity* (1884), in Stone, *op. cit.*, p. 19. Hyde, citing a debate in the House of Lords on July 7, 1937, also comments that as late as this (and probably much later), the prevailing view on homosexuality was that it was not a disease, but rather "the result of wicked impulses which, like other wicked impulses, are capable of being controlled ... they can be checked by advice and by resolution." Hyde, *op. cit.*, p. 258.

15. Philippa Levine, *Feminist Lives in Victorian England: Private Roles and Public Commitment*, Oxford: Basil Blackwell, 1990, p. 87; Sheila Jeffries, *The Spinster and Her Enemies: Feminism and Sexuality 1880–1930*, London, Boston, and Henley: Pandora, 1985, p. 6. Jeffries says that "the social purity movement

reached through hundreds of societies into the lives of a considerable proportion of the male and female population."

16. Jeffries, *op. cit.*, pp. 6, 7.

17. Stead described himself as a "child of the revival of 1859–60." Bristow, *op. cit.*, p. 4.

18. Josephine Butler founded the Ladies National Association for the Repeal of the CD Acts (LNA) in 1869. The LNA was concerned as much with political issues concerning women as with moral issues concerning men. Butler in particular championed the human dignity of prostitutes, and opposed legislation, such as the CD Acts, that restricted the civil liberties of women while ostensibly trying to contain men's lust. Jeffries, *op. cit.*, pp. 8, 9. Barbara Caine argues that Butler's moral fervor was more suited to liberal reform campaigns than to the social purity movement, and that her orientation was essentially political rather than moral. Barbara Caine, *Victorian Feminists*, Oxford: Oxford University Press, 1991, p. 193. In a telling letter written just days after the conclusion of the trials, Butler expressed her confusion regarding Wilde's sexuality, and her Christian concern for Wilde's soul: "I am so sorry for Oscar Wilde. ... What must solitary confinement be for such a man? He who loved praise and was much flattered by a certain set has now to sit and brood over the general loathing and contempt which has been poured upon him. ... I hope they will treat him mercifully. ... As you say there are others worse than he, and 'society' seems lately very diseased this way. ... I pity the criminal on whose head society's vials of wrath are poured. ... I pray for him constantly—that God will tell him

that He does not despise him."
Letter to Stanley Butler, June 4,
1895. *Ibid.*, p. 192.

19. Ellice Hopkins founded the White
Cross Army (1883), a barnstorming
movement lacking central direction
and having no church affiliation,
whose purpose was to modify
moral behavior. It had five central
tenets: "1. To treat all women with
respect, and endeavor to protect
them from wrong and degradation.
2. To use every possible means to
fulfill the command: 'Keep thyself
pure.' 3. To endeavor to put down
all indecent language and coarse
jests. 4. To maintain the law of
purity as equally binding upon men
and women. 5. To endeavor to
spread these principles among my
companions, and to try and help
my younger brothers." Bristow, *op.
cit.*, p. 103.

20. *Ibid.*, pp. 4, 5.

21. The 1864 Contagious Diseases Act,
which extended to a number of
selected naval ports and garrison
towns, empowered both police and
medical practitioners to notify a
justice of the peace if they even *suspected* a woman of being a common
prostitute. The woman could then
be taken to a certified hospital for a
forced medical examination (a pro-
cedure that feminist historians such
as Philippa Levine and Lucy Bland
have equated with legalized "medical rape"). The women could be
detained for up to three months
and were often under police surveillance afterwards. They could be
imprisoned for up to two months
for disobeying hospital rules or for
leaving without proper medical
consent. Brothel keepers were also
penalized. The 1866 and 1869 CD
Acts enlarged upon the 1864 Act—
including mandatory detention for
up to six months, moral and reli-

gious instruction for the women,
and regular fortnightly inspections
of previous detainees—and extended its geographical boundaries. Frank Mort, *Dangerous
Sexualities: Medico-moral Politics
in England since 1830*, London:
Routledge & Kegan Paul, 1987, pp.
69–76.

22. Levine, *op. cit.*, pp. 79–102; Lucy
Bland, "Purity, Motherhood,
Pleasure or Threat? Definitions of
Female Sexuality, 1900–1970s," in
Sue Cartledge and Joanna Ryan,
eds., *Sex and Love: New Thoughts on
Old Contradictions*, London: The
Women's Press, 1983, pp. 13–16;
Judith Walkowitz, "Male Vice and
Feminist Virtue: Feminism and the
Politics of Prostitution in Nine-
teenth Century Britain," *History
Workshop*, 1982, no. 13, 89.

23. Bland, *op. cit.*, pp. 12–15.

24. Judith R. Walkowitz, *City of
Dreadful Delight: Narratives of
Sexual Danger in Late-Victorian
London*, Chicago: University of
Chicago Press, 1992, p. 103.

25. *Ibid.*, pp. 120–21. For the effectiveness of the NVA in pressuring the
government in a variety of ways,
Mort, *op. cit.*, pp. 130–36.

26. *Ibid.*, p. 105.

27. Levine, *op. cit.*, p. 97.

28. Jeffries, *op. cit.*, p. 6.

29. Mort, *op. cit.*, p. 118.

30. *Ibid.*, pp. 149–50.

31. Anthony F.C. Wallace, "Revitalization Movements," in *American
Anthropologist* (58, 1956), pp. 264–81.
Types of revitalization movements
include nativistic movements, cargo
cults, religious revivals, reform
movements, messianic movements,
charismatic movements, utopian
communities, relgious sects, and
revolutions.

32. *Ibid.*, p. 265.

33. *Ibid.*, pp. 269, 279.

34. Bristow, *op. cit.*, p. 6.
35. Wilde, *De Profundis*, in Isobel Murray, ed., *The Soul of Man and Prison Writings*, Oxford: Oxford University Press, 1991, p. 139.
36. Walter E. Houghton, *The Victorian Frame of Mind, 1830–1870*, New Haven: Yale University Press, 1985, p. 54.
37. Matei Calinescu, *Five Faces of Modernity*, Durham: Duke University Press, 1987, pp. 192–3.
38. Weeks, *Sex, Politics and Society*, *op. cit.*, pp. 86, 87.
39. Alan Sked, *Britain's Decline: Problems and Perspectives*, New York: Basil Blackwell, 1987, pp. 13–21.
40. Gareth Stedman Jones, *Outcast London: A Study in the Relationship between Classes in Victorian London*, Oxford: Clarendon Press, 1971, especially Chapters 14–16.
41. Martin J. Weiner, *English Culture and the Decline of the Industrial Spirit, 1850–1980*, New York: Cambridge University Press, 1990, *passim*.
42. Keith Robbins, *The Eclipse of a Great Power: Modern Britain 1870–1975*, New York: Longman, 1989, pp. 8–34.
43. Elie Halévy, *History of the English People, Volume 5, Imperialism and the Rise of Labour, 1895–1905*, trans. E.I. Watkin, New York: Barnes & Noble, 1961, pp. vii–xi.
44. Michael Freeden, "The New Liberalism and Its Aftermath," in Richard Bellamy, ed., *Victorian Liberalism: Nineteenth-century Political Thought and Practice*, London: Routledge, 1990, p. 183.
45. This fact seemed to be well-hidden from the public. From reading *The Times*, the most politically and governmentally oriented of the major London papers, one gains no sense that anything is seriously amiss in the Cabinet. Allusions to a crisis in the Rosebery Cabinet appeared only in the political diaries of those privileged insiders who mixed socially with its members, such as Beatrice Webb, and those who had access to the highest circles of government in an official capacity, such as Sir Edward Walter Hamilton, a Treasury Clerk and confidant of Rosebery's. David Brooks, ed., *The Destruction of Lord Rosebery: From the Diary of Sir Edward Hamilton, 1894–1895*, London: The Historians' Press, 1986, pp. 110–274.
46. Beatrice Webb, diary entry January 20, 1895 (admittedly unsympathetic to the Liberal Party), in *Our Partnership* (London, 1948), p. 121, quoted in Peter Stansky, *Ambitions & Strategies: The Struggle for the Leadership of the Liberal Party in the 1890's*, Oxford: Clarendon Press, 1964, p. 147.
47. Philippa Levine, for one, argues that issues of sexuality and morality were conflated in the Victorian mind. Levine, *op. cit.*, p. 92.
48. Karl Pearson's "Men's and Women's Club" can be seen as an example of the latter phenomenon. Judith Walkowitz, "Science, Feminism, and Romance: The Men and Women's Club, 1885–1889," *History Workshop Journal* (April 1986), pp. 37–59.
49. Freeden, *op. cit.*, pp. 179–81.
50. *Ibid.*, p. 179.
51. L.T. Hobhouse, *Liberalism*, London: Thornton Butterworth, 1934, pp. 138–66. See also Alan Bullock and Maurice Shock, eds., *The Liberal Tradition: From Fox to Keynes*, Oxford: Clarendon, 1967, pp. xlii–xliii.
52. Thomas Hill Green, *Lectures on the Principles of Political Obligation*, London: Longmans, 1911, pp. 206–10.

53. D.G. Ritchie, *Philosophical Studies,* p. 267, in Michael Freeden, *The New Liberalism: An Ideology of Social Reform,* Oxford: Clarendon Press, 1978, p. 98.

54. Freeden, "The New Liberalism and its Aftermath," p. 179.

55. Steven Lukes, *Emile Durkheim: His Life and Work,* Stanford: Stanford University Press, 1985. In this fascinating intellectual biography, Lukes points out Spencer's influence on Durkheim (pp. 82–4), similarities between Green's and Durkheim's views of morality and the interventionist State (pp. 271–2), and Hobhouse's discussion of Durkheim's views (p. 397).

56. Emile Durkheim, *Sociology and Philosophy,* trans. D.F. Pocock, New York: The Free Press, 1974, p. xvii n.

57. "The Determination of Moral Facts," in *ibid.,* p. 43.

58. *Ibid.,* p. 61.

59. *Ibid.,* p. xxvi.

60. *Ibid.,* p. 60.

61. Lukes, *The New Liberalism: An Ideology of Social Reform,* p. 19.

62. Freeden, *The New Liberalism: An Ideology of Social Reform,* p. 114.

63. Brougham Villiers, *The Opportunity of Liberalism,* 1904, in Freeden, *The New Liberalism: An Ideology of Social Reform,* p. 114. Brougham Villiers, the pseudonym for Frederick John Shaw, was a prominent social critic and advocate of social and political reforms.

64. D.G. Ritchie, *The Moral Function of the State,* 1887, in Freeden, *The New Liberalism: An Ideology of Social Reform,* p. 58.

65. Durkheim, *op. cit.,* pp. x–xvi.

66. Canguilhem, *op. cit.,* pp. 125, 240.

67. *Ibid.,* p. 263.

68. *Ibid.,* p. 237.

69. *Daily Telegraph,* April 6, 1895.

70. *Star,* April 6, 1895.

71. Hyde, *op. cit.,* p. 213.

72. *Ibid.,* p. 264.

73. *Star,* April 25, 1895.

74. *Morning,* May 2, 1895.

75. *Daily Telegraph,* May 27, 1895.

76. Canguilhem discusses the process of labelling and stigmatization of people suffering from AIDS, and the social death that frequently preceded physical death. Canguilhem, *op. cit.,* p. 63.

77. Robert Sherard, *Oscar Wilde: The Story of an Unhappy Friendship,* privately printed, 1902, pp. 218–19.

78. Sander L. Gilman, "Sexology, Psychoanalysis, and Degeneration: From a Theory of Race to a Race to Theory," in Chamberlin and Gilman, eds., *Degeneration: The Dark Side of Progress,* pp. 88–9. Gilman says that "the power possessed by society in defining the Other was ... linked to the power of the explanatory model of human biology and its 'scientific' authority." While I agree with Gilman that society's power was linked to the authority of science, I do not think biological models can offer a convincing explanation of the Other, as I have argued.

79. Mary Douglas, *Purity and Danger: An Analysis of the Concepts of Pollution and Taboo,* London: ARK, 1966, p. 5.

80. *Ibid.,* p. 2.

81. *Ibid.,* p. 3. Similar ideas are expressed in Durkheim, *op. cit.,* p. xvii, and in Canguilhem, *op. cit.,* p. 52.

82. Canguilhem, *op. cit.,* pp. 100, 121.

83. Susan Sontag, *Illness as Metaphor,* New York: Farrar, Straus and Giroux, 1978, p. 58.

84. Canguilhem, *op. cit.,* p. 41.

85. Sontag, *op. cit.,* pp. 63–8.

86. *Daily Telegraph,* May 27, 1895, in Jonathan Goodman, ed., *The Oscar Wilde Files,* London: Allison and Busby, 1989, pp. 133–4.

87. *Ibid.*

88. Buchanan's letter appeared in the *Star*, April 20, 1895, and the letter from COMMON-SENSE appeared the following day.

89. In *De Profundis*, Wilde detailed the debts he accumulated in order to maintain a lifestyle that was beyond even his relatively extensive means. Wilde, *De Profundis, op. cit.*, pp. 43–4.

90. Sherard, *op. cit.*, p. 187.

91. *Daily Telegraph*, May 6, 1895.

92. *Daily Telegraph*, May 27, 1895.

93. W.H. Auden referred to Wilde, inaccurately I believe, as the first "homintern martyr." In Richard Ellmann, "The Uses of Decadence: Wilde, Yeats, Joyce," in Richard Ellmann, *a long the riverrun: selected essays*, New York: Vintage, 1990, p. 9.

94. David Hilliard, "UnEnglish and Unmanly: Anglo Catholicism and Homosexuality," *Victorian Studies*, 25, no. 2 (Winter, 1982) p. 184.

95. Hyde, *op. cit.*, p. 349.

96. At the end of "A Study in Modern Ethics," J.A. Symonds discusses the prevalence of "homosexual" behavior in English public school, in part tracing it to the classical curriculum "impregnated with *paederastia.*" John Addington Symonds, *Studies in Sexual Inversion*, privately printed, 1928, p. 200. In "A Study in Greek Ethics," Symonds develops the ancient Athenian cultural context and social conditions in which the practice of pederasty developed. According to Symonds, the prevalence of war fostered a spirit of physical cultivation which manifested itself in sport, especially gymnastics, which was performed naked. He posits that continual sight of the male form led to the appreciation of various qualities. The lack of possibility of forming intellectual relationships with women, due to their lack of formal education and confinement to the household economy, the commonality of interests in sport and war of all male society, and the absence of religious prohibitions, all contributed to the encouragement of the formation of close emotional bonds between men, within which physical love could be expressed as well. *Ibid.*, p. 84. Although Symonds does not similarly develop the parallel between social conditions of the ancient Athenians and those of the English public school system, one can easily be constructed. A similar scenario might read: within the cloistered world of the boys' public schools in Britain grew up close associations between boys and men. Encouraged by a classical curriculum, whose literature, "impregnated with *paederastia*" as it was, provided within the closed communities of the schools the intellectual authority which temporarily overrode the social prohibitions against homosexual contacts. Some such contacts might also have been intended as acts of adolescent rebellion against social norms. There was also the element of necessity, which was compounded by a lack of female alternatives. Once one left the sanctuary of the public schools, however, the intellectual authority of the ancient texts clashed with social prohibitions and cultural norms, resulting in the creation of a homosexual subculture which idealized masculine love and whose rhetoric espoused a nobility of manly virtues, but whose real-world encounters were characterized by secrecy, danger, furtiveness, concealment, anxiety, and fear of exposure.

97. Richard Jenkyns notes that "the classics were the staple of educa-

tion, but they were always subversive." Richard Jenkyns, *The Victorians and Ancient Greece*, Cambridge: Harvard University Press, 1980, p. 280.

98. Weiner, *op. cti.*, p. 11.

99. According to Ellmann, Wilde's own first homosexual experience occurred in 1886, when he allowed himself to be seduced by Robert Ross, then a seventeen-year-old Cambridge student whom he met at Oxford. Richard Ellmann, *Oscar Wilde*, New York: Alfred A. Knopf, 1988, p. 275. Lord Alfred Douglas had just completed his second year at Oxford and was already involved in "rough trade" when Wilde met him in the summer of 1891. *Ibid.*, pp. 324, 389.

100. This characterization of *fin-de-siècle* is Nordau's. Max Nordau, *Degeneration*, 6th edn., New York: Capricorn, 1913, pp. 1–30. Holbrook Jackson, among others, characterizes the eighteen-nineties as "the age of Wilde." Holbrook Jackson, *The Eighteen Nineties*, New York: Capricorn, 1913, *passim*. Richard Ellmann states that of all the writers associated with eighteen-nineties, "Wilde is the only one whom everyone still reads."

101. In *De Profundis*, Wilde wrote that prison time was reflective and reconstitutive. He discovered that suffering was the only mode of being which confirms one's identity. Wilde, *De Profundis*, *op. cit.*, p. 54.

102. Oscar Wilde, letter from H.M. Prison, Reading, addressed to the Home Secretary, dated July 2, 1896, in Rupert Hart-Davis, ed., *Letters*, Oxford: Oxford University Press, pp. 142–5.

103. Wilde, *De Profundis*, *op. cit.*, pp. 80–81.

104. *Ibid.*, p. 96.

105. *Ibid.*, p. 149.

BIBLIOGRAPHY

Primary Sources

Allen, Grant, "The New Hedonism," *Fortnightly Review*, March 1894, pp. 377–92.

Gladstone, William Ewart, "Locksley Hall and the Jubilee," in *The Nineteenth Century*, No. CXIX, Jan. 1887.

Grolleau, Charles, ed., *The Trial of Oscar Wilde*, Paris: privately printed, 1906.

Jackson, Holbrook, *The Eighteen Nineties*, New York: Capricorn, 1913.

Mason, Stuart (pseudonym for Christopher Sclater Millard), *Art and Morality: A Defense of "The Picture of Dorian Gray,"* London: J. Jacobs, 1908.

——, *Oscar Wilde Three Times Tried*, London: privately printed, 1912.

Nordau, Max, *Degeneration*, New York: D. Appleton and Co., 1895.

Shaw, George Bernard, *The Sanity of Art*, New York: Wm. Wise & Company, 1931.

Sherard, Robert, *Oscar Wilde: The Story of an Unhappy Friendship*, privately printed, 1902.

Symonds, John Addington, *Studies in Sexual Inversion*, London: privately printed, 1928.

Tennyson, Alfred, "Locksley Hall" (1886), in *The Poems of Tennyson*, ed. C. Ricks, London, 1969.

Wilde, Oscar, *Letters of Oscar Wilde*, ed. Rupert Hart-Davis, New York: Harcourt, 1962.

——, *The Complete Works of Oscar Wilde*, ed. Vyvyan Holland, London: Collins, 1966.

——, *Selected Letters of Oscar Wilde*, ed. Rupert Hart-Davis, Oxford: Oxford University Press, 1979.

——, *The Artist as Critic: Critical Writings of Oscar Wilde*, ed. Richard Ellmann, Chicago: University of Chicago Press, 1982.

——, *The Picture of Dorian Gray*, ed. Donald L. Lawler, New York: W.W. Norton & Company, 1988.

——, *The Soul of Man and Prison Writings*, ed. Isobel Murray, Oxford: Oxford University Press, 1991.

Young, Dalhousie, *Apologia pro Oscar Wilde*, London: privately printed, 1895.

Secondary Works

Adorno, Theodor W., *Kierkegaard: Construction of the Aesthetic*, ed. and trans. Robert Hullot-Kentor, Minneapolis: University of Minnesota Press, 1989.

Arnold, Matthew, *Culture and Anarchy*, in *Culture and Anarchy and Other Writings*, ed. Stefan Collini, Cambridge: Cambridge University Press, 1993.

Bakhtin, Mikhail, *The Dialogic Imagination: Four Essays*, ed. Michael Holquist, trans. Caryl Emerson and Michael Holquist, Austin: University of Texas Press, 1990.

Bartlett, Neil, *Who Was That Man? A Present for Mr. Oscar Wilde*, London: Serpent's Tail, 1988.

Baudelaire, Charles, *The Flowers of Evil*, ed. Marthiel and Jackson Mathews, New York: New Directions, 1989.

Beckson, Karl, *London in the 1890s: A Cultural History*, New York: W. W. Norton & Company, 1992.

Bell, Daniel, *The Cultural Contradictions of Capitalism*, New York: Basic Books, 1976.

——, *The Winding Passage: Essays and Sociological Journeys, 1960–1980*, New York: Basic Books, 1980.

Bellamy, Richard, ed., *Victorian Liberalism: Nineteenth-century Political Thought and Practice*, London: Routledge, 1990.

Berman, Marshall, *All That Is Solid Melts Into Air: The Experience of Modernity*, New York: Simon & Schuster, 1982.

Bourdieu, Pierre, *Distinction: A Social Critique of the Judgement of Taste*, trans. Richard Nice, Cambridge: Harvard University Press, 1984.

Bowler, Peter, *Darwinism*, New York: Twayne, 1993.

Boyce, George, James Curran, and Pauline Wingate, eds., *Newspaper History: from the Seventeenth Century to the Present Day*, London: Constable; Beverly Hills: Sage Publications, 1978.

Bristow, Edward J., *Vice and Vigilance: Purity Movements in Britain since 1700*, Bristol: Gill and MacMillan, 1977.

Brooks, David, *The Destruction of Lord Rosebery*, London: The Historians' Press, 1986.

Buck-Morss, Susan, *The Dialectics of Seeing: Walter Benjamin and the Arcades Project*, Cambridge: MIT Press, 1991.

Bullock, Alan, and Maurice Shock, eds., *The Liberal Tradition: From Fox to Keynes*, Oxford: Clarendon, 1967.

Caine, Barbara, *Victorian Feminists*, Oxford: Oxford University Press, 1991.

Calinescu, Matei, *The Five Faces of Modernity*, Bloomington and Indianapolis: University of Indiana Press, 1977.

Canguilhem, Georges, *The Normal and the Pathological*, trans. Carolyn R. Fawcett, New York: Zone Books, 1991.

Cartledge, Sue and Joanna Ryan, eds., *Sex & Love: New Thoughts on Old Contradictions*, London: The Women's Press, 1983.

Chamberlin, J. Edward, and Sander L. Gilman, eds., *Degeneration: The Dark Side of Progress*, New York, Columbia University Press, 1985.

Chiari, Joseph, *Symbolism from Poe to Mallarmé: The Growth of a Myth*, New York: Gordian Press, 1970.

Chibnall, Steve, "Chronicles of the Gallows: The Social History of Crime

Reporting," in *The Social History of Journalism and the Press*, Sociological Review Monograph 29, (October 1980).

Cohen, Ed, *Talk on the Wilde Side: Towards a Genealogy of a Discourse on Male Sexualities*, London: Routledge, 1993.

Croft-Cooke, Rupert, *Bosie: The Story of Lord Alfred Douglas, His Friends and Enemies*, London: W.H. Allen, 1963.

Crossick, Geoffrey, ed., *The Lower Middle Class in Britain, 1870–1914*, New York: St. Martin's Press, 1977.

Debon, Günther, *Oscar Wilde und der Taoismus*, Bern: Peter Lang, 1986.

Debord, Guy, *Society of the Spectacle*, Detroit: Black & Red, 1983.

Deleuze, Gilles, *Nietzsche & Philosophy*, trans. Hugh Tomlinson, New York: Columbia University Press, 1983.

——, *The Deleuze Reader*, ed. Constantin V. Boundas, New York: Columbia University Press, 1993.

——, and F. Guattari, *Anti-Oedipus: Capitalism and Schizophrenia*, Minneapolis: University of Minneapolis Press, 1984.

Dollimore, Jonathan, *Sexual Dissidence: Augustine to Wilde, Freud to Foucault*, Oxford: Clarendon Press, 1991.

Douglas, Mary, *Purity and Danger: An Analysis of the Concepts of Pollution and Taboo*, London: Ark, 1988.

Dover, K. J., *Greek Homosexuality*, Cambridge: Harvard University Press, 1989.

Durkheim, Emile, *Sociology and Philosophy*, trans. D.F. Pocock, New York: The Free Press, 1974.

——, *The Rules of Sociological Method: and Selected Texts on Sociology and Its Method*, trans. W.D. Halls, New York: The Free Press, 1982.

Eckhardt, Wolf von, Sander L. Gilman, J. Edward Chamberlin, *Oscar Wilde's London*, Garden City: Anchor Press, 1987.

Ellmann, Richard, *Oscar Wilde*, New York: Knopf, 1988.

——, *a long the riverrun: selected essays*, New York: Vintage, 1990.

Emerson, Ralph Waldo, *The Complete Essays and Other Writings of Ralph Waldo Emerson*, ed. Brooks Atkinson, New York: The Modern Library, 1950.

Foster, Hal, *The Anti-Aesthetic*, Port Townsend: Bay Press, 1984.

Foucault, Michel, *The Order of Things: An Archaeology of the Human Sciences*, New York: Vintage, 1973.

——, *The Birth of the Clinic: An Archaeology of Medical Perception*, trans. A.M. Sheridan Smith, New York: Vintage, 1975.

——, *The Foucault Reader*, ed. Paul Rabinow, New York: Pantheon, 1984.

——, *The History of Sexuality*, 3 vols., trans. Robert Hurley, New York: Vintage, 1985.

Freeden, Michael, ed., *The New Liberalism: An Ideology of Social Reform*, Oxford: Clarendon Press, 1978.

——, *J.A. Hobson: A Reader*, London: Unwin Hyman, 1988.

Freud, Sigmund, *The Basic Writings of Sigmund Freud*, trans. and ed. A. A. Brill, New York: Modern Library, 1938.

——, *Civilization and Its Discontents*, trans. James Strachey, New York: W.W. Norton & Company, 1962.

——, *General Psychological Theory*, New York: Collier, 1963.

Frye, Northrop, *Anatomy of Criticism: Four Essays*, Princeton: Princeton University Press, 1990.

Fryer, Peter, *Mrs. Grundy: Studies in English Prudery*, New York: London House & Maxwell, 1963.

Gadamer, Hans-Georg, *Truth and Method*, New York: Crossroad, 1988.

Gagnier, Regenia, *Idylls of the Marketplace: Oscar Wilde and the Victorian Public*, Stanford: Stanford University Press, 1986.

Gay, Peter, *The Bourgeois Experience: From Victoria to Freud*, Vol.2, *The Tender Passion*, New York: Oxford University Press, 1986.

Gilman, Richard, *Decadence: The Strange Life of an Epithet*, New York: Farrar, Straus and Giroux, 1979.

Goodman, Jonathan, ed., *The Oscar Wilde File*, London: Allison & Busby, 1989.

Green, Thomas Hill, *Lectures on the Principles of Political Obligation*, London: Longmans, 1941.

Habermas, Jürgen, *The Philosophical Discourse of Modernity*, trans. Frederic Lawrence, Cambridge: MIT Press, 1987.

Halévy, Elie, *History of the English People, Vol.5, Imperialism and the Rise of Labour, 1895–1905*, trans. E.I. Watkin, New York: Barnes & Noble, 1961.

Halperin, David M., *One Hundred Years of Homosexuality: And Other Essays on Greek Love*, London: Routledge, 1990.

Harris, Frank, *Oscar Wilde*, New York: Carroll & Graf, 1992.

Harris, Jose, *Private Lives, Public Spirit: Britain 1870–1917*, New York: Penguin, 1994.

Harvey, David, *The Condition of Postmodernity*, Oxford: Blackwell, 1989.

Hichens, Robert, *The Green Carnation*, Lincoln: University of Nebraska Press, 1970.

Hilliard, David, "UnEnglish and UnManly," *Victorian Studies*, 25, No. 2 (Winter, 1982).

Hobhouse, L. T., *Liberalism*, London: Thornton Butterworth Ltd, 1934.

Holland, Vyvyan, *Son of Oscar Wilde*, New York: Hart-Davis, 1954.

Horkheimer, Max, and Theodor W. Adorno, *Dialectic of Enlightenment*, trans. John Cumming, New York: Continuum, 1989.

Horney, Karen, *The Neurotic Personality of Our Time*, New York: W. W. Norton & Company, 1937.

Houghton, Walter E., *The Victorian Frame of Mind, 1830-1870*, New Haven and London: Yale University Press, 1985.

Huysmans, J. K., *Against the Grain (A Rebours)*, New York, Dover, 1969.

Huyssen, Andreas, *After the Great Divide: Modernism, Mass Culture, Post-modernism*, Bloomington and Indianapolis: University of Indiana Press, 1986.

Hyde, H. Montgomery, *Carson: The Life of Sir Edward Carson, Lord Carson of Duncairn*, London: William Heinemann Ltd, 1953.

——, *Lord Alfred Douglas: A Biography*, London: Methuen, 1984.

——, *Oscar Wilde*, New York: Da Capo Press, 1975.

——, *The Trials of Oscar Wilde*, New York: Dover, 1962.

Iser, Wolfgang, *The Act of Reading: A Theory of Aesthetic Response*, Baltimore: Johns Hopkins University Press, 1978.

Jameson, Fredric, *The Prison House of Language*, Princeton: Princeton University Press, 1972.

——, *The Political Unconscious: Narrative as a Socially Symbolic Act*, Ithaca: Cornell University Press, 1981.

Jeffries, Sheila, *The Spinster and Her Enemies: Feminism and Sexuality 1880–1930*, London, Boston, and Henley: Pandora, 1990.

Jenkyns, Richard, *The Victorians and Ancient Greece*, Cambridge: Harvard University Press, 1980.

Jones, Gareth Stedman, *Outcast London: A Study in the Relationship between Classes in Victorian London*, Oxford: Clarendon, 1971.

——, *The Languages of Class: Studies in English Working Class History, 1832–1982*, Cambridge: Cambridge University Press, 1983.

Kierkegaard, Søren, *The Present Age*, trans. Alexander Dru, New York: Harper, 1962.

Klossowski, Pierre, *Sade, My Neighbor*, trans. Alphonso Lingis, Evanston: Northwestern University Press, 1991.

Knox, Melissa, *Oscar Wilde: A Long and Lovely Suicide*, New Haven and London: Yale University Press, 1994.

Kohl, Norbert, *Oscar Wilde: The Works of a Conformist Rebel*, Cambridge: Cambridge University Press, 1989.

Kohut, Heinz, *The Restoration of the Self*, New York: International Universities Press, 1977.

Lee, Alan J., *The Origins of the Popular Press in England, 1855–1914*, London: Croom Helm.

Levine, Philippa, *Feminist Lives in Victorian England: Private Roles and Public Commitment*, Oxford: Blackwell, 1990.

Lukes, Steven, *Emile Durkheim, His Life and Work: A Historical and Critical Study*, Stanford: Stanford University Press, 1985.

Lyotard, Jean-François, *The Postmodern Condition*, Minneapolis: University of Minnesota Press, 1984.

Marcus, Steven, *The Other Victorians*, New York: Norton, 1985.

Marcuse, Herbert, *Negations: Essays in Critical Theory*, trans. Jeremy J. Shapiro, London: Free Association Books, 1988.

Megill, Alan, *Prophets of Extremity: Nietzsche, Heidegger, Foucault, Derrida*, Berkeley and Los Angeles: The University of California Press, 1987.

Mikhail, E.H., *Oscar Wilde: Interviews and Recollections*, 2 vols., New York: Barnes & Noble, 1979.

Morris, Andrew R., "Oscar Wilde and the Eclipse of Darwinism: Aestheticism, Degeneration, and Moral Reaction in Late Victorian Ideology," *Studies in History and Philosophy of Science* (October 1993), Vol. 24, No. 4, pp. 513–40.

Mort, Frank, *Dangerous Sexualities: Medico-Moral Politics in England since 1830*, New York: Routledge & Kegan Paul, 1987.

Nietzsche, Friedrich, *The Birth of Tragedy and The Case of Wagner*, trans. Walter Kaufmann, New York: Vintage, 1967.

——, *Twilight of the Idols and The Anti-Christ*, trans. R.J. Hollingdale, New York: Penguin, 1978.

——, *Joyful Wisdom*, trans. Thomas Common, New York: Frederick Ungar, 1981.

——, *The Will To Power*, ed. Walter Kaufmann, trans. Walter Kaufmann and R. J. Hollingdale, New York: Vintage, 1967.

Pater, Walter, *Essays on Literature and Art*, ed. Jennifer Uglow, Everyman's Library, London: J. M. Dent & Sons, 1990.

Pearsall, Ronald, *The Worm in the Bud: The World of Victorian Sexuality*, London: Weidenfeld and Nicolson, 1969.

Perkin, Harold, *The Rise of Professional Society: England since 1880*, London and New York: Routledge, 1989.

Pick, Daniel, *Faces of Degeneration*, Cambridge UK: Cambridge University Press, 1993.

Pierrot, Jean, *The Decadent Imagination, 1880–1900*, trans. Derek Coltman, Chicago: University of Chicago Press, 1981.

Plato, *The Symposium*, trans. Walter Hamilton, New York: Penguin, 1951.

Porter, Bernard, *The Lion's Share: A Short History of British Imperialism, 1850–1970*, London: Longman, 1975.

——, *Britain, Europe and the World, 1850–1986: Delusions of Grandeur*, London: Unwin Hyman, 1987.

Poulet, Georges, "Phenomenology of Reading," *New Literary History*, 1, 53–68.

Praz, Mario, *The Romantic Agony*, trans. Angus Davidson, Cleveland: World Publishing Company, 1968.

Queensberry, Francis Archibald Kelhead Douglas, *Oscar Wilde and the Black Douglas*, with Percy Colson, London: Hutchinson, 1949.

Rieff, Philip, "The Impossible Culture: Wilde as a Modern Prophet," *Salamagundi*, 58–9, (1982–3), 406–26.

Robbins, Keith, *The Eclipse of a Great Power: Modern Britain 1870–1975*, New York: Longman, 1989.

Sade, Marquis de, *Justine, Philosophy in the Bedroom, and Other Writings*, trans. Richard Seaver and Austryn Wainhouse, New York: Grove Weidenfeld, 1990.

Schmidgall, Gary, *The Stranger Wilde: Interpreting Oscar*, New York: Dutton, 1994.

Schneewind, J. B., ed., *Mill: A Collection of Critical Essays*, Garden City: Anchor Books, 1968.

Sedgwick, Eve Kosofsky, *Between Men: English Literature and Male Homosocial Desire*, New York: Columbia University Press, 1985.

——, *Epistemology of the Closet*, Berkeley and Los Angeles: University of California Press, 1990.

Sewell, Brocard, *Footnote to the Nineties: A Memoir of John Gray and André Raffalovich*, London: Cecil and Amelia Woolf, 1968.

Showalter, Elaine, *Sexual Anarchy: Gender and Culture at the Fin-de-Siècle*, New York: Penguin, 1990.

Simmel, Georg, *On Individuality and Social Forms*, ed. Donald N. Levine, Chicago: University of Chicago Press, 1971.

——, *The Sociology of Georg Simmel*, ed. and trans. Kurt H. Wolff, New York: The Free Press, 1971.

——, *Schopenhauer and Nietzsche*, trans. Helmut Loiskandl, Deena Weinstein, and Michael Weinstein, Urbana and Chicago: University of Illinois Press, 1991.

Sked, Alan, *Britain's Decline: Problems and Perspectives*, New York: Blackwell, 1987.

Sontag, Susan, *Illness as Metaphor*, New York: Farrar Straus and Giroux, 1978.

——, *Against Interpretation*, New York: Anchor, 1990.

Sorel, Georges, *The Illusions of Progress*, trans. John and Charlotte Stanley, Berkeley and Los Angeles: University of California Press, 1972.

Spencer, Herbert, *Herbert Spencer: Selected Writings*, ed. J.D.Y. Peel, Chicago: University of Chicago Press, 1972.

Stansky, Peter, *Ambitions and Strategies: The Struggle for the Leadership of the Liberal Party in the 1890's*, Oxford: Clarendon, 1964.

——, *Gladstone: A Progress in Politics*, Boston: Little, Brown and Company, 1979.

Stokes, John, "Wilde at Bay: The Diaries of George Ives," *Literature in Transition, 1880–1920*, 26 (1983), 175–86.

——, *In the Nineties*, Chicago: University of Chicago Press, 1989.

Stone, Michael, ed., *Essential Papers on Borderline Disorders: One Hundred Years at the Border*, New York: NYU Press, 1986.

Symonds, John Addington, *Studies in Sexual Inversion*, London: privately printed, 1928.

Taylor, Charles, *The Ethics of Authenticity*, Cambridge: Harvard University Press, 1992.

Thorlby, A. K., *The Romantic Movement*, London: Longmans, 1966.

Toulmin, Stephen, *Cosmopolis: The Hidden Agenda of Modernity*, New York: The Free Press, 1990.

Trilling, Lionel, *Sincerity and Authenticity*, Cambridge: Harvard University Press, 1971.

Tuchman, Gaye, *Making News: A Study in the Construction of Reality*, New York: The Free Press, 1978.

Vattimo, Gianni, *The End of Modernity: Nihilism and Hermeneutics in Postmodern Culture*, Baltimore: Johns Hopkins University Press, 1991.

Walkowitz, Judith R., *City of Dreadful Delight: Narratives of Sexual Danger in Late-Victorian London*, Chicago: University of Chicago Press, 1992.

Weber, Max, *The Protestant Ethic and the Spirit of Capitalism*, trans. Talcott Parsons, New York: Charles Scribner's Sons, 1958.

Weeks, Jeffrey, *Coming Out: Homosexual Politics in Britain, from the Nineteenth Century to the Present*, London: Quartet, 1977.

——, "Inverts, Perverts, and Mary-Annes," *Journal of Homosexuality*, Vol. 6, Nos. 1 and 2, 1981.

——, *Sexuality and Its Discontents: Meanings, Myths & Modern Sexualities*, London: Routledge, 1985.

——, *Sex, Politics, and Society: The Regulation of Sexuality since 1800*, London: Longman, 1989.

——, *Against Nature: Essays on History, Sexuality, and Identity*, London: Rivers Oram Press, 1991.

Weiner, Martin, *English Culture and the Decline of the Industrial Spirit, 1850–1980*, New York: Longman, 1989.

Williams, Raymond, *The Long Revolution*, New York: Columbia University Press, 1961.

——, *Culture and Society: 1780–1950*, New York: Columbia University Press, 1983.

Williams, Rosalind, *Dream Worlds: Mass Consumption in Late Nineteenth-Century France*, Berkeley and Los Angeles: University of California Press, 1991.

Wratislaw, Theodore, *Oscar Wilde: A Memoir*, London: The Eighteen-Nineties Society, 1979.

Index